1996 Musky Hunter's Almanac

1996 Musky Hunter's Almanac

Editor:
Bill Hamblin

Editor:
Larry Ramsell

Published By
Musky Hunter Publications
Minocqua, Wisconsin

© 1995 Bill Hamblin and Larry Ramsell

All rights reserved. No part of this book may be reproduced or transmitted in any form by any means, electronic or mechanical, including photocopying, recording, or by any information storage and retrieval system, without permission in writing from the publisher.

All correspondence should be addressed to:
MUSKY HUNTER'S ALMANAC
c/o Musky Hunter Magazine
#1 51 Centre, Minocqua, WI 54548

or

Bill Hamblin, 718 Dunbar Road, Kitchener, Ontario, Canada N2M 2X6
Larry Ramsell, P.O. Box 306, Knoxville, Illinois 61448

Contributions are welcome, but *Musky Hunter's Almanac* assumes no responsibility for unsolicited manuscripts or illustrative materials. All submissions must be accompanied by a self-addressed, stamped envelope.

ISBN 1-57223-036-3

Contents

What Is An Almanac? 9
First Thoughts 11

Astronomical Phenomena
All About The Moon 17
    Apogee and Perigee; Phases of the Moon 18
    Moonrise and Moonset 20
All About The Sun 29
    Sunrise and Sunset 30
Latitudes and Longitudes 36

Calendars
Monthly Calendars 44
Yearly Calendars 62

Features
Do You Know Your Musky Biology? 66
Estimated Weight Chart 70
Good Advice! 81
Gweedo the Guide Sez 85
Hedrick Wachelka
    The Armchair Musky Angler 88
How to Determine the Sex of a Musky 94
How to Make Your Own Secchi Disk 96
Interview — John Parry 99

CONTENTS *(Continued)*

Larry Ramsell's Chronological
    Listing of the World Records 108
Pros' Pointers 112
Profile of a Musky Legend — Homer LeBlanc 118
The Cleithrum Project 122
The 50-Pound Club 129
The 45-Pound Release Club 136
The 40-Pound Hybrid Club 138
The Great Debate 140
The State & Provincial Records 150
The World Records 153
Facts You May Not Have Known 163
Tips on Establishing a "Kept" Fish Record Catch 166
United States Minimum Size and Possession Limits 168
Is This the Forerunner of Today's Bucktail? 170
Where Are They Now? 174

HUMOR AND POETRY
A Fisherman to his Son 180
Crazy Musky Fishermen 182
Murphy's Law of Random Perversity 183

MUSKY CLUBS
Directory of Musky Clubs 188
Muskies Canada 190

CONTENTS *(Continued)*

Muskies, Inc. 194

STORIES AND ARTICLES
1895 — The Technique of Fishing 202
Are All The Big Muskies Gone? 206
Coast Guard Helps Land a Musky 208
Difficulties of the Old Days 210
Did You Ever Dream? 214
Fish Knocks Out Woman 216
Lightning Strikes Twice in the Same Place 217
Musky Jumps into the Boat 220
Muskyology 222
Old Musky Ads 226
Superstition — It's Garbage 230
The Musky Trip of a Lifetime 232
The Field Trip 238
The Musky That Couldn't Stop Eating 242
Would You Believe a Huge Pet Musky? 244
Musky Crossword Puzzle 246

LAST THOUGHTS 251
ABOUT THE EDITORS 252

WHAT IS AN ALMANAC?

An almanac is a book or pamphlet, usually published once a year, that contains many kinds of information. It often includes a calendar, dates of related events and activities, and, among other things, facts about history, geography and weather.

Almanacs originally provided a calendar of the months, with eclipses, the movements of the planets, and the rising and setting times of the sun, moon, and stars. People believed that this information would be useful to farmers and to navigators. Through time, fisherman have come to learn that this information is also an invaluable aid in establishing peak activity times of fish and successful fishing patterns.

First Thoughts

Few if any other anglers have a thirst for knowledge that rivals that of a musky fisherman. This may be more to the fish's credit than the fisherman's. Oh, make no mistake, musky fishermen are truly unique individuals, but it is really the fish that accounts for the distinction, for this compulsion to learn. In the "few and far between" life of the musky fisherman we must rely on the experiences of others as much as our own to satisfy our need to learn. For many, this means delving into the sport's rich history to tap the experience of those who have worked the waters before us; for others, it means maintaining meticulous documentation on modern day catches in search of clues that provide an insight into the musky's behavior. In any event, it makes for a unique relationship between man and fish. Bodies of water become legendary, fish become as famous as the fishermen and the fishermen become the focus of the musky fishing community's praise and scrutiny.

A consequence of this unique relationship is that musky fishermen are inclined to want to *discover* their sport as much as partake of it. With this in mind, Larry and I have written the *Musky Hunter's Almanac* to not only provide you with some effective tools to use on the water but as a guide to assist you in these discoveries as you explore the world of musky fishing. Within these pages you may take

1996 Musky Hunter's Almanac

a trip in search of Louie Spray's memoirs or venture back to 1883 on the St. Lawrence River and the capture of the first world record. You can peruse Larry's new "45 Pound Release Club" or learn from the top musky anglers of the day what they feel is the single most important piece of advice for a novice angler. Read on and relive the trials of fishing in the old days or learn where you can find and view some of history's most outstanding musky mounts. There's lots to discover.

As important as the muskellunge is, we must be careful not to get carried away with its mystique and make it something that it is not. For after all, it is man who has elevated the fish to its current high regard, not the other way around. Fishermen should always put people above all else. Sometimes I think we lose sight of this. Time on the water is about enriching friendships and exploring our inner selves as much as anything. It's as though the fish know we need time to sort out life's problems and clear the clutter from our minds. God knows they oblige us often enough.

During slow times on the water I am often reminded of a trip I shared with a client from New York a number of years ago. I was to guide Ron, a truly remarkable individual, for five days on the Moon River area of Georgian Bay. Despite our best efforts we didn't see a fish until the last hour of the last day. It was a magnificent fish that followed in from a distance and smashed a figure-8 on the very first turn. Completely clearing the water on her assault, she wasn't hooked. This failure, after five hard days of fishing, was very disappointing yet rarely have I spent more personally fulfilling days or a more enjoyable time on the water. Ron and I spent many hours discussing our personal dreams and aspirations. For him, his sculpting, and me, my fishing. (Ron — the "helping hands" theory is still at work.)

First Thoughts

Even now, this experience remains a constant reminder of how this passionate pastime can rise above the fish itself if you let it. Musky fishing represents a wonderful opportunity to build bridges between fishermen, communities, states, provinces and countries; but, most importantly, between people. With this almanac, Larry and I hope, if only in a small way, to seize this opportunity and share it with as many people as possible. We hope you enjoy the *Almanac* and that it enriches your fishing experiences this coming year.

Sincerely,
Bill "Hambug" Hamblin

More than any other angling pursuit, musky fishing is built on a mutual respect between the fisherman and the fish. Out of this respect has evolved not only a sport but a philosophy. "Catch and Release" found its roots in musky fishing long before being adopted by the fishing community at large. Musky fishermen are to be thanked and congratulated.

• • •

Hambug's Hint — Would you like find out what the musky are feeding on in your neck of the woods? Talk to a local taxidermist. They should be able to tell you what the musky are feeding on and how feeding habits may change by season. You may also get a clue as to what depth they are feeding in.

1996 Musky Hunter's Almanac

Astronomical Phenomena

ALL ABOUT THE MOON

*H*ere are definitions about the moon that you'll need to know when determining moon phases and planning your fishing trips according to them.

- First Quarter: The right half of the moon is illuminated by the sun
- Full Moon: The moon is fully illuminated by the sun
- Last Quarter: The left half of the moon is illuminated by the sun
- New Moon: The moon is not illuminated by the sun
- Apogee: The point in the moon's orbit when it is farthest from the Earth
- Perigee: The point in the moon's orbit when it is closest to the Earth
- Moon's Age: the number of days since the previous new moon
- Moonrise and Moonset: The times of moonrise and moonset are the instants when the upper edge of the moon appears to lie on the horizon for an observer at sea level.

APOGEE & PERIGEE; PHASES OF THE MOON

*T*he times expressed in the table below are expressed in the scale of universal time or (UT). This is also known as Greenwich mean time or (GMT). In other words, these are the times at 0 degrees longitude. To calculate the time for your time zone make the following simple calculation:

    For: Eastern time zone deduct 5 hours
        Central time zone deduct 6 hours
        Mountain time zone deduct 7 hours.

Times have already been adjusted for daylight savings time.

Moon At Apogee (Farthest from Earth)			Moon At Perigee (Closest to Earth)		
1996	**Day**	**Hour**	**1996**	**Day**	**Hour**
January	05	12 p.m.	January	19	11 p.m.
February	01	4 p.m.	February	17	9 a.m.
February	29	7 a.m.	March	16	6 a.m.
March	28	3 a.m.	April	11	4 a.m.
April	24	11 p.m.	May	06	11 p.m.
May	22	5 p.m.	June	03	5 p.m.
June	19	7 a.m.	July	01	11 p.m.
July	16	3 p.m.	July	30	9 a.m.
August	12	5 p.m.	August	27	6 p.m.
September	09	3 a.m.	September	24	11 p.m.
October	06	7 p.m.	October	22	10 a.m.
November	03	2 p.m.	November	16	5 a.m.
December	01	11 a.m.	December	13	4 a.m.
December	29	5 a.m.			

New Moon

1996	Day	Hour
January	20	12:50 p.m.
February	18	11:30 p.m.
March	19	10:45 a.m.
April	17	11:49 p.m.
May	17	12:46 a.m.
June	16	2:36 p.m.
July	15	5:15 p.m.
August	14	8:34 a.m.
September	12	12:07 a.m.
October	12	3:14 p.m.
November	11	4:16 a.m.
December	10	4:56 p.m.

First Quarter

1996	Day	Hour
January	27	11:14 a.m.
February	26	5:52 a.m.
March	27	1:31 a.m.
April	25	9:40 p.m.
May	25	3:13 p.m.
June	24	6:23 p.m.
July	23	6:49 p.m.
August	22	8:34 a.m.
September	12	4:36 a.m.
October	19	7:09 p.m.
November	18	1:09 a.m.
December	17	9:31 a.m.

Full Moon

1996	Day	Hour
January	05	8:51 p.m.
February	04	3:58 p.m.
March	05	9:23 a.m.
April	04	12:07 a.m.
May	03	12:48 p.m.
June	01	9:47 p.m.
July	01	4:58 a.m.
July	30	11:35 a.m.
August	28	6:52 p.m.
September	27	3:51 a.m.
October	26	3:11 p.m.
November	25	4:10 a.m.
December	24	8:41 p.m.

Last Quarter

1996	Day	Hour
January	13	8:45 p.m.
February	12	8:37 a.m.
March	12	5:15 p.m.
April	10	12:36 a.m.
May	10	6:04 a.m.
June	08	12:05 p.m.
July	07	7:55 p.m.
August	06	6:25 a.m.
September	04	8:06 p.m.
October	04	1:04 a.m.
November	03	7:50 a.m.
December	03	5:06 a.m.

MOONRISE AND MOONSET

*T*he times of moonrise and moonset are the instants when the upper edge of the moon appears to lie on the horizon for an observer at sea level. The accompanying tables identify these times for varying degrees of latitude. The tables list times for 40 degrees latitude through 52 degrees of latitude in 2 degree increments. Longitude has no significant effect on moonrise and moonset times for our purpose.

Times are listed at daily intervals. Unlike the Earth's slow orbit of the sun, the moon orbits the Earth at a relatively fast rate of speed. Consequently, the times change significantly from one day to the next. You may note that the change in times of moonrise from January 1, 1996 to January 2, 1996 at 40 degrees is 40 minutes.

All times listed are already adjusted for local time zones but not daylight savings time. Clocks are turned ahead one hour on April 7, 1996 and back one hour October 27, 1996.

If you would like to determine the time for a latitude that is not specifically listed, say 43 degrees on January 1, 1996, simply extrapolate the midway point for the times listed at 42 degrees and 44 degrees for the same day. For example:

January 1, 1996 at 42 degrees latitude moonrise happens at 13:45 p.m. January 1, 1996 at 44 degrees latitude moonrise occurs at 13:41 p.m.

The moonrise occurs four minutes earlier at 44 degrees. We can conclude from this that at 43 degrees (halfway between 42 and 44) the moon would rise at 13:43 p.m.

Moonrise

Lat.	+40°	+42°	+44°	+46°	+48°	+50°	+52°
	h m	h m	h m	h m	h m	h m	h m
Jan. 0	13 12	13 09	13 05	13 01	12 56	12 52	12 46
1	13 50	13 45	13 41	13 36	13 30	13 25	13 18
2	14 30	14 25	14 20	14 15	14 09	14 02	13 55
3	15 14	15 09	15 04	14 58	14 51	14 44	14 36
4	16 02	15 57	15 51	15 45	15 39	15 32	15 24
5	16 53	16 48	16 43	16 37	16 31	16 24	16 17
6	17 46	17 42	17 37	17 32	17 27	17 21	17 14
7	18 42	18 38	18 34	18 30	18 25	18 20	18 15
8	19 38	19 35	19 32	19 29	19 25	19 22	19 18
9	20 35	20 33	20 31	20 29	20 27	20 24	20 22
10	21 33	21 32	21 31	21 30	21 29	21 28	21 27
11	22 32	22 32	22 32	22 33	22 33	22 34	22 34
12	23 32	23 34	23 35	23 37	23 39	23 40	23 43
13	.. ..	.. ..	.. ..	.. ..	.. ..	.. ..	.. ..
14	0 35	0 37	0 40	0 43	0 46	0 49	0 53
15	1 39	1 43	1 47	1 51	1 55	2 00	2 05
16	2 45	2 50	2 55	3 00	3 05	3 11	3 18
17	3 52	3 57	4 02	4 08	4 14	4 21	4 29
18	4 56	5 01	5 07	5 13	5 19	5 27	5 35
19	5 55	6 00	6 06	6 12	6 18	6 25	6 32
20	6 49	6 53	6 58	7 03	7 08	7 14	7 21
21	7 36	7 40	7 43	7 47	7 51	7 56	8 01
22	8 18	8 20	8 23	8 25	8 28	8 31	8 34
23	8 56	8 57	8 58	8 59	9 01	9 02	9 04
24	9 31	9 31	9 31	9 31	9 31	9 31	9 30

Lat.	+40°	+42°	+44°	+46°	+48°	+50°	+52°
	h m	h m	h m	h m	h m	h m	h m
Jan. 23	8 56	8 57	8 58	8 59	9 01	9 02	9 04
24	9 31	9 31	9 31	9 31	9 31	9 31	9 30
25	10 05	10 04	10 02	10 01	10 00	9 58	9 56
26	10 39	10 37	10 34	10 32	10 29	10 26	10 23
27	11 14	11 10	11 07	11 03	10 59	10 55	10 50
28	11 50	11 46	11 42	11 38	11 33	11 27	11 21
29	12 30	12 25	12 20	12 15	12 09	12 03	11 56
30	13 13	13 08	13 02	12 56	12 50	12 43	12 36
31	13 59	13 54	13 48	13 42	13 36	13 29	13 21
Feb. 1	14 48	14 43	14 38	14 32	14 26	14 19	14 12
2	15 41	15 36	15 31	15 26	15 20	15 14	15 07
3	16 35	16 32	16 27	16 23	16 18	16 13	16 07
4	17 32	17 29	17 25	17 22	17 18	17 14	17 09
5	18 29	18 27	18 24	18 22	18 19	18 16	18 13
6	19 27	19 26	19 25	19 23	19 22	19 20	19 19
7	20 26	20 26	20 26	20 26	20 25	20 25	20 25
8	21 26	21 27	21 28	21 29	21 30	21 32	21 33
9	22 27	22 29	22 31	22 34	22 36	22 39	22 42
10	23 30	23 33	23 36	23 40	23 43	23 48	23 52
11	.. ..	.. ..	.. ..	.. ..	.. ..	.. ..	.. ..
12	0 33	0 37	0 41	0 46	0 51	0 57	1 03
13	1 37	1 42	1 47	1 52	1 58	2 05	2 12
14	2 40	2 45	2 50	2 56	3 03	3 10	3 18
15	3 39	3 44	3 50	3 56	4 02	4 09	4 17
16	4 34	4 39	4 44	4 49	4 55	5 01	5 08

Moonset

Lat.	+40°	+42°	+44°	+46°	+48°	+50°	+52°
	h m	h m	h m	h m	h m	h m	h m
Jan. 0	2 21	2 24	2 27	2 31	2 35	2 40	2 44
1	3 18	3 22	3 27	3 31	3 36	3 42	3 48
2	4 13	4 18	4 23	4 29	4 34	4 41	4 48
3	5 06	5 11	5 16	5 22	5 29	5 36	5 43
4	5 55	6 00	6 06	6 12	6 18	6 25	6 33
5	6 40	6 45	6 51	6 57	7 03	7 10	7 17
6	7 22	7 26	7 31	7 37	7 42	7 48	7 55
7	8 00	8 04	8 08	8 12	8 17	8 22	8 28
8	8 34	8 37	8 41	8 44	8 48	8 52	8 57
9	9 07	9 09	9 11	9 14	9 16	9 19	9 22
10	9 37	9 39	9 40	9 41	9 43	9 44	9 46
11	10 08	10 08	10 08	10 08	10 09	10 09	10 09
12	10 38	10 38	10 37	10 36	10 35	10 34	10 32
13	11 11	11 09	11 07	11 05	11 02	11 00	10 57
14	11 46	11 43	11 40	11 37	11 33	11 29	11 25
15	12 26	12 22	12 18	12 14	12 09	12 04	11 58
16	13 12	13 07	13 02	12 57	12 51	12 45	12 38
17	14 05	14 00	13 54	13 48	13 42	13 35	13 27
18	15 06	15 01	14 55	14 49	14 43	14 35	14 27
19	16 14	16 09	16 04	15 58	15 52	15 45	15 38
20	17 25	17 21	17 17	17 12	17 07	17 02	16 56
21	18 38	18 35	18 32	18 29	18 25	18 21	18 17
22	19 50	19 48	19 46	19 44	19 42	19 40	19 37
23	20 59	20 59	20 58	20 58	20 57	20 56	20 56
24	22 06	22 07	22 07	22 08	22 09	22 10	22 11

Lat.	+40°	+42°	+44°	+46°	+48°	+50°	+52°
	h m	h m	h m	h m	h m	h m	h m
Jan. 23	20 59	20 59	20 58	20 58	20 57	20 56	20 56
24	22 06	22 07	22 07	22 08	22 09	22 10	22 11
25	23 10	23 12	23 14	23 16	23 18	23 20	23 23
26	.. ..	.. ..	.. ..	.. ..	.. ..	.. ..	.. ..
27	0 11	0 14	0 17	0 20	0 24	0 28	0 32
28	1 10	1 14	1 18	1 22	1 27	1 32	1 38
29	2 07	2 11	2 16	2 21	2 27	2 33	2 40
30	3 01	3 06	3 11	3 17	3 23	3 29	3 37
31	3 51	3 56	4 02	4 08	4 14	4 21	4 29
Feb. 1	4 38	4 43	4 48	4 54	5 00	5 07	5 15
2	5 21	5 25	5 30	5 36	5 42	5 48	5 55
3	6 00	6 04	6 08	6 13	6 18	6 24	6 30
4	6 36	6 39	6 43	6 47	6 51	6 56	7 01
5	7 09	7 12	7 15	7 17	7 21	7 24	7 28
6	7 41	7 43	7 44	7 46	7 48	7 50	7 52
7	8 12	8 12	8 13	8 14	8 14	8 15	8 16
8	8 43	8 42	8 42	8 41	8 41	8 40	8 39
9	9 14	9 13	9 11	9 09	9 08	9 06	9 04
10	9 48	9 46	9 43	9 40	9 37	9 34	9 30
11	10 25	10 22	10 18	10 14	10 10	10 05	10 00
12	11 07	11 03	10 59	10 54	10 48	10 42	10 36
13	11 56	11 51	11 45	11 40	11 34	11 27	11 19
14	12 51	12 45	12 40	12 27	12 20	12 12	12 12
15	13 53	13 48	13 42	13 36	13 30	13 23	13 16
16	15 00	14 56	14 51	14 46	14 40	14 34	14 27

21

1996 Musky Hunter's Almanac

Moonrise

Lat.	+40°	+42°	+44°	+46°	+48°	+50°	+52°
	h m	h m	h m	h m	h m	h m	h m
Feb. 15	3 39	3 44	3 50	3 56	4 02	4 09	4 17
16	4 34	4 39	4 44	4 49	4 55	5 01	5 08
17	5 23	5 27	5 32	5 36	5 41	5 46	5 52
18	6 08	6 11	6 14	6 17	6 21	6 24	6 29
19	6 48	6 50	6 52	6 54	6 56	6 58	7 01
20	7 25	7 26	7 26	7 27	7 28	7 28	7 29
21	8 01	8 00	8 00	7 59	7 58	7 57	7 56
22	8 36	8 34	8 32	8 30	8 28	8 26	8 23
23	9 11	9 09	9 06	9 03	8 59	8 56	8 52
24	9 48	9 45	9 41	9 37	9 32	9 27	9 22
25	10 28	10 23	10 19	10 14	10 08	10 02	9 56
26	11 10	11 05	11 00	10 54	10 48	10 41	10 34
27	11 55	11 50	11 44	11 38	11 32	11 25	11 17
28	12 43	12 38	12 33	12 27	12 21	12 14	12 06
29	13 34	13 30	13 25	13 19	13 13	13 07	13 00
Mar. 1	14 28	14 24	14 19	14 15	14 09	14 04	13 58
2	15 23	15 20	15 16	15 13	15 08	15 04	14 59
3	16 20	16 18	16 15	16 12	16 09	16 06	16 02
4	17 19	17 17	17 16	17 14	17 12	17 10	17 08
5	18 18	18 17	18 17	18 16	18 16	18 15	18 15
6	19 18	19 19	19 20	19 20	19 21	19 22	19 23
7	20 20	20 22	20 24	20 25	20 28	20 30	20 32
8	21 23	21 26	21 28	21 32	21 35	21 39	21 43
9	22 26	22 30	22 34	22 38	22 43	22 48	22 53
10	23 30	23 34	23 39	23 44	23 50	23 56	.. ..
Mar. 9	22 26	22 30	22 34	22 38	22 43	22 48	22 53
10	23 30	23 34	23 39	23 44	23 50	23 56	.. ..
11	.. ..	.. ..	.. ..	.. ..	.. ..	.. ..	0 03
12	0 32	0 37	0 42	0 48	0 54	1 01	1 09
13	1 31	1 36	1 41	1 47	1 54	2 01	2 09
14	2 26	2 30	2 36	2 41	2 47	2 54	3 01
15	3 15	3 20	3 24	3 29	3 34	3 40	3 46
16	4 00	4 04	4 07	4 11	4 15	4 20	4 24
17	4 41	4 43	4 46	4 48	4 51	4 54	4 58
18	5 19	5 20	5 21	5 23	5 24	5 26	5 27
19	5 55	5 55	5 55	5 55	5 55	5 55	5 55
20	6 30	6 29	6 28	6 27	6 25	6 24	6 22
21	7 06	7 04	7 01	6 59	6 56	6 53	6 50
22	7 43	7 40	7 36	7 33	7 29	7 25	7 20
23	8 22	8 18	8 14	8 09	8 04	7 59	7 53
24	9 04	8 59	8 54	8 49	8 43	8 37	8 30
25	9 48	9 43	9 38	9 32	9 26	9 19	9 12
26	10 36	10 31	10 25	10 20	10 13	10 06	9 59
27	11 26	11 21	11 16	11 11	11 05	10 58	10 51
28	12 19	12 14	12 10	12 05	11 59	11 53	11 47
29	13 13	13 10	13 06	13 02	12 57	12 52	12 47
30	14 09	14 07	14 04	14 00	13 57	13 53	13 49
31	15 07	15 05	15 03	15 01	14 59	14 56	14 53
Apr. 1	16 06	16 05	16 04	16 03	16 02	16 01	16 00
2	17 06	17 07	17 07	17 07	17 07	17 07	17 08

Moonset

Lat.	+40°	+42°	+44°	+46°	+48°	+50°	+52°
	h m	h m	h m	h m	h m	h m	h m
Feb. 15	13 53	13 48	13 42	13 36	13 30	13 23	13 16
16	15 00	14 56	14 51	14 46	14 40	14 34	14 27
17	16 11	16 08	16 04	16 00	15 55	15 51	15 45
18	17 23	17 21	17 18	17 15	17 12	17 09	17 06
19	18 34	18 33	18 32	18 30	18 29	18 27	18 26
20	19 44	19 44	19 44	19 44	19 44	19 44	19 44
21	20 51	20 52	20 53	20 55	20 56	20 58	21 00
22	21 55	21 58	22 00	22 03	22 06	22 09	22 12
23	22 57	23 00	23 04	23 08	23 12	23 16	23 21
24	23 56	.. ..	.. ..	.. ..	.. ..	.. ..	.. ..
25	.. ..	0 00	0 05	0 09	0 15	0 20	0 26
26	0 52	0 57	1 02	1 07	1 13	1 20	1 27
27	1 44	1 49	1 55	2 00	2 07	2 14	2 21
28	2 33	2 38	2 43	2 49	2 55	3 02	3 10
29	3 17	3 22	3 27	3 33	3 39	3 45	3 52
Mar. 1	3 58	4 02	4 07	4 12	4 17	4 23	4 29
2	4 35	4 39	4 43	4 47	4 51	4 56	5 02
3	5 10	5 12	5 15	5 19	5 22	5 26	5 30
4	5 42	5 44	5 46	5 48	5 51	5 53	5 56
5	6 14	6 15	6 16	6 17	6 18	6 19	6 20
6	6 45	6 45	6 45	6 45	6 45	6 45	6 44
7	7 17	7 16	7 15	7 13	7 12	7 10	7 09
8	7 51	7 48	7 46	7 44	7 41	7 38	7 35
9	8 27	8 24	8 21	8 17	8 13	8 09	8 04
10	9 08	9 04	8 59	8 55	8 50	8 44	8 38
Mar. 9	8 27	8 24	8 21	8 17	8 13	8 09	8 04
10	9 08	9 04	8 59	8 55	8 50	8 44	8 38
11	9 53	9 49	9 44	9 38	9 32	9 26	9 19
12	10 45	10 40	10 35	10 29	10 22	10 15	10 08
13	11 43	11 38	11 32	11 27	11 20	11 13	11 05
14	12 46	12 41	12 36	12 31	12 25	12 19	12 12
15	13 53	13 49	13 45	13 41	13 36	13 30	13 24
16	15 02	14 59	14 56	14 53	14 49	14 45	14 41
17	16 12	16 10	16 08	16 06	16 04	16 02	15 59
18	17 21	17 21	17 20	17 19	17 19	17 18	17 17
19	18 29	18 30	18 30	18 31	18 32	18 33	18 34
20	19 35	19 37	19 39	19 41	19 43	19 45	19 48
21	20 39	20 42	20 45	20 48	20 52	20 56	21 00
22	21 41	21 45	21 49	21 53	21 58	22 03	22 08
23	22 39	22 44	22 49	22 54	22 59	23 05	23 12
24	23 34	23 39	23 44	23 50	23 56	.. ..	.. ..
25	.. ..	.. ..	.. ..	.. ..	.. ..	0 03	0 10
26	0 25	0 30	0 35	0 41	0 48	0 55	1 02
27	1 11	1 16	1 22	1 27	1 33	1 40	1 48
28	1 54	1 58	2 03	2 08	2 14	2 20	2 27
29	2 32	2 36	2 40	2 45	2 50	2 55	3 01
30	3 08	3 11	3 14	3 18	3 22	3 26	3 31
31	3 41	3 43	3 46	3 48	3 51	3 54	3 58
Apr. 1	4 13	4 14	4 16	4 17	4 19	4 21	4 23
2	4 44	4 45	4 45	4 45	4 46	4 46	4 47

Moonrise And Moonset

Moonrise

Lat.	+40°	+42°	+44°	+46°	+48°	+50°	+52°
	h m	h m	h m	h m	h m	h m	h m
Apr. 1	16 06	16 05	16 04	16 03	16 02	16 01	16 00
2	17 06	17 07	17 07	17 07	17 07	17 07	17 08
3	18 08	18 10	18 11	18 13	18 14	18 16	18 18
4	19 12	19 14	19 17	19 20	19 23	19 26	19 29
5	20 17	20 20	20 24	20 28	20 32	20 36	20 41
6	21 22	21 26	21 30	21 35	21 41	21 46	21 53
7	22 25	22 30	22 35	22 41	22 47	22 54	23 01
8	23 26	23 31	23 37	23 42	23 49	23 56	.. ..
9	.. ..	.. ..	.. ..	.. ..	.. ..	.. ..	0 04
10	0 22	0 27	0 32	0 38	0 44	0 51	0 59
11	1 13	1 17	1 22	1 27	1 33	1 39	1 45
12	1 58	2 02	2 06	2 10	2 14	2 19	2 25
13	2 39	2 42	2 45	2 48	2 51	2 55	2 58
14	3 17	3 19	3 20	3 22	3 24	3 26	3 28
15	3 53	3 53	3 53	3 54	3 54	3 55	3 56
16	4 27	4 27	4 26	4 25	4 24	4 23	4 22
17	5 02	5 00	4 58	4 56	4 54	4 52	4 49
18	5 38	5 35	5 32	5 29	5 26	5 22	5 18
19	6 16	6 12	6 09	6 04	6 00	5 55	5 49
20	6 57	6 52	6 48	6 43	6 37	6 31	6 25
21	7 41	7 36	7 31	7 25	7 19	7 12	7 05
22	8 27	8 22	8 17	8 11	8 05	7 58	7 50
23	9 17	9 12	9 07	9 01	8 55	8 48	8 41
24	10 09	10 04	10 00	9 54	9 49	9 42	9 35
25	11 03	10 59	10 54	10 50	10 45	10 40	10 34

Lat.	+40°	+42°	+44°	+46°	+48°	+50°	+52°
	h m	h m	h m	h m	h m	h m	h m
Apr. 24	10 09	10 04	10 00	9 54	9 49	9 42	9 35
25	11 03	10 59	10 54	10 50	10 45	10 40	10 34
26	11 58	11 55	11 51	11 48	11 44	11 39	11 34
27	12 54	12 52	12 49	12 47	12 44	12 41	12 37
28	13 52	13 51	13 49	13 48	13 46	13 44	13 42
29	14 51	14 51	14 51	14 50	14 50	14 49	14 49
30	15 52	15 53	15 54	15 55	15 56	15 57	15 58
May 1	16 55	16 57	16 59	17 01	17 04	17 06	17 09
2	18 00	18 03	18 07	18 10	18 14	18 18	18 22
3	19 07	19 11	19 15	19 20	19 24	19 30	19 36
4	20 13	20 18	20 23	20 28	20 34	20 41	20 48
5	21 17	21 22	21 28	21 33	21 40	21 47	21 55
6	22 17	22 22	22 27	22 33	22 39	22 46	22 54
7	23 10	23 15	23 20	23 25	23 31	23 38	23 45
8	23 58	.. ..	.. ..	.. ..	.. ..	.. ..	.. ..
9	.. ..	0 02	0 06	0 11	0 16	0 21	0 27
10	0 41	0 44	0 47	0 50	0 54	0 58	1 02
11	1 19	1 21	1 23	1 25	1 27	1 30	1 33
12	1 54	1 55	1 56	1 57	1 58	1 59	2 00
13	2 28	2 28	2 28	2 27	2 27	2 27	2 26
14	3 02	3 01	2 59	2 58	2 56	2 54	2 52
15	3 37	3 34	3 32	3 29	3 26	3 23	3 19
16	4 13	4 10	4 06	4 02	3 58	3 54	3 49
17	4 52	4 48	4 44	4 39	4 34	4 28	4 22
18	5 34	5 30	5 25	5 19	5 13	5 07	5 00

Moonset

Lat.	+40°	+42°	+44°	+46°	+48°	+50°	+52°
	h m	h m	h m	h m	h m	h m	h m
Apr. 1	4 13	4 14	4 16	4 17	4 19	4 21	4 23
2	4 44	4 45	4 45	4 45	4 46	4 46	4 47
3	5 16	5 16	5 15	5 14	5 13	5 12	5 11
4	5 50	5 48	5 46	5 44	5 42	5 40	5 37
5	6 26	6 23	6 20	6 17	6 14	6 10	6 06
6	7 06	7 02	6 58	6 54	6 50	6 45	6 39
7	7 51	7 47	7 42	7 37	7 31	7 25	7 18
8	8 42	8 37	8 31	8 25	8 19	8 12	8 05
9	9 38	9 33	9 27	9 21	9 15	9 08	9 00
10	10 39	10 34	10 29	10 24	10 18	10 11	10 04
11	11 44	11 40	11 36	11 31	11 26	11 20	11 14
12	12 51	12 48	12 44	12 41	12 37	12 32	12 27
13	13 59	13 57	13 54	13 52	13 49	13 46	13 43
14	15 06	15 05	15 04	15 03	15 01	15 00	14 59
15	16 13	16 13	16 13	16 13	16 13	16 13	16 14
16	17 18	17 20	17 21	17 22	17 24	17 26	17 28
17	18 23	18 25	18 28	18 30	18 33	18 36	18 40
18	19 25	19 29	19 32	19 36	19 40	19 45	19 50
19	20 26	20 30	20 34	20 39	20 44	20 50	20 56
20	21 23	21 27	21 31	21 38	21 44	21 50	21 57
21	22 16	22 21	22 26	22 32	22 38	22 45	22 53
22	23 05	23 10	23 15	23 21	23 27	23 34	23 42
23	23 49	23 54	23 59	.. ..	.. ..	.. ..	.. ..
24	.. ..	.. ..	.. ..	0 04	0 10	0 16	0 24
25	0 29	0 33	0 38	0 43	0 48	0 53	1 00

Lat.	+40°	+42°	+44°	+46°	+48°	+50°	+52°
	h m	h m	h m	h m	h m	h m	h m
Apr. 24	0 04	0 10	0 16	0 24			
25	0 29	0 33	0 38	0 43	0 48	0 53	1 00
26	1 06	1 09	1 13	1 17	1 21	1 26	1 31
27	1 39	1 42	1 45	1 48	1 51	1 55	1 59
28	2 11	2 13	2 15	2 17	2 19	2 22	2 24
29	2 43	2 43	2 44	2 45	2 46	2 47	2 48
30	3 14	3 14	3 14	3 13	3 13	3 13	3 12
May 1	3 47	3 45	3 44	3 43	3 41	3 39	3 37
2	4 22	4 19	4 17	4 14	4 11	4 08	4 05
3	5 00	4 57	4 54	4 50	4 46	4 41	4 36
4	5 44	5 40	5 35	5 31	5 25	5 20	5 13
5	6 34	6 29	6 24	6 18	6 12	6 05	5 58
6	7 30	7 25	7 19	7 13	7 07	6 59	6 52
7	8 31	8 26	8 21	8 15	8 09	8 02	7 54
8	9 36	9 32	9 27	9 22	9 16	9 10	9 02
9	10 44	10 40	10 36	10 32	10 27	10 23	10 17
10	11 51	11 48	11 46	11 43	11 40	11 36	11 32
11	12 58	12 56	12 55	12 53	12 51	12 50	12 47
12	14 03	14 03	14 03	14 03	14 02	14 02	14 02
13	15 08	15 09	15 10	15 11	15 12	15 13	15 14
14	16 11	16 13	16 16	16 18	16 20	16 23	16 26
15	17 14	17 17	17 20	17 23	17 27	17 31	17 36
16	18 14	18 18	18 22	18 27	18 32	18 37	18 43
17	19 12	19 17	19 22	19 27	19 33	19 39	19 46
18	20 07	20 12	20 18	20 23	20 30	20 36	20 44

1996 Musky Hunter's Almanac

Moonrise

Lat.	+40°	+42°	+44°	+46°	+48°	+50°	+52°
	h m	h m	h m	h m	h m	h m	h m
May 17	4 52	4 48	4 44	4 39	4 34	4 28	4 22
18	5 34	5 30	5 25	5 19	5 13	5 07	5 00
19	6 20	6 15	6 10	6 04	5 57	5 51	5 43
20	7 09	7 04	6 58	6 52	6 46	6 39	6 31
21	8 00	7 55	7 50	7 44	7 38	7 32	7 25
22	8 53	8 49	8 44	8 39	8 34	8 28	8 22
23	9 48	9 44	9 40	9 36	9 32	9 27	9 22
24	10 43	10 40	10 37	10 34	10 31	10 27	10 23
25	11 39	11 38	11 36	11 34	11 32	11 29	11 26
26	12 37	12 36	12 35	12 34	12 32	12 31	
27	13 36	13 36	13 37	13 37	13 37	13 38	13 38
28	14 37	14 39	14 40	14 42	14 43	14 45	14 47
29	15 41	15 43	15 46	15 49	15 52	15 55	15 58
30	16 46	16 50	16 54	16 58	17 02	17 07	17 12
31	17 53	17 58	18 02	18 07	18 13	18 19	18 25
June 1	19 00	19 05	19 10	19 16	19 22	19 29	19 37
2	20 03	20 09	20 14	20 20	20 27	20 34	20 42
3	21 02	21 07	21 12	21 18	21 24	21 31	21 38
4	21 54	21 58	22 03	22 08	22 13	22 19	22 25
5	22 40	22 43	22 47	22 51	22 55	22 59	23 04
6	23 20	23 23	23 25	23 28	23 31	23 34	23 37
7	23 57	23 58					
8	.. ..	.. ..	0 00	0 01	0 03	0 04	0 06
9	0 32	0 32	0 32	0 32	0 32	0 32	0 32
10	1 05	1 04	1 03	1 02	1 01	1 00	0 58

Moonrise

Lat.	+40°	+42°	+44°	+46°	+48°	+50°	+52°
	h m	h m	h m	h m	h m	h m	h m
June 8	.. ..	.. ..	0 00	0 01	0 03	0 04	0 06
9	0 32	0 32	0 32	0 32	0 32	0 32	0 32
10	1 05	1 04	1 03	1 02	1 01	1 00	0 58
11	1 39	1 37	1 35	1 33	1 30	1 27	1 24
12	2 14	2 11	2 08	2 05	2 01	1 57	1 52
13	2 52	2 48	2 44	2 39	2 35	2 29	2 24
14	3 32	3 28	3 23	3 18	3 12	3 06	2 59
15	4 16	4 11	4 06	4 00	3 54	3 47	3 39
16	5 03	4 58	4 52	4 47	4 40	4 33	4 25
17	5 53	5 48	5 43	5 37	5 31	5 24	5 17
18	6 46	6 41	6 36	6 31	6 25	6 19	6 12
19	7 40	7 36	7 32	7 27	7 22	7 17	7 11
20	8 35	8 32	8 28	8 25	8 21	8 17	8 12
21	9 30	9 28	9 26	9 23	9 21	9 18	9 14
22	10 27	10 26	10 24	10 23	10 21	10 20	10 18
23	11 24	11 24	11 24	11 23	11 23	11 23	11 23
24	12 23	12 24	12 25	12 26	12 27	12 28	12 29
25	13 24	13 26	13 28	13 30	13 32	13 35	13 37
26	14 27	14 30	14 33	14 36	14 40	14 44	14 48
27	15 32	15 36	15 40	15 44	15 49	15 55	16 00
28	16 38	16 43	16 48	16 53	16 59	17 05	17 12
29	17 43	17 48	17 54	18 00	18 06	18 13	18 21
30	18 45	18 51	18 56	19 02	19 08	19 15	19 23
July 1	19 42	19 47	19 52	19 57	20 03	20 09	20 16
2	20 32	20 36	20 40	20 45	20 50	20 55	21 01

Moonset

Lat.	+40°	+42°	+44°	+46°	+48°	+50°	+52°
	h m	h m	h m	h m	h m	h m	h m
May 17	19 12	19 17	19 22	19 27	19 33	19 39	19 46
18	20 07	20 12	20 18	20 23	20 30	20 36	20 44
19	20 58	21 03	21 09	21 15	21 21	21 28	21 36
20	21 45	21 49	21 55	22 00	22 06	22 13	22 21
21	22 26	22 31	22 36	22 41	22 46	22 52	22 59
22	23 04	23 08	23 12	23 17	23 21	23 27	23 32
23	23 39	23 42	23 45	23 49	23 53	23 57	
24	.. ..	.. ..	.. ..	.. ..	.. ..	.. ..	0 01
25	0 11	0 14	0 16	0 18	0 21	0 24	0 27
26	0 42	0 44	0 45	0 46	0 48	0 49	0 51
27	1 13	1 13	1 13	1 14	1 14	1 14	1 15
28	1 44	1 43	1 42	1 42	1 41	1 40	1 38
29	2 17	2 15	2 13	2 11	2 09	2 07	2 04
30	2 53	2 51	2 48	2 44	2 41	2 37	2 33
31	3 34	3 31	3 26	3 22	3 17	3 12	3 07
June 1	4 21	4 17	4 12	4 06	4 01	3 54	3 48
2	5 15	5 10	5 05	4 59	4 52	4 45	4 38
3	6 16	6 11	6 05	5 59	5 53	5 46	5 38
4	7 22	7 17	7 12	7 07	7 01	6 54	6 47
5	8 31	8 27	8 23	8 18	8 13	8 08	8 02
6	9 41	9 38	9 34	9 31	9 27	9 23	9 19
7	10 49	10 47	10 45	10 43	10 41	10 39	10 36
8	11 56	11 55	11 55	11 54	11 53	11 52	11 51
9	13 01	13 02	13 02	13 03	13 03	13 04	13 05
10	14 05	14 06	14 08	14 10	14 12	14 14	14 16

Moonset

Lat.	+40°	+42°	+44°	+46°	+48°	+50°	+52°
	h m	h m	h m	h m	h m	h m	h m
June 8	11 56	11 55	11 55	11 54	11 53	11 52	11 51
9	13 01	13 02	13 02	13 03	13 03	13 04	13 05
10	14 05	14 06	14 08	14 10	14 12	14 14	14 16
11	15 07	15 09	15 12	15 15	15 18	15 22	15 26
12	16 07	16 11	16 14	16 19	16 23	16 28	16 33
13	17 05	17 10	17 14	17 19	17 25	17 31	17 37
14	18 01	18 06	18 11	18 17	18 23	18 29	18 37
15	18 53	18 58	19 04	19 09	19 16	19 23	19 31
16	19 41	19 46	19 51	19 57	20 04	20 10	20 18
17	20 25	20 29	20 34	20 40	20 46	20 52	20 59
18	21 04	21 08	21 13	21 18	21 23	21 28	21 34
19	21 40	21 43	21 47	21 51	21 55	22 00	22 05
20	22 13	22 16	22 18	22 21	22 25	22 28	22 32
21	22 44	22 46	22 48	22 50	22 52	22 54	22 56
22	23 14	23 15	23 16	23 17	23 17	23 18	23 19
23	23 44	23 44	23 43	23 43	23 43	23 43	23 42
24	.. ..	.. ..	.. ..	.. ..	.. ..	.. ..	.. ..
25	0 16	0 14	0 13	0 11	0 10	0 08	0 06
26	0 49	0 47	0 45	0 42	0 39	0 36	0 33
27	1 27	1 23	1 20	1 16	1 12	1 08	1 03
28	2 10	2 05	2 01	1 56	1 51	1 45	1 39
29	2 59	2 54	2 49	2 43	2 37	2 31	2 23
30	3 56	3 51	3 45	3 39	3 33	3 26	3 18
July 1	5 00	4 55	4 50	4 44	4 38	4 31	4 23
2	6 10	6 05	6 01	5 55	5 50	5 44	5 37

Moonrise And Moonset

Moonrise

Lat.	+40°	+42°	+44°	+46°	+48°	+50°	+52°
	h m	h m	h m	h m	h m	h m	h m
July 1	19 42	19 47	19 52	19 57	20 03	20 09	20 16
2	20 32	20 36	20 40	20 45	20 50	20 55	21 01
3	21 17	21 20	21 23	21 26	21 30	21 33	21 37
4	21 57	21 58	22 00	22 02	22 04	22 07	22 09
5	22 33	22 34	22 34	22 35	22 36	22 36	22 37
6	23 08	23 07	23 07	23 06	23 05	23 05	23 04
7	23 42	23 41	23 39	23 37	23 35	23 33	23 30
8	..	..	..	..	..	..	23 58
9	0 17	0 14	0 12	0 09	0 05	0 02	..
10	0 54	0 50	0 46	0 42	0 38	0 33	0 28
11	1 33	1 28	1 24	1 19	1 14	1 08	1 01
12	2 15	2 10	2 05	1 59	1 53	1 47	1 40
13	3 00	2 55	2 50	2 44	2 38	2 31	2 23
14	3 49	3 44	3 39	3 33	3 27	3 20	3 12
15	4 41	4 36	4 31	4 25	4 19	4 13	4 06
16	5 34	5 30	5 25	5 21	5 15	5 10	5 04
17	6 29	6 25	6 22	6 18	6 13	6 09	6 04
18	7 24	7 22	7 19	7 16	7 13	7 09	7 06
19	8 20	8 18	8 17	8 15	8 13	8 11	8 08
20	9 17	9 16	9 15	9 15	9 14	9 13	9 12
21	10 14	10 14	10 15	10 15	10 16	10 16	10 17
22	11 13	11 14	11 16	11 17	11 19	11 21	11 23
23	12 13	12 16	12 18	12 21	12 24	12 27	12 31
24	13 15	13 19	13 22	13 26	13 31	13 35	13 41
25	14 19	14 23	14 28	14 33	14 38	14 44	14 51

Lat.	+40°	+42°	+44°	+46°	+48°	+50°	+52°
	h m	h m	h m	h m	h m	h m	h m
July 24	13 15	13 19	13 22	13 26	13 31	13 35	13 41
25	14 19	14 23	14 28	14 33	14 38	14 44	14 51
26	15 23	15 28	15 33	15 39	15 45	15 52	15 59
27	16 26	16 31	16 36	16 42	16 49	16 56	17 04
28	17 25	17 30	17 35	17 41	17 47	17 54	18 01
29	18 19	18 23	18 28	18 33	18 38	18 44	18 50
30	19 07	19 11	19 14	19 18	19 22	19 27	19 32
31	19 50	19 53	19 55	19 58	20 01	20 04	20 07
Aug. 1	20 30	20 31	20 32	20 33	20 35	20 36	20 38
2	21 07	21 07	21 06	21 06	21 06	21 06	21 06
3	21 42	21 41	21 40	21 38	21 37	21 35	21 34
4	22 18	22 16	22 13	22 11	22 08	22 05	22 02
5	22 55	22 51	22 48	22 44	22 40	22 36	22 31
6	23 33	23 29	23 25	23 20	23 15	23 10	23 04
7	..	..	..	..	..	23 54	23 48	23 41
8	0 15	0 10	0 05	0 00	..	..	..
9	0 59	0 54	0 49	0 43	0 37	0 30	0 23
10	1 46	1 41	1 36	1 30	1 24	1 17	1 09
11	2 37	2 32	2 27	2 21	2 15	2 09	2 01
12	3 29	3 25	3 20	3 15	3 10	3 04	2 57
13	4 23	4 20	4 16	4 12	4 07	4 02	3 57
14	5 19	5 16	5 13	5 10	5 06	5 02	4 58
15	6 15	6 13	6 11	6 08	6 06	6 03	6 01
16	7 11	7 10	7 09	7 08	7 07	7 06	7 04
17	8 08	8 08	8 08	8 09	8 09	8 09	8 09

Moonset

Lat.	+40°	+42°	+44°	+46°	+48°	+50°	+52°
	h m	h m	h m	h m	h m	h m	h m
July 1	5 00	4 55	4 50	4 44	4 38	4 31	4 23
2	6 10	6 05	6 01	5 55	5 50	5 44	5 37
3	7 22	7 18	7 14	7 10	7 06	7 01	6 56
4	8 33	8 31	8 29	8 26	8 23	8 20	8 16
5	9 44	9 42	9 41	9 40	9 38	9 37	9 35
6	10 51	10 51	10 51	10 51	10 51	10 52	10 52
7	11 57	11 58	11 59	12 01	12 02	12 04	12 05
8	13 00	13 02	13 05	13 07	13 10	13 13	13 17
9	14 01	14 04	14 08	14 12	14 16	14 20	14 25
10	15 00	15 04	15 08	15 13	15 18	15 24	15 30
11	15 56	16 01	16 06	16 11	16 17	16 24	16 31
12	16 49	16 54	17 00	17 05	17 12	17 19	17 26
13	17 38	17 43	17 49	17 55	18 01	18 08	18 16
14	18 23	18 28	18 33	18 39	18 45	18 52	18 59
15	19 04	19 09	19 13	19 18	19 24	19 30	19 36
16	19 42	19 45	19 49	19 53	19 58	20 03	20 08
17	20 16	20 19	20 22	20 25	20 29	20 32	20 37
18	20 49	20 49	20 52	20 54	20 56	20 59	21 02
19	21 18	21 19	21 20	21 21	21 23	21 24	21 26
20	21 48	21 48	21 48	21 48	21 48	21 48	21 48
21	22 17	22 16	22 15	22 14	22 13	22 12
22	22 50	22 48	22 46	22 44	22 41	22 39	22 36
23	23 24	23 21	23 18	23 15	23 12	23 08	23 04
24	..	..	23 59	23 55	23 51	23 46	23 41	23 36
25	0 03	..	..	..	..	..	..

Lat.	+40°	+42°	+44°	+46°	+48°	+50°	+52°
	h m	h m	h m	h m	h m	h m	h m
July 24		23 59	23 55	23 51	23 46	23 41	23 36
25	0 03	..	..	..	..	..	..
26	0 48	0 43	0 38	0 33	0 28	0 21	0 15
27	1 39	1 34	1 29	1 23	1 17	1 10	1 02
28	2 39	2 34	2 28	2 22	2 16	2 09	2 01
29	3 45	3 40	3 35	3 29	3 23	3 17	3 10
30	4 56	4 52	4 48	4 43	4 38	4 32	4 26
31	6 09	6 06	6 03	5 59	5 56	5 52	5 47
Aug. 1	7 22	7 20	7 18	7 16	7 14	7 12	7 09
2	8 33	8 33	8 32	8 31	8 31	8 30	8 29
3	9 42	9 43	9 43	9 44	9 45	9 46	9 47
4	10 48	10 50	10 52	10 54	10 56	10 59	11 01
5	11 52	11 55	11 58	12 01	12 05	12 08	12 13
6	12 53	12 56	13 00	13 05	13 09	13 14	13 20
7	13 50	13 55	14 00	14 05	14 10	14 16	14 23
8	14 45	14 50	14 55	15 01	15 07	15 13	15 21
9	15 35	15 40	15 46	15 51	15 58	16 05	16 12
10	16 22	16 27	16 32	16 37	16 44	16 50	16 58
11	17 04	17 08	17 13	17 18	17 24	17 30	17 37
12	17 42	17 46	17 51	17 55	18 00	18 05	18 11
13	18 18	18 21	18 24	18 28	18 32	18 36	18 41
14	18 50	18 53	18 55	18 58	19 01	19 04	19 07
15	19 21	19 23	19 24	19 26	19 28	19 30	19 32
16	19 52	19 52	19 53	19 53	19 54	19 54	19 55
17	20 22	20 21	20 21	20 20	20 19	20 19	20 18

1996 Musky Hunter's Almanac

Moonrise

Lat.	+40°	+42°	+44°	+46°	+48°	+50°	+52°
	h m	h m	h m	h m	h m	h m	h m
Aug. 16	7 11	7 10	7 09	7 08	7 07	7 06	7 04
17	8 08	8 08	8 08	8 09	8 09	8 09	8 09
18	9 06	9 08	9 09	9 10	9 11	9 13	9 14
19	10 06	10 08	10 10	10 12	10 15	10 18	10 21
20	11 06	11 09	11 12	11 16	11 20	11 24	11 28
21	12 08	12 12	12 16	12 20	12 25	12 31	12 36
22	13 10	13 14	13 19	13 24	13 30	13 37	13 44
23	14 11	14 16	14 21	14 27	14 33	14 40	14 48
24	15 09	15 15	15 20	15 26	15 32	15 39	15 47
25	16 04	16 09	16 14	16 19	16 25	16 31	16 38
26	16 55	16 58	17 03	17 07	17 12	17 17	17 23
27	17 40	17 43	17 46	17 49	17 53	17 57	18 01
28	18 22	18 23	18 25	18 27	18 29	18 32	18 34
29	19 00	19 01	19 01	19 02	19 03	19 03	19 04
30	19 38	19 37	19 36	19 35	19 35	19 34	19 33
31	20 14	20 13	20 11	20 09	20 06	20 04	20 02
Sept. 1	20 52	20 49	20 46	20 43	20 39	20 36	20 32
2	21 31	21 27	21 23	21 19	21 14	21 09	21 04
3	22 12	22 08	22 03	21 58	21 52	21 46	21 40
4	22 56	22 51	22 46	22 40	22 34	22 28	22 21
5	23 43	23 38	23 32	23 27	23 20	23 13	23 06
6	.. ..	.. ..	.. ..	.. ..	.. ..	.. ..	23 56
7	0 32	0 27	0 22	0 16	0 10	0 04	.. ..
8	1 24	1 19	1 15	1 09	1 04	0 58	0 51
9	2 17	2 14	2 09	2 05	2 00	1 55	1 49

Lat.	+40°	+42°	+44°	+46°	+48°	+50°	+52°
	h m	h m	h m	h m	h m	h m	h m
Sept. 8	1 24	1 19	1 15	1 09	1 04	0 58	0 51
9	2 17	2 14	2 09	2 05	2 00	1 55	1 49
10	3 12	3 09	3 06	3 02	2 58	2 54	2 50
11	4 08	4 06	4 03	4 01	3 58	3 55	3 52
12	5 05	5 03	5 02	5 01	4 59	4 57	4 55
13	6 02	6 02	6 02	6 01	6 01	6 00	6 00
14	7 00	7 01	7 02	7 03	7 04	7 05	7 06
15	8 00	8 02	8 03	8 05	8 08	8 10	8 13
16	9 00	9 03	9 06	9 09	9 12	9 16	9 20
17	10 01	10 05	10 09	10 13	10 18	10 22	10 28
18	11 02	11 07	11 12	11 17	11 22	11 28	11 35
19	12 03	12 08	12 13	12 19	12 25	12 31	12 39
20	13 01	13 06	13 11	13 17	13 23	13 30	13 38
21	13 55	14 00	14 05	14 11	14 17	14 23	14 31
22	14 46	14 50	14 54	14 59	15 04	15 10	15 16
23	15 31	15 35	15 38	15 42	15 46	15 51	15 56
24	16 14	16 16	16 18	16 21	16 24	16 27	16 30
25	16 53	16 54	16 55	16 57	16 58	16 59	17 01
26	17 30	17 30	17 30	17 30	17 30	17 30	17 30
27	18 07	18 06	18 05	18 04	18 02	18 01	17 59
28	18 45	18 43	18 40	18 38	18 35	18 32	18 29
29	19 24	19 21	19 17	19 14	19 10	19 05	19 00
30	20 05	20 01	19 57	19 52	19 47	19 42	19 36
Oct. 1	20 49	20 44	20 39	20 34	20 28	20 22	20 15
2	21 36	21 31	21 25	21 20	21 14	21 07	20 59

Moonset

Lat.	+40°	+42°	+44°	+46°	+48°	+50°	+52°
	h m	h m	h m	h m	h m	h m	h m
Aug. 16	19 52	19 52	19 53	19 53	19 54	19 54	19 55
17	20 22	20 21	20 21	20 20	20 19	20 19	20 18
18	20 53	20 51	20 50	20 48	20 46	20 44	20 42
19	21 26	21 24	21 21	21 18	21 15	21 12	21 08
20	22 03	21 59	21 56	21 52	21 47	21 43	21 38
21	22 44	22 39	22 35	22 30	22 25	22 19	22 13
22	23 31	23 26	23 21	23 15	23 09	23 03	22 55
23	.. ..	.. ..	.. ..	.. ..	.. ..	23 55	23 47
24	0 24	0 19	0 14	0 08	0 02	.. ..	.. ..
25	1 25	1 20	1 15	1 09	1 03	0 56	0 49
26	2 32	2 28	2 23	2 18	2 12	2 06	1 59
27	3 43	3 39	3 36	3 31	3 27	3 22	3 17
28	4 56	4 53	4 51	4 48	4 45	4 41	4 38
29	6 08	6 07	6 06	6 04	6 03	6 01	6 00
30	7 20	7 20	7 20	7 20	7 20	7 20	7 20
31	8 29	8 30	8 31	8 33	8 34	8 36	8 38
Sept. 1	9 36	9 38	9 41	9 43	9 46	9 49	9 53
2	10 40	10 43	10 47	10 50	10 55	10 59	11 04
3	11 40	11 44	11 49	11 54	11 59	12 04	12 11
4	12 37	12 42	12 47	12 52	12 58	13 05	13 12
5	13 30	13 35	13 40	13 46	13 52	13 59	14 06
6	14 18	14 23	14 28	14 34	14 40	14 47	14 54
7	15 02	15 06	15 11	15 17	15 23	15 29	15 36
8	15 42	15 46	15 50	15 55	16 00	16 06	16 12
9	16 18	16 22	16 25	16 29	16 33	16 38	16 43

Lat.	+40°	+42°	+44°	+46°	+48°	+50°	+52°
	h m	h m	h m	h m	h m	h m	h m
Sept. 8	15 42	15 46	15 50	15 55	16 00	16 06	16 12
9	16 18	16 22	16 25	16 29	16 33	16 38	16 43
10	16 52	16 54	16 57	17 00	17 03	17 07	17 11
11	17 24	17 25	17 27	17 29	17 31	17 33	17 36
12	17 54	17 55	17 56	17 57	17 58	17 59	18 00
13	18 25	18 25	18 24	18 24	18 24	18 24	18 23
14	18 56	18 55	18 53	18 52	18 51	18 49	18 47
15	19 29	19 27	19 24	19 22	19 19	19 16	19 13
16	20 04	20 01	19 58	19 54	19 50	19 46	19 42
17	20 44	20 40	20 36	20 31	20 26	20 21	20 15
18	21 28	21 23	21 19	21 13	21 08	21 01	20 54
19	22 18	22 13	22 08	22 02	21 56	21 49	21 42
20	23 15	23 10	23 04	22 59	22 52	22 45	22 38
21	.. ..	.. ..	.. ..	.. ..	.. ..	23 56	23 50
22	0 17	0 12	0 07	0 02	.. ..	.. ..	.. ..
23	1 24	1 20	1 16	1 11	1 06	1 01	0 55
24	2 33	2 30	2 27	2 24	2 20	2 16	2 12
25	3 44	3 42	3 41	3 38	3 36	3 34	3 31
26	4 55	4 55	4 54	4 53	4 53	4 52	4 51
27	6 05	6 06	6 07	6 07	6 08	6 09	6 10
28	7 14	7 16	7 18	7 20	7 22	7 25	7 27
29	8 21	8 24	8 27	8 30	8 34	8 37	8 42
30	9 24	9 28	9 32	9 37	9 41	9 47	9 52
Oct. 1	10 25	10 29	10 34	10 39	10 45	10 51	10 57
2	11 20	11 25	11 30	11 36	11 42	11 49	11 56

Moonrise And Moonset

Moonrise

Lat.	+40°	+42°	+44°	+46°	+48°	+50°	+52°
	h m	h m	h m	h m	h m	h m	h m
Oct. 1	20 49	20 44	20 39	20 34	20 28	20 22	20 15
2	21 36	21 31	21 25	21 20	21 14	21 07	20 59
3	22 25	22 20	22 15	22 09	22 03	21 56	21 49
4	23 16	23 12	23 07	23 01	22 56	22 49	22 42
5	.. ..	.. ..	.. ..	23 56	23 51	23 45	23 39
6	0 09	0 05	0 01	.. ..	.. ..	.. ..	.. ..
7	1 04	1 00	0 57	0 53	0 49	0 44	0 39
8	1 59	1 57	1 54	1 51	1 48	1 44	1 40
9	2 56	2 54	2 52	2 50	2 48	2 46	2 43
10	3 53	3 52	3 51	3 51	3 50	3 49	3 48
11	4 51	4 51	4 52	4 52	4 53	4 53	4 54
12	5 51	5 52	5 54	5 55	5 57	5 59	6 01
13	6 52	6 54	6 57	7 00	7 03	7 06	7 09
14	7 54	7 57	8 01	8 05	8 09	8 13	8 18
15	8 56	9 00	9 05	9 10	9 15	9 21	9 27
16	9 57	10 02	10 07	10 13	10 19	10 25	10 33
17	10 57	11 02	11 07	11 13	11 19	11 26	11 34
18	11 52	11 57	12 02	12 08	12 14	12 21	12 28
19	12 43	12 47	12 52	12 57	13 02	13 08	13 15
20	13 29	13 32	13 36	13 40	13 45	13 50	13 55
21	14 10	14 13	14 16	14 19	14 22	14 26	14 30
22	14 49	14 51	14 53	14 55	14 56	14 59	15 01
23	15 26	15 27	15 27	15 28	15 28	15 29	15 30
24	16 02	16 02	16 01	16 00	15 59	15 59	15 58
25	16 39	16 37	16 35	16 33	16 31	16 29	16 26

Lat.	+40°	+42°	+44°	+46°	+48°	+50°	+52°
	h m	h m	h m	h m	h m	h m	h m
Oct. 24	16 02	16 02	16 01	16 00	15 59	15 59	15 58
25	16 39	16 37	16 35	16 33	16 31	16 29	16 26
26	17 17	17 14	17 11	17 08	17 04	17 01	16 56
27	17 57	17 53	17 49	17 45	17 40	17 35	17 30
28	18 40	18 35	18 31	18 26	18 20	18 14	18 08
29	19 26	19 21	19 16	19 10	19 04	18 58	18 50
30	20 15	20 10	20 05	19 59	19 53	19 46	19 38
31	21 06	21 01	20 56	20 51	20 45	20 38	20 31
Nov. 1	21 59	21 55	21 50	21 45	21 40	21 34	21 27
2	22 53	22 50	22 46	22 41	22 37	22 32	22 26
3	23 48	23 45	23 42	23 39	23 35	23 31	23 27
4	.. ..	.. ..	.. ..	.. ..	.. ..	.. ..	.. ..
5	0 44	0 42	0 40	0 37	0 35	0 32	0 29
6	1 41	1 39	1 38	1 37	1 36	1 34	1 33
7	2 38	2 38	2 38	2 38	2 38	2 38	2 37
8	3 37	3 38	3 39	3 40	3 41	3 43	3 44
9	4 38	4 40	4 42	4 44	4 47	4 49	4 52
10	5 40	5 43	5 46	5 50	5 54	5 58	6 02
11	6 44	6 48	6 52	6 56	7 01	7 07	7 13
12	7 47	7 52	7 57	8 02	8 08	8 15	8 22
13	8 49	8 54	9 00	9 06	9 12	9 19	9 26
14	9 48	9 53	9 58	10 04	10 10	10 17	10 25
15	10 41	10 45	10 50	10 56	11 02	11 08	11 15
16	11 29	11 33	11 37	11 41	11 46	11 52	11 58
17	12 12	12 15	12 18	12 21	12 25	12 29	12 34

Moonset

Lat.	+40°	+42°	+44°	+46°	+48°	+50°	+52°
	h m	h m	h m	h m	h m	h m	h m
Oct. 1	10 25	10 29	10 34	10 39	10 45	10 51	10 57
2	11 20	11 25	11 30	11 36	11 42	11 49	11 56
3	12 11	12 16	12 22	12 27	12 34	12 40	12 48
4	12 58	13 02	13 07	13 13	13 19	13 25	13 32
5	13 39	13 43	13 48	13 53	13 58	14 04	14 11
6	14 17	14 21	14 25	14 29	14 33	14 38	14 44
7	14 52	14 54	14 58	15 01	15 05	15 08	15 13
8	15 24	15 26	15 28	15 31	15 33	15 36	15 39
9	15 55	15 56	15 57	15 59	16 00	16 01	16 03
10	16 26	16 26	16 26	16 26	16 26	16 27	16 27
11	16 57	16 56	16 55	16 54	16 53	16 52	16 51
12	17 29	17 27	17 26	17 23	17 21	17 19	17 16
13	18 04	18 02	17 59	17 55	17 52	17 48	17 44
14	18 43	18 39	18 35	18 31	18 27	18 22	18 16
15	19 26	19 22	19 17	19 12	19 07	19 01	18 54
16	20 15	20 10	20 05	19 59	19 53	19 47	19 39
17	21 10	21 05	20 59	20 53	20 47	20 40	20 33
18	22 10	22 05	22 00	21 54	21 48	21 41	21 34
19	23 14	23 09	23 05	23 00	22 55	22 49	22 43
20	.. ..	.. ..	.. ..	.. ..	.. ..	.. ..	23 56
21	0 20	0 17	0 14	0 10	0 06	0 01	.. ..
22	1 29	1 26	1 24	1 21	1 19	1 16	1 12
23	2 37	2 36	2 35	2 34	2 32	2 31	2 29
24	3 46	3 46	3 46	3 46	3 46	3 46	3 47
25	4 54	4 55	4 56	4 58	5 00	5 01	5 03

Lat.	+40°	+42°	+44°	+46°	+48°	+50°	+52°
	h m	h m	h m	h m	h m	h m	h m
Oct. 24	3 46	3 46	3 46	3 46	3 46	3 46	3 47
25	4 54	4 55	4 56	4 58	5 00	5 01	5 03
26	6 01	6 03	6 06	6 08	6 11	6 15	6 18
27	7 06	7 09	7 13	7 17	7 21	7 26	7 31
28	8 09	8 13	8 17	8 22	8 27	8 33	8 39
29	9 07	9 12	9 17	9 23	9 29	9 35	9 42
30	10 02	10 07	10 12	10 18	10 24	10 31	10 38
31	10 51	10 56	11 01	11 07	11 13	11 19	11 27
Nov. 1	11 35	11 39	11 44	11 50	11 55	12 01	12 08
2	12 14	12 18	12 23	12 27	12 32	12 38	12 44
3	12 50	12 54	12 57	13 01	13 05	13 09	13 14
4	13 23	13 26	13 28	13 31	13 34	13 38	13 41
5	13 55	13 56	13 58	14 00	14 02	14 04	14 06
6	14 25	14 26	14 26	14 27	14 28	14 28	14 29
7	14 56	14 55	14 55	14 54	14 54	14 53	14 53
8	15 27	15 26	15 25	15 23	15 21	15 19	15 17
9	16 01	15 59	15 56	15 54	15 51	15 48	15 44
10	16 39	16 36	16 32	16 28	16 24	16 20	16 15
11	17 21	17 17	17 12	17 08	17 02	16 57	16 51
12	18 09	18 04	17 59	17 53	17 47	17 41	17 34
13	19 03	18 58	18 52	18 46	18 40	18 33	18 25
14	20 02	19 57	19 52	19 46	19 40	19 33	19 26
15	21 06	21 02	20 57	20 52	20 46	20 40	20 33
16	22 13	22 09	22 05	22 01	21 56	21 51	21 46
17	23 20	23 18	23 15	23 12	23 08	23 05	23 01

1996 Musky Hunter's Almanac

Moonrise

Lat.	+40°	+42°	+44°	+46°	+48°	+50°	+52°
	h m	h m	h m	h m	h m	h m	h m
Nov. 16	11 29	11 33	11 37	11 41	11 46	11 52	11 58
17	12 12	12 15	12 18	12 21	12 25	12 29	12 34
18	12 51	12 53	12 55	12 57	13 00	13 02	13 05
19	13 27	13 28	13 29	13 30	13 31	13 32	13 34
20	14 02	14 02	14 02	14 02	14 01	14 01	14 01
21	14 37	14 36	14 35	14 33	14 31	14 30	14 28
22	15 13	15 11	15 09	15 06	15 03	15 00	14 56
23	15 52	15 48	15 45	15 41	15 37	15 32	15 27
24	16 33	16 28	16 24	16 19	16 14	16 09	16 02
25	17 17	17 12	17 07	17 02	16 56	16 49	16 42
26	18 05	18 00	17 54	17 49	17 42	17 35	17 28
27	18 55	18 50	18 45	18 39	18 33	18 26	18 19
28	19 48	19 44	19 39	19 33	19 27	19 21	19 14
29	20 42	20 38	20 34	20 29	20 24	20 19	20 12
30	21 37	21 34	21 30	21 27	21 22	21 18	21 13
Dec. 1	22 33	22 30	22 27	22 25	22 21	22 18	22 14
2	23 28	23 27	23 25	23 23	23 21	23 19	23 17
3	.. ..	.. ..	.. ..	.. ..	.. ..	.. ..	.. ..
4	0 25	0 24	0 23	0 23	0 22	0 21	0 20
5	1 22	1 23	1 23	1 23	1 24	1 25	1 25
6	2 21	2 23	2 24	2 26	2 28	2 30	2 32
7	3 22	3 25	3 27	3 30	3 33	3 37	3 40
8	4 25	4 29	4 32	4 36	4 41	4 45	4 50
9	5 29	5 34	5 38	5 43	5 49	5 55	6 01
10	6 33	6 38	6 44	6 49	6 56	7 02	7 10

Lat.	+40°	+42°	+44°	+46°	+48°	+50°	+52°
	h m	h m	h m	h m	h m	h m	h m
Dec. 9	5 29	5 34	5 38	5 43	5 49	5 55	6 01
10	6 33	6 38	6 44	6 49	6 56	7 02	7 10
11	7 35	7 41	7 46	7 52	7 58	8 05	8 13
12	8 33	8 38	8 43	8 49	8 55	9 02	9 09
13	9 25	9 29	9 34	9 39	9 44	9 50	9 57
14	10 11	10 15	10 18	10 22	10 27	10 31	10 36
15	10 53	10 55	10 57	11 00	11 03	11 06	11 10
16	11 30	11 32	11 33	11 34	11 36	11 38	11 40
17	12 06	12 06	12 06	12 06	12 06	12 07	12 07
18	12 40	12 39	12 38	12 37	12 36	12 35	12 34
19	13 15	13 13	13 11	13 09	13 06	13 04	13 01
20	13 52	13 49	13 46	13 42	13 38	13 34	13 30
21	14 31	14 27	14 23	14 18	14 13	14 08	14 03
22	15 13	15 08	15 03	14 58	14 52	14 46	14 40
23	15 58	15 53	15 48	15 42	15 36	15 29	15 22
24	16 47	16 42	16 37	16 31	16 25	16 18	16 10
25	17 39	17 34	17 29	17 23	17 17	17 11	17 03
26	18 33	18 28	18 24	18 19	18 13	18 07	18 00
27	19 28	19 24	19 20	19 16	19 11	19 06	19 00
28	20 23	20 20	20 17	20 13	20 10	20 06	20 02
29	21 18	21 16	21 14	21 12	21 09	21 07	21 04
30	22 14	22 13	22 12	22 11	22 09	22 08	22 06
31	23 10	23 10	23 10	23 10	23 10	23 10	23 10
32	.. ..	.. ..	.. ..	.. ..	.. ..	.. ..	.. ..
33	0 07	0 08	0 09	0 10	0 11	0 13	0 14

Moonset

Lat.	+40°	+42°	+44°	+46°	+48°	+50°	+52°
	h m	h m	h m	h m	h m	h m	h m
Nov. 16	22 13	22 09	22 05	22 01	21 56	21 51	21 46
17	23 20	23 18	23 15	23 12	23 08	23 05	23 01
18	.. ..	.. ..	.. ..	.. ..	.. ..	.. ..	.. ..
19	0 28	0 26	0 25	0 23	0 21	0 19	0 17
20	1 35	1 34	1 34	1 34	1 33	1 33	1 32
21	2 41	2 42	2 43	2 44	2 45	2 46	2 47
22	3 47	3 49	3 51	3 53	3 55	3 58	4 01
23	4 51	4 54	4 57	5 01	5 04	5 08	5 13
24	5 54	5 58	6 02	6 06	6 11	6 17	6 22
25	6 54	6 59	7 04	7 09	7 15	7 21	7 28
26	7 51	7 56	8 01	8 07	8 13	8 20	8 27
27	8 43	8 48	8 53	8 59	9 05	9 12	9 20
28	9 29	9 34	9 39	9 45	9 51	9 57	10 05
29	10 11	10 16	10 20	10 25	10 31	10 36	10 43
30	10 49	10 53	10 57	11 01	11 05	11 10	11 15
Dec. 1	11 23	11 26	11 29	11 32	11 36	11 40	11 44
2	11 55	11 57	11 59	12 01	12 04	12 06	12 09
3	12 25	12 26	12 27	12 29	12 30	12 31	12 33
4	12 55	12 55	12 55	12 55	12 55	12 56	12 56
5	13 26	13 25	13 24	13 23	13 22	13 20	13 19
6	13 58	13 56	13 54	13 52	13 49	13 47	13 44
7	14 33	14 30	14 27	14 24	14 20	14 16	14 12
8	15 13	15 09	15 05	15 00	14 56	14 51	14 45
9	15 58	15 53	15 48	15 43	15 37	15 31	15 24
10	16 50	16 45	16 39	16 33	16 27	16 20	16 13

Lat.	+40°	+42°	+44°	+46°	+48°	+50°	+52°
	h m	h m	h m	h m	h m	h m	h m
Dec. 9	15 58	15 53	15 48	15 43	15 37	15 31	15 24
10	16 50	16 45	16 39	16 33	16 27	16 20	16 13
11	17 48	17 43	17 38	17 32	17 25	17 18	17 11
12	18 53	18 48	18 43	18 37	18 31	18 25	18 18
13	20 01	19 57	19 52	19 48	19 43	19 37	19 31
14	21 10	21 07	21 04	21 00	20 56	20 52	20 48
15	22 19	22 17	22 15	22 13	22 11	22 08	22 05
16	23 27	23 26	23 25	23 25	23 24	23 23	23 22
17	.. ..	.. ..	.. ..	.. ..	.. ..	.. ..	.. ..
18	0 34	0 34	0 34	0 35	0 35	0 36	0 37
19	1 39	1 40	1 42	1 44	1 46	1 48	1 50
20	2 42	2 45	2 48	2 51	2 54	2 58	3 01
21	3 45	3 48	3 52	3 56	4 01	4 05	4 11
22	4 45	4 49	4 54	4 59	5 04	5 10	5 17
23	5 42	5 47	5 52	5 58	6 04	6 10	6 18
24	6 35	6 40	6 46	6 52	6 58	7 05	7 13
25	7 24	7 29	7 34	7 40	7 46	7 53	8 01
26	8 08	8 13	8 18	8 23	8 29	8 35	8 42
27	8 48	8 52	8 56	9 01	9 06	9 11	9 17
28	9 24	9 27	9 30	9 34	9 38	9 42	9 47
29	9 56	9 59	10 01	10 04	10 07	10 10	10 14
30	10 27	10 28	10 30	10 32	10 34	10 36	10 38
31	10 57	10 58	10 58	10 59	11 00	11 00	11 01
32	11 26	11 26	11 25	11 25	11 24	11 24	11 23
33	11 57	11 55	11 54	11 52	11 50	11 49	11 47

All About The Sun

*H*ere are definitions about the sun that you'll need to know about the sun and its rising and setting, and how this may apply to your musky fishing.

- Sunrise and Sunset Times: The instant in time of the visible rising or setting of the sun's upper edge by someone standing at sea level with an unobstructed view of the horizon.

- Latitude: Describes the position of a point on the earth's surface in relation to the equator.
  These imaginary lines are measured in degrees. The equator is 0 degrees rising to 90 degrees at the North Pole. Most musky waters lie between 35 and 55 degrees latitude.

- Longitude: Describes the position of a point on the earth's surface in relation to the Meridian of Greenwich. These imaginary lines that run north-south are measured in degrees. Greenwich is 0 degrees. A point halfway around the world is 180 degrees.

SUNRISE AND SUNSET

*T*he times of sunrise and sunset are the instants when the upper edge of the sun appears to lie on the horizon for an observer at sea level. The accompanying tables identify these times for varying degrees of latitude. The tables list times for 35 degrees latitude and then 40 degrees latitude through 52 degrees of latitude in 2 degree increments. Longitude has no significant effect on sunrise and sunset times for our purpose.

Times are listed at three- to four-day intervals. Because the Earth orbits the sun at a relatively slow rate of speed the change in times on a daily basis is insignificant from the fisherman's point of view. You may note that the difference in sunrise times at 35 degrees from January 1, 1996 to January 3, 1996 is only 1 minute. To the contrary, the tables that list moonrise and moonset times (elsewhere in the *Almanac*) do so on a daily basis because the daily changes can be hours as opposed to minutes. This is because the moon orbits the earth at a relatively fast rate of speed.

All times listed are already adjusted for local time zones but not daylight savings time. Clocks are turned ahead 1 hour on April 7, 1996 and back 1 hour October 27, 1996.

If you would like to determine the time for a latitude that is not specifically listed, say 43 degrees on January 1, 1996, simply extrapolate the midway point for the times listed at 42 degrees and 44 degrees for the same day. For example:

January 1, 1996 at 42 degrees latitude sunrise happens at 7:28 a.m.

January 1, 1996 at 44 degrees latitude sunrise happens at 7:34

a.m.

The sunrise occurs 6 minutes later at 44 degrees. We can conclude from this that at 43 degrees (halfway between 42 and 44) the sun would rise at 7:31 a.m. (halfway between 7:28 a.m. and 7:34 a.m.)

• • •

Larry's Lesson — If your released musky has trouble going down after you let it go (you can tell if they try to dive and are unable to do so), you can "BURP" them by simply regaining control of them, pull them gently to the side of the boat and while steadying the fish with one hand use the other to push the stomach from the rear toward the head, thereby forcing out excess air. Muskies that I have used this technique on have immediately been able to swim off and dive.

• • •

Did You Know — An unscientific but nonetheless very reliable way of differentiating between pike and muskies is a quick visual check of the fish's color pattern. Pike have light spots on a dark background while muskies will have dark markings on a light background. Except for very rare cases (the silver pike) fish with no markings will also be muskies.

1996 Musky Hunter's Almanac

1996 Sunrise Times - A.M.

Latitude		35°		40°		42°		44°		46°		48°		50°		52°	
		h	m	h	m	h	m	h	m	h	m	h	m	h	m	h	m
January	1	7	07	7	21	7	28	7	34	7	42	7	50	7	59	8	08
	3	7	08	7	22	7	28	7	35	7	42	7	50	7	58	8	08
	7	7	09	7	22	7	28	7	35	7	42	7	49	7	58	8	07
	11	7	08	7	22	7	27	7	34	7	40	7	48	7	56	8	05
	15	7	08	7	20	7	26	7	32	7	38	7	46	7	53	8	02
	19	7	07	7	19	7	24	7	30	7	36	7	43	7	50	7	58
	23	7	05	7	16	7	21	7	27	7	33	7	39	7	46	7	54
	27	7	03	7	14	7	18	7	23	7	29	7	35	7	41	7	48
	31	7	00	7	10	7	15	7	19	7	25	7	30	7	36	7	43
February	4	6	57	7	06	7	11	7	15	7	20	7	25	7	30	7	36
	8	6	54	7	02	7	06	7	10	7	14	7	19	7	24	7	30
	12	6	50	6	58	7	01	7	05	7	09	7	13	7	17	7	22
	16	6	46	6	53	6	56	6	59	7	02	7	06	7	10	7	15
	20	6	41	6	47	6	50	6	53	6	56	6	59	7	03	7	07
	24	6	37	6	42	6	44	6	47	6	49	6	52	6	55	6	58
	28	6	32	6	36	6	38	6	40	6	42	6	45	6	47	6	50
March	3	6	27	6	30	6	32	6	33	6	35	6	37	6	39	6	41
	7	6	21	6	24	6	25	6	26	6	28	6	29	6	30	6	32
	11	6	16	6	18	6	18	6	19	6	20	6	21	6	22	6	23
	15	6	10	6	11	6	12	6	12	6	12	6	13	6	13	6	14
	19	6	05	6	05	6	05	6	05	6	05	6	05	6	05	6	05
	23	5	59	5	58	5	58	5	58	5	57	5	56	5	56	5	55
	27	5	54	5	52	5	51	5	50	5	49	5	48	5	47	5	46
	31	5	48	5	45	5	44	5	43	5	42	5	40	5	39	5	37
April	4	5	43	5	39	5	37	5	36	5	34	5	32	5	30	5	28
	8	6	37	6	33	6	31	6	29	6	26	6	24	6	21	6	19
	12	6	32	6	27	6	24	6	22	6	19	6	16	6	13	6	10
	16	6	27	6	20	6	18	6	15	6	12	6	08	6	05	6	01
	20	6	22	6	15	6	12	6	08	6	05	6	01	5	57	5	52
	24	6	17	6	09	6	06	6	02	5	58	5	54	5	49	6	44
	28	6	12	6	04	6	00	5	56	5	51	5	47	5	41	5	36
May	2	6	08	5	59	5	54	5	50	5	45	5	40	5	34	5	28
	6	6	04	5	54	5	49	5	45	5	39	5	34	5	28	5	21
	10	6	00	5	50	5	45	5	40	5	34	5	28	5	21	5	14
	14	5	57	5	46	5	40	5	35	5	29	5	22	5	15	5	07
	18	5	54	5	42	5	37	5	31	5	24	5	17	5	10	5	01
	22	5	52	5	39	5	33	5	27	5	20	5	13	5	05	4	56
	26	5	50	5	36	5	30	5	24	5	17	5	09	5	01	4	51
	30	5	48	5	34	5	28	5	21	5	14	5	06	5	57	4	47
June	3	5	47	5	32	5	26	5	19	5	12	5	03	4	54	4	44
	7	5	46	5	31	5	25	5	18	5	10	5	02	4	52	4	42
	11	5	45	5	31	5	24	5	17	5	09	5	00	4	51	4	40
	15	5	46	5	31	5	24	5	16	5	09	5	00	4	50	4	39
	19	5	46	5	31	5	24	5	17	5	09	5	00	4	50	4	39
	23	5	47	5	32	5	25	5	18	5	10	5	01	4	51	4	40

Sunrise And Sunset

1996 Sunrise Times continued....

Latitude		35°		40°		42°		44°		46°		48°		50°		52°	
		h	m	h	m	h	m	h	m	h	m	h	m	h	m	h	m
June	27	5	48	5	33	5	26	5	19	5	11	5	02	4	53	4	42
July	1	5	50	5	35	5	28	5	21	5	13	5	05	4	55	4	44
	5	5	52	5	37	5	30	5	23	5	16	5	07	4	58	4	48
	9	5	54	5	40	5	33	5	26	5	19	5	11	5	01	4	51
	13	5	56	5	42	5	36	5	29	5	22	5	14	5	05	4	56
	17	5	59	5	45	5	39	5	33	5	26	5	18	5	10	5	01
	21	6	01	5	49	5	43	5	37	5	30	5	23	5	15	5	06
	25	6	04	5	52	5	47	5	41	5	34	5	28	5	20	5	12
	29	6	07	5	56	5	51	5	45	5	39	5	32	5	25	5	17
August	2	6	10	5	59	5	55	5	49	5	44	5	38	5	31	5	24
	6	6	13	6	03	5	59	5	54	5	49	5	43	5	37	5	30
	10	6	16	6	07	6	03	5	58	5	53	5	48	5	42	5	36
	14	6	19	6	11	6	07	6	03	5	58	5	54	5	48	5	43
	18	6	22	6	15	6	11	6	07	6	03	5	59	5	54	5	49
	22	6	25	6	18	6	15	6	12	6	08	6	04	6	00	5	56
	26	6	28	6	22	6	19	6	16	6	13	6	10	6	06	6	02
	30	6	31	6	26	6	24	6	21	6	18	6	15	6	12	6	09
September	3	6	34	6	30	6	28	6	26	6	23	6	21	6	08	6	15
	7	6	37	6	33	6	32	6	30	6	28	6	26	6	24	6	22
	11	6	40	6	37	6	36	6	35	6	33	6	32	6	30	6	28
	15	6	43	6	41	6	40	6	39	6	38	6	37	6	36	6	35
	19	6	46	6	45	6	44	6	44	6	43	6	43	6	42	6	41
	23	6	49	6	49	6	49	6	48	6	48	6	48	6	48	6	48
	27	6	52	6	52	6	53	6	53	6	53	6	54	6	54	6	54
October	1	6	55	6	56	6	57	6	58	6	59	6	59	7	00	7	01
	5	6	58	7	00	7	01	7	03	7	04	7	05	7	06	7	08
	9	7	01	7	04	7	06	7	07	7	09	7	11	7	13	7	15
	13	7	04	7	09	7	10	7	12	7	14	7	17	7	19	7	22
	17	7	08	7	13	7	15	7	17	7	20	7	22	7	25	7	29
	21	7	11	7	17	7	20	7	22	7	25	7	28	7	32	7	36
	25	7	15	7	21	7	24	7	27	7	31	7	34	7	38	7	43
	29	6	18	6	26	6	29	6	33	6	36	6	41	6	45	6	50
November	2	6	22	6	30	6	34	6	38	6	42	6	47	6	52	6	57
	6	6	26	6	35	6	39	6	43	6	48	6	53	6	58	7	04
	10	6	30	6	40	6	44	6	49	6	54	6	59	7	05	7	11
	14	6	34	6	44	6	49	6	54	6	59	7	05	7	11	7	18
	18	6	38	6	49	6	54	6	59	7	05	7	11	7	18	7	25
	22	6	41	6	53	6	59	7	04	7	10	7	17	7	24	7	32
	26	6	45	6	58	7	03	7	09	7	15	7	22	7	30	7	39
	30	6	49	7	02	7	08	7	14	7	20	7	28	7	36	7	45
December	4	6	52	7	06	7	12	7	18	7	25	7	33	7	41	7	50
	8	6	56	7	09	7	15	7	22	7	29	7	37	7	45	7	55
	12	6	59	7	13	7	19	7	26	7	33	7	41	7	50	7	59
	16	7	01	7	16	7	22	7	29	7	36	7	44	7	53	8	03
	20	7	04	7	18	7	24	7	31	7	39	7	47	7	56	8	05
	24	7	06	7	20	7	26	7	33	7	40	7	48	7	57	8	07
	28	7	07	7	21	7	27	7	34	7	42	7	50	7	58	8	08

1996 Musky Hunter's Almanac

1996 Sunset Times - P.M.

Latitude		35°		40°		42°		44°		46°		48°		50°		52°	
		h	m	h	m	h	m	h	m	h	m	h	m	h	m	h	m
January	1	4	57	4	43	4	37	4	30	4	23	4	15	4	06	3	57
	3	5	00	4	47	4	40	4	34	4	27	4	19	4	10	4	01
	7	5	04	4	50	4	44	4	38	4	31	4	23	4	15	4	06
	11	5	07	4	54	4	48	4	42	4	35	4	28	4	20	4	11
	15	5	11	4	58	4	53	4	47	4	40	4	33	4	26	4	17
	19	5	15	5	03	4	58	4	52	4	46	4	39	4	32	4	24
	23	5	19	5	07	5	02	4	57	4	51	4	45	4	38	4	30
	27	5	23	5	12	5	07	5	02	4	57	4	51	4	45	4	37
	31	5	27	5	17	5	13	5	08	5	03	4	57	4	51	4	45
February	4	5	31	5	22	5	18	5	13	5	09	5	04	5	58	4	52
	8	5	35	5	27	5	23	5	19	5	15	5	10	5	05	5	00
	12	5	39	5	31	5	28	5	24	5	21	5	16	5	12	5	07
	16	5	43	5	36	5	33	5	30	5	27	5	23	5	19	5	14
	20	5	47	5	41	5	38	5	35	5	32	5	29	5	26	5	22
	24	5	50	5	45	5	43	5	41	5	38	5	35	5	32	5	29
	28	5	54	5	50	5	48	5	46	5	44	5	42	5	39	5	37
March	3	5	58	5	54	5	53	5	51	5	50	5	48	5	46	5	44
	7	6	01	5	59	5	58	5	56	5	55	5	54	5	52	5	51
	11	6	04	6	03	6	02	6	01	6	01	6	00	5	59	5	58
	15	6	08	6	07	6	07	6	06	6	06	6	06	6	05	6	05
	19	6	11	6	11	6	11	6	11	6	11	6	12	6	12	6	12
	23	6	14	6	15	6	16	6	16	6	17	6	17	6	18	6	19
	27	6	17	6	19	6	20	6	21	6	22	6	23	6	24	6	26
	31	6	21	6	23	6	25	6	26	6	27	6	29	6	31	6	33
April	4	6	24	6	28	6	25	6	31	6	33	6	35	6	37	6	39
	8	7	27	7	32	7	34	7	36	7	38	7	41	7	43	7	46
	12	7	30	7	36	7	38	7	41	7	43	7	46	7	49	7	53
	16	7	33	7	40	7	42	7	45	7	49	7	52	7	56	8	00
	20	7	37	7	44	7	47	7	50	7	54	7	58	8	02	8	07
	24	7	40	7	48	7	51	7	55	7	59	8	03	8	08	8	13
	28	7	43	7	52	7	56	8	00	8	04	8	09	8	14	8	20
May	2	7	46	7	56	8	00	8	05	8	10	8	15	8	21	8	27
	6	7	50	8	00	8	04	8	09	8	15	8	20	8	27	8	34
	10	7	53	8	04	8	09	8	14	8	20	8	26	8	33	8	40
	14	7	56	8	08	8	13	8	18	8	25	8	31	8	38	8	46
	18	7	59	8	11	8	17	8	23	8	29	8	36	8	44	8	52
	22	8	02	8	15	8	21	8	27	8	34	8	41	8	49	8	58
	26	8	05	8	18	8	24	8	31	8	38	8	46	8	54	9	03
	30	8	08	8	21	8	28	8	34	8	42	8	50	8	59	9	08
June	3	8	10	8	24	8	31	8	38	8	45	8	53	9	03	9	13
	7	8	12	8	27	8	33	8	40	8	48	8	57	9	06	9	16
	11	8	14	8	29	8	36	8	43	8	51	8	59	9	09	9	20
	15	8	16	8	31	8	37	8	45	8	53	9	01	9	11	9	22
	19	8	17	8	32	8	39	8	46	8	54	9	03	9	13	9	23
	23	8	18	8	33	8	39	8	47	8	55	9	04	9	13	9	24

Sunrise And Sunset

1996 Sunset Times continued....

Latitude		35°		40°		42°		44°		46°		48°		50°		52°	
		h	m	h	m	h	m	h	m	h	m	h	m	h	m	h	m
June	27	8	18	8	33	8	40	8	47	8	55	9	04	9	13	9	24
July	1	8	18	8	33	8	39	8	47	8	54	9	03	9	12	9	23
	5	8	17	8	32	8	38	8	45	8	53	9	02	9	11	9	21
	9	8	16	8	31	8	37	8	44	8	51	8	59	9	08	9	18
	13	8	15	8	29	8	35	8	42	8	49	8	57	9	05	9	15
	17	8	13	8	26	8	32	8	39	8	46	8	53	9	02	9	11
	21	8	11	8	24	8	29	8	35	8	42	8	49	8	57	9	06
	25	8	08	8	20	8	26	8	32	8	38	8	45	8	52	9	01
	29	8	05	8	17	8	22	8	27	8	33	8	40	8	47	8	54
August	2	8	02	8	12	8	17	8	22	8	28	8	34	8	41	8	48
	6	7	58	8	08	8	12	8	17	8	22	8	28	8	34	8	41
	10	7	54	8	03	8	07	8	12	8	16	8	21	8	27	8	33
	14	7	49	7	58	8	02	8	06	8	10	8	15	8	20	8	25
	18	7	45	7	52	7	56	7	59	8	03	8	08	8	12	8	17
	22	7	40	7	47	7	50	7	53	7	56	8	00	8	04	8	09
	26	7	35	7	41	7	43	7	46	7	49	7	52	7	56	8	00
	30	7	29	7	34	7	37	7	39	7	42	7	45	7	48	7	51
September	3	7	24	7	28	7	30	7	32	7	34	7	37	7	39	7	42
	7	7	18	7	22	7	23	7	25	7	27	7	29	7	31	7	33
	11	7	12	7	15	7	16	7	17	7	19	7	20	7	22	7	24
	15	7	07	7	08	7	09	7	10	7	11	7	12	7	13	7	14
	19	7	01	7	02	7	02	7	03	7	03	7	04	7	04	7	05
	23	6	55	6	55	6	55	6	55	6	55	6	55	6	55	6	56
	27	6	49	6	49	6	48	6	48	6	48	6	47	6	47	6	46
October	1	6	44	6	42	6	41	6	41	6	40	6	39	6	38	6	37
	5	6	38	6	36	6	35	6	33	6	32	6	31	6	29	6	28
	9	6	33	6	29	6	28	6	26	6	25	6	23	6	21	6	19
	13	6	27	6	23	6	21	6	19	6	17	6	15	6	13	6	10
	17	6	22	6	17	6	15	6	13	6	10	6	07	6	04	6	01
	21	6	18	6	12	6	09	6	06	6	03	6	00	5	57	5	53
	25	6	13	6	06	6	03	6	00	5	57	5	53	5	49	5	45
	29	5	09	5	01	4	58	4	54	4	50	4	46	4	42	4	37
November	2	5	05	4	56	4	53	4	49	4	44	4	40	4	35	4	29
	6	5	01	4	52	4	48	4	43	4	39	4	34	4	28	4	22
	10	4	58	4	48	4	44	4	39	4	34	4	28	4	22	4	16
	14	4	55	4	44	4	40	4	35	4	29	4	23	4	17	4	10
	18	4	53	4	41	4	36	4	31	4	25	4	19	4	12	4	05
	22	4	51	4	39	4	34	4	28	4	22	4	15	4	08	4	00
	26	4	49	4	37	4	31	4	25	4	19	4	12	4	04	3	56
	30	4	48	4	36	4	30	4	24	4	17	4	10	4	02	3	53
December	4	4	48	4	35	4	29	4	22	4	15	4	08	4	00	3	50
	8	4	48	4	35	4	28	4	22	4	15	4	07	3	58	3	49
	12	4	49	4	35	4	29	4	22	4	15	4	07	3	58	3	48
	16	4	50	4	36	4	30	4	23	4	16	4	07	3	59	3	49
	20	4	52	4	38	4	31	4	24	4	17	4	09	4	00	3	50
	24	4	54	4	40	4	33	4	27	4	19	4	11	4	02	3	52
	28	4	56	4	42	4	36	4	29	4	22	4	14	4	05	3	55

LATITUDES & LONGITUDES

*K*nowing the latitudes and longitudes for all your favorite musky holes can help you establish exact sunrise, sunset, moonrise and moonset times.

What They Are:

Latitude: Describes the position of a point on the earth's surface in relation to the equator.

These imaginary lines are measured in degrees. The equator is 0 degrees rising to +90 degrees at the North Pole and -90 degrees at the South Pole. Most musky waters lie between 35 and 55 degrees latitude.

Longitude: Describes the position of a point on the earth's surface in relation to the Meridian of Greenwich. These imaginary lines that run north-south are measured in degrees. Greenwich is 0 degrees. A point halfway around the world is 180 degrees.

Both latitude and longitude are measured in degrees and expressed as (°). Fractions of degrees are expressed in minutes and expressed as ('). Eagle Lake in northwest Ontario has a latitude of 49 degrees and 42 minutes. This would be expressed as 49° 42'.

Why You Need Them:

To determine the sunrise/sunset times and moonrise/moonset times for a specific location you will need to know the approximate latitude. The latitudes for the most common bodies of water used by musky fishermen may be found on the following table. If the body of water you are planning to fish is not listed select the latitude for the next closest body of water or you may find latitudes in most atlases.

Fractions of degrees (minutes) will not change the times significantly. Consequently, minutes have only been listed on the following table for areas that this information was specifically available. Longitudes will not affect times but are listed for your information.

Lines of Latitude   Lines of Longitude

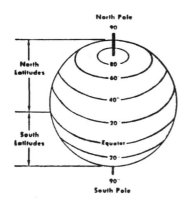
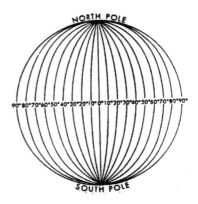

1996 Musky Hunter's Almanac

Table of Latitudes & Longitudes

State/Province	Location	Latitude	Longitude
Colorado	Denver	40	105
Illinois			
	Fox Chain of Lakes	42	88
	Lake Shabbona	42	89
	Lake Shelbyville	40	88
	Spring Lake	40	90
Iowa			
	W. Okoboji Lake	43.5	95
	Spirit Lake	43.5	95
Kentucky			
	Cave Run Lake	38	83
	Green River Lake	37.5	85
Michigan			
	Houghton Lake	44.5	85
	Lake St. Clair	42.5	82
	Torch Lake	45	85
Minnesota			
	Grand Rapids	47	94
	Leech Lake	47	94.5
	Mille Lacs	46	93.5
	Minneapolis/St. Paul	45	93
	Winnie & Cass Lakes	47.5	94.5
Missouri			
	Pomme de	38	93
Nebraska			
	Merrit Reservoir	43	101
New Jersey			
	Delaware Water Gap	41	75

Latitudes & Longitudes

Table of Latitudes & Longitudes

State/Province	Location	Latitude	Longitude
New York			
	Lake Chautauqua	42	79
	Lake George	43	73.5
	St. Lawrence River at:		
	Clayton	44	76
	Lake Champlain	44 to 45	75.5
	Massena	45	75
	Morristown	44.5	75.5
	Ogdensberg	44.75	75.5
	Waddington	45	75
	Niagara River	43	79
North Dakota			
	Spiritwood Lake	47	99
Ohio			
	Berlin Lake	41	81
	Lake Milton	41	81
	Leesville Lake	40.5	81
	Piedmont Lake	40.25	81
	Pymatuning	41	80.5
	Salt Fork	40	81.5
	West Branch Reservoir	41	81
Ontario			
	Balsam Lake	44° 38'	78° 52'
	Buckhorn / Chemong Lakes	44° 29'	78° 23'
	Eagle Lake	49° 42'	93° 13'
	Lake Scugog	44° 10'	78° 50'
	Lake Simcoe	44° 25'	79° 20'
	Lake St. Clair	42° 28'	82° 40'

1996 Musky Hunter's Almanac

State/Province	Location	Latitude	Longitude
Ontario cont.	Georgian Bay at:		
	Blind River	46° 11'	82° 58'
	Byng Inlet	45° 46'	80° 32'
	French River Main Channel	46° 02'	80° 30'
	French River Main Outlet	45° 56'	80° 54'
	French River North Channel	46° 05'	80° 23'
	French River Western Channel	46° 00'	80° 56'
	Honey Harbour	44° 52'	79° 49'
	Key Harbour	45° 53'	80° 45'
	Killarney Harbour	45° 58'	81° 31'
	McGregor Bay	46° 05'	81° 40'
	Moon River	45° 08'	79° 59'
	Parry Sound Harbour	45° 20'	80° 03'
	Pointe Au Baril Harbour	45° 33'	80° 31'
	Port Severn	44° 48'	79° 43'
	Sault Ste. Marie	46° 31'	84° 20'
	Pigeon Lake	44° 27'	78° 30'
	Rainy Lake	48° 45'	92° 56'
	Lac Seul	50° 15'	92° 15'
	Lake Nipissing	46° 20'	79° 45'
	Lake of the Woods at:		
	North	49° 30'	94° 50'
	South	49° 13'	94° 25'
	Niagara River	43° 16'	79° 03'
	Ottawa River at:		
	Carillon	45° 33'	74° 26'
	Ottawa	45° 25'	75° 42'
	Rice Lake	44° 12'	78° 10'
	St. Lawrence River at:		
	Brockville	44° 35'	75° 41'
	Cornwall	45° 01'	74° 48'
	Kingston Harbour	44° 14'	76° 28'
	Lake St. Francis / St. Louis	48° 08'	74° 25'
	Morrisburg	44° 54'	75° 11'
	Prescott/Ogdensburg	44° 43'	75° 31'

Latitudes & Longitudes

State/Province	Location	Latitude	Longitude
	Stony Lake	44° 33'	78° 06'
	Wabigoon Lake	49° 44'	92° 44'
Pennsylvania			
	Allegheny Reservoir	42	79
	Conneaut Lake	41	80.5
	Pymatuning	41	80.5
	Susquehanna River	41 to 42	76 to 76.5
Vermont			
	Lake Champlain - North End	45	73.5
	Missisquoi River	45	73
Virginia			
	New River		
	Smith Mountain Lake	37	79.5
West. Virginia			
	Elk River	39	81
	Middle Is. Creek	39	81
Wisconsin			
	Forest County	45.75	89
	Iron County	46.5	90
	Oneida County	43.75	89.5
	Sawyer County	46	41
	Vilas County	46	89.5

1996 Musky Hunter's Almanac

Calendars

Monthly Calendars

*P*lanning is an integral part of any musky hunter's fishing experience. The monthly calendars that follow are designed to provide an aid to fisherman in planning both their on- and off-season fishing activities.

A unique feature of these calendars is that the weeks begin with Monday rather than the typical Sunday. Because most fishing events or activities encompass full weekends, we have made this change so that the Saturday and Sunday of the same weekend may appear together on the same line. Hopefully you will find this a useful aid that will simplify your planning.

The 16 monthly calendars included in the *Musky Hunter's Almanac* cover the last four months of 1995, September through December, and the entire 1996 calendar year. The information to be found on the calendars may be broken down in to the four following categories.

1. Moon Phases — The moon phases: full moon, new moon, first quarter and last quarter are depicted graphically on each monthly calendar. The moon phases and their definitions also appear elsewhere in the *Almanac* in the feature "All About The Moon."

2. Periods of Apogee and Perigee — The periods of moon

apogee and perigee are listed on the calendars on the day that they occur each month. Each will occur at least once a month and periodically twice a month. There is no correlation between the moon phases and apogee and perigee. The periods of apogee and perigee and their definitions also appear elsewhere in the *Almanac* in the feature "All About The Moon."

3. Musky Events — During the course of the year many different activities and events take place in the musky fishing community. Many of these are listed on the calendars including: all musky fishing shows, major sports shows, musky tournaments and significant dates for organizations such as Muskies Canada and Muskies, Inc. If you or your organization would like to have a significant date added to the *1997 Musky Hunter's Almanac* we would be happy to consider your request provided it is received no later than March 15, 1996.

4. American and Canadian Holidays — Often fishermen plan fishing trips and activities around long weekends and/or statutory holidays. These have been included for your easy reference. Dates such as Valentine's and Mother's Day have also been included so that you know when not to schedule fishing-related activities.

• • •

Due to the short deadline and a preponderance of material for this first issue of the Musky Hunter's Almanac, *some items received from readers were not used. These items will receive first consideration for next year's* Almanac. *In addition, we will expand the "dates" section of the calendar to include a full explanation of "what," "when" and "why" and "where." Input must be received by March 15, 1996.*

1996 Musky Hunter's Almanac

September 1995
MUSKY HUNTER'S MONTHLY PLANNER

Monday	Tuesday	Wednesday	Thursday	Friday	Saturday	Sunday
				1	2	3
4 Labor Day	5	6	7	8	9	10
11	12	13	14	15	16	17 Apogee
18	19	20	21	22	23 Autumn Begins — Can Am Challunge — Guide For A Day, Pomme de Terre, MO	24
25 Rosh Hashanah	26	27	28	29	30 Perigee	

Dates for musky events to be listed in the 1997 Almanac must be received by March 15, 1996

Calendars

October 1995
MUSKY HUNTER'S MONTHLY PLANNER

Monday	Tuesday	Wednesday	Thursday	Friday	Saturday	Sunday
						1
2	*3*	*4* Yom Kippur	*5*	*6*	*7* Hayward Lakes Chapter Muskies, Inc. Fall Tournament	*8*
					Pomme de Terre Muskies Inc. Open Tournament	
9 Columbus Day (observed) Thanksgiving (Canada)	*10*	*11*	*12*	*13*	*14* Muskies Canada Honey Harbour Outing	*15* Apogee
16	*17*	*18*	*19*	*20* Muskies, Inc. Fall International Board Meeting	*21*	*22*
23	*24*	*25*	*26* Perigee	*27*	*28*	*29* Daylight savings — set back one hour
30	*31* Halloween					

Dates for musky events to be listed in the 1997 Almanac must be received by March 15, 1996

1996 Musky Hunter's Almanac

November 1995
MUSKY HUNTER'S MONTHLY PLANNER

Monday	Tuesday	Wednesday	Thursday	Friday	Saturday	Sunday
		1	2	3	4	5
6	7 ○ Election Day	8	9	10	11 Veterans Day Remembrance Day	12
13	14	15 ◐	16	17	18	19
20	21	22 ●	23 Perigee Thanksgiving	24	25	26
27	28	29 ◐	30			

Dates for musky events to be listed in the 1997 Almanac must be received by March 15, 1996

Calendars

December 1995

MUSKY HUNTER'S MONTHLY PLANNER

Monday	Tuesday	Wednesday	Thursday	Friday	Saturday	Sunday
				1	*2*	*3*
4	*5*	*6*	*7*	*8*	*9* Apogee	*10*
11	*12*	*13*	*14*	*15*	*16*	*17*
18 Hanukkah	*19*	*20*	*21*	*22* Perigee Winter begins	*23*	*24*
25 Christmas	*26*	*27*	*28*	*29*	*30*	*31* New Year's Eve

Dates for musky events to be listed in the 1997 Almanac must be received by March 15, 1996

1996 Musky Hunter's Almanac

January 1996
MUSKY HUNTER'S MONTHLY PLANNER

Monday	Tuesday	Wednesday	Thursday	Friday	Saturday	Sunday
1 New Year's Day	2	3	4	5 Apogee	6	7
8	9	10	11	12	13	14
15 Martin Luther King Jr. Day	16	17	18	19 Perigee	20 — Muskies Canada Annl Meet; Chicago Musky Expo, Kane Co. Fairgrounds; Chicago Musky Show, Inland Expo Center	21
22	23	24	25	26	27 — Chicago Fishing, Travel & Outdoors Show	28
29	30	31 — Chicago Fishing, Travel & Outdoors Show				

Dates for musky events to be listed in the 1997 Almanac must be received by March 15, 1996

Calendars

February 1996
MUSKY HUNTER'S MONTHLY PLANNER

Monday	Tuesday	Wednesday	Thursday	Friday	Saturday	Sunday
			1 Apogee	**2** Groundhog Day	**3**	**4** ○
				Chicago Fishing, Travel & Outdoors Show		
5	**6**	**7**	**8**	**9**	**10**	**11** "Let's Talk Fishing" sport show, 12 Apostles Musky Club, Stevens Point, WI
12 ◐ Lincoln's B-Day	**13**	**14** Valentine's Day	**15**	**16**	**17** Perigee	**18** ●
					Milwaukee Musky Expo	
			Chicago Fishing Tackle Expo			
19 President's Day	**20**	**21** Ash Wednesday	**22** Washington's B-Day	**23**	**24**	**25** ◑
26	**27**	**28**	**29** Apogee			

Dates for musky events to be listed in the 1997 Almanac must be received by March 15, 1996

1996 Musky Hunter's Almanac

March 1996
MUSKY HUNTER'S MONTHLY PLANNER

Monday	Tuesday	Wednesday	Thursday	Friday	Saturday	Sunday
				1	2	3
4	5 ○	6	7	8	9	10 Musky Hunter Winter Musky Symposium
					Toronto Sportsmen's Show	
11	12 ◐	13	14	15	16 Muskies Can. Awards Perigee	17 St. Patrick's Day
					Minnesota Musky Expo	
	Toronto Sportsmen's Show					
18	19 ●	20 Spring Begins	21	22	23	24
25	26 ◑	27	28 Apogee	29	30	31 Palm Sunday

Dates for musky events to be listed in the 1997 Almanac must be received by March 15, 1996

Calendars

April 1996

MUSKY HUNTER'S MONTHLY PLANNER

Monday	Tuesday	Wednesday	Thursday	Friday	Saturday	Sunday
1 April Fool's Day	**2**	**3** ◯	**4** Passover	**5** Good Friday	**6**	**7** Easter; Daylight savings ends — set ahead one hour
8 Easter Monday	**9**	**10** ◐	**11** Perigee	**12**	**13**	**14**
15	**16**	**17** ●	**18**	**19**	**20**	**21**
22	**23**	**24** Apogee	**25** ◑	**26**	**27**	**28**
29	**30**					

Dates for musky events to be listed in the 1997 Almanac must be received by March 15, 1996

1996 Musky Hunter's Almanac

May 1996
MUSKY HUNTER'S MONTHLY PLANNER

Monday	Tuesday	Wednesday	Thursday	Friday	Saturday	Sunday
		1	2	3 ○	4	5
6 Perigee	7	8	9 ◐	10	11	12 Mother's Day
13	14	15	16 Ascension Day	17 ●	18 Armed Forces Day	19
20 Victoria Day	21	22 Apogee	23	24	25 ◑	26 Pentecost; Wisconsin musky season opens
27 Memorial Day (observed)	28	29	30	31		

Dates for musky events to be listed in the 1997 Almanac must be received by March 15, 1996

Calendars

June 1996

MUSKY HUNTER'S MONTHLY PLANNER

Monday	Tuesday	Wednesday	Thursday	Friday	Saturday	Sunday
					1	2
3 Perigee	4	5	6 Corpus Christi	7	8	9
10	11	12	13	14 Flag Day; Season opens: Eagle L., Lake Of The Woods, Lac Seul, Ottawa River	15 Season opens: Georgian Bay, St. Lawrence R	16 Father's Day
17	18	19 Apogee	20 Summer begins	21	22	23
24	25	26	27	28	29	30

Dates for musky events to be listed in the 1997 Almanac must be received by March 15, 1996

1996 Musky Hunter's Almanac

July 1996

MUSKY HUNTER'S MONTHLY PLANNER

Monday	Tuesday	Wednesday	Thursday	Friday	Saturday	Sunday
1 Canada Day; Perigee	2	3	4 Independence Day	5	6	7
8	9	10	11	12	13	14
15	16 Apogee	17	18	19	20	21
22	23	24	25	26	27	28
29	30 Perigee	31				

Dates for musky events to be listed in the 1997 Almanac must be received by March 15, 1996

Calendars

August 1996
MUSKY HUNTER'S MONTHLY PLANNER

Monday	Tuesday	Wednesday	Thursday	Friday	Saturday	Sunday
			1	2	3	4
5 Civic Holiday	6	7	8	9	10	11
12 Apogee	13	14	15	16	17 Nat'l Champ. Musky Open — Eagle River, WI	18
19	20	21	22	23	24 World Musky Hunt — Minocqua, WI	25
26	27 Perigee	28	29	30	31	

Dates for musky events to be listed in the 1997 Almanac must be received by March 15, 1996

1996 Musky Hunter's Almanac

September 1996
MUSKY HUNTER'S MONTHLY PLANNER

Monday	Tuesday	Wednesday	Thursday	Friday	Saturday	Sunday
						1
2 Labor Day Labour Day	3	4	5	6	7	8
9 Apogee	10	11	12	13	14 Rosh Hashanah	15
16	17	18	19	20	21 Guide For A Day, Pomme de Terre, MO Can Am Challunge Cup	22 Autumn begins
23 Yom Kippur	24 Perigee	25	26	27	28	29
30						

Dates for musky events to be listed in the 1997 Almanac must be received by March 15, 1996

Calendars

October 1996
MUSKY HUNTER'S MONTHLY PLANNER

Monday	Tuesday	Wednesday	Thursday	Friday	Saturday	Sunday
	1	2	3	4	5	6 Apogee
					Pomme de Terre Muskies Inc. Open Tournament	
7	8	9	10	11	12	13
14 Columbus Day (observed) Thanksgiving Day (Canada	15	16	17	18	19	20
21	22 Perigee	23	24	25	26	27 Daylight savings — set back one hour
28	29	30	31 Halloween			

Dates for musky events to be listed in the 1997 Almanac must be received by March 15, 1996

1996 Musky Hunter's Almanac

November 1996
MUSKY HUNTER'S MONTHLY PLANNER

Monday	Tuesday	Wednesday	Thursday	Friday	Saturday	Sunday
				1	2	3 Apogee
4	5 Election Day	6	7	8	9	10
11 Remembrance Day; Veterans Day	12	13	14	15	16 Perigee	17
18	19	20	21	22	23	24
25	26	27	28 Thanksgiving	29	30 Season close: Georgian Bay, Lake O' Woods, Eagle L., Lac Seul, Ottawa R., St. Lawrence R., Wisconsin	

Dates for musky events to be listed in the 1997 Almanac must be received by March 15, 1996

Calendars

December 1996
MUSKY HUNTER'S MONTHLY PLANNER

Monday	Tuesday	Wednesday	Thursday	Friday	Saturday	Sunday
						1 Apogee
2	3	4	5	6 Hanukkah	7	8
9	10	11	12	13 Perigee	14	15
16	17	18	19	20	21 Winter begins	22
23	24	25 Christmas	26	27	28	29 Apogee
30	31 New Year's Eve					

Dates for musky events to be listed in the 1997 Almanac must be received by March 15, 1996

1996 Musky Hunter's Almanac

1996
MUSKY HUNTER'S YEARLY PLANNER

January						
S	M	T	W	T	F	S
	1	2	3	4	5	6
7	8	9	10	11	12	13
14	15	16	17	18	19	20
21	22	23	24	25	26	27
28	29	30	31			

February						
S	M	T	W	T	F	S
				1	2	3
4	5	6	7	8	9	10
11	12	13	14	15	16	17
18	19	20	21	22	23	24
25	26	27	28	29		

March						
S	M	T	W	T	F	S
					1	2
3	4	5	6	7	8	9
10	11	12	13	14	15	16
17	18	19	20	21	22	23
24	25	26	27	28	29	30
31						

April						
S	M	T	W	T	F	S
	1	2	3	4	5	6
7	8	9	10	11	12	13
14	15	16	17	18	19	20
21	22	23	24	25	26	27
28	29	30				

May						
S	M	T	W	T	F	S
			1	2	3	4
5	6	7	8	9	10	11
12	13	14	15	16	17	18
19	20	21	22	23	24	25
26	27	28	29	30	31	

June						
S	M	T	W	T	F	S
						1
2	3	4	5	6	7	8
9	10	11	12	13	14	15
16	17	18	19	20	21	22
23	24	25	26	27	28	29
30						

July						
S	M	T	W	T	F	S
	1	2	3	4	5	6
7	8	9	10	11	12	13
14	15	16	17	18	19	20
21	22	23	24	25	26	27
28	29	30	31			

August						
S	M	T	W	T	F	S
				1	2	3
4	5	6	7	8	9	10
11	12	13	14	15	16	17
18	19	20	21	22	23	24
25	26	27	28	29	30	31

September						
S	M	T	W	T	F	S
1	2	3	4	5	6	7
8	9	10	11	12	13	14
15	16	17	18	19	20	21
22	23	24	25	26	27	28
29	30					

October						
S	M	T	W	T	F	S
		1	2	3	4	5
6	7	8	9	10	11	12
13	14	15	16	17	18	19
20	21	22	23	24	25	26
27	28	29	30	31		

November						
S	M	T	W	T	F	S
					1	2
3	4	5	6	7	8	9
10	11	12	13	14	15	16
17	18	19	20	21	22	23
24	25	26	27	28	29	30

December						
S	M	T	W	T	F	S
1	2	3	4	5	6	7
8	9	10	11	12	13	14
15	16	17	18	19	20	21
22	23	24	25	26	27	28
29	30	31				

Calendars

1997
MUSKY HUNTER'S YEARLY PLANNER

January						
S	M	T	W	T	F	S
			1	2	3	4
5	6	7	8	9	10	11
12	13	14	15	16	17	18
19	20	21	22	23	24	25
26	27	28	29	30	31	

February						
S	M	T	W	T	F	S
						1
2	3	4	5	6	7	8
9	10	11	12	13	14	15
16	17	18	19	20	21	22
23	24	25	26	27	28	

March						
S	M	T	W	T	F	S
						1
2	3	4	5	6	7	8
9	10	11	12	13	14	15
16	17	18	19	20	21	22
23	24	25	26	27	28	29
30	31					

April						
S	M	T	W	T	F	S
		1	2	3	4	5
6	7	8	9	10	11	12
13	14	15	16	17	18	19
20	21	22	23	24	25	26
27	28	29	30			

May						
S	M	T	W	T	F	S
				1	2	3
4	5	6	7	8	9	10
11	12	13	14	15	16	17
18	19	20	21	22	23	24
25	26	27	28	29	30	31

June						
S	M	T	W	T	F	S
1	2	3	4	5	6	7
8	9	10	11	12	13	14
15	16	17	18	19	20	21
22	23	24	25	26	27	28
29	30					

July						
S	M	T	W	T	F	S
		1	2	3	4	5
6	7	8	9	10	11	12
13	14	15	16	17	18	19
20	21	22	23	24	25	26
27	28	29	30	31		

August						
S	M	T	W	T	F	S
					1	2
3	4	5	6	7	8	9
10	11	12	13	14	15	16
17	18	19	20	21	22	23
24	25	26	27	28	29	30
31						

September						
S	M	T	W	T	F	S
	1	2	3	4	5	6
7	8	9	10	11	12	13
14	15	16	17	18	19	20
21	22	23	24	25	26	27
28	29	30				

October						
S	M	T	W	T	F	S
			1	2	3	4
5	6	7	8	9	10	11
12	13	14	15	16	17	18
19	20	21	22	23	24	25
26	27	28	29	30	31	

November						
S	M	T	W	T	F	S
						1
2	3	4	5	6	7	8
9	10	11	12	13	14	15
16	17	18	19	20	21	22
23	24	25	26	27	28	29
30						

December						
S	M	T	W	T	F	S
	1	2	3	4	5	6
7	8	9	10	11	12	13
14	15	16	17	18	19	20
21	22	23	24	25	26	27
28	29	30	31			

1996 Musky Hunter's Almanac

Features

DO YOU KNOW YOUR MUSKY BIOLOGY?

QUESTIONS
1. True or False — Male muskies grow larger than female muskies.

2. T or F — A hybrid is a cross between a female musky and a male pike.

3. T or F — Muskellunge are fractional spawners. They deposit their eggs in two distinct clutches. In younger muskies the first clutch has a greater hatching success rate.

4. T or F — In the spring, after spawning, newly-hatched musky fry like to feed on newly hatched pike fry.

5. T or F — A tiger musky has a growth rate nearly twice that of a natural musky.

6. T or F — As the water begins to warm, the muskies' metabolism increases.

7. T or F — The tiger musky has a fully scaled cheek, whereas the natural musky has scales only on the top half of the cheek.

8. T or F — Young of the year tiger muskies can be raised on a diet of manufactured food.

9. T or F — The muskellunge is considered to be a fall spawner by most biologists.

10. T or F — Female muskies are usually first to appear on the spawning site and the last to leave.

11. T or F — On female muskellunge the urogenital region is shaped like a keyhole.

12. T or F — On male muskies the urogenital region is shaped like an egg.

13. T or F — Muskellunge may actively spawn for up to one month.

14. T or F — Fertilized muskellunge eggs are 2.5 to 3.5 mm in diameter, clear and amber in color.

15. T or F — A female muskellunge produces three clutches of eggs each year.

16. T or F — Muskellunge are considered to be single spawners.

17. T or F — Female hybrid muskies can sometimes be fertile.

18. T or F A large, mature female from big waters has the potential to produce over 450,000 eggs.

1996 Musky Hunter's Almanac

19. T or F — The differences in structure of the sexual anatomy between pike and musky reflects the differences in spawning behavior in these two species.

20. T or F — Muskies in excess of 20 years of age have been known to suffer from senility.

21. T or F — There are two species of muskies.

Answers
1. False — The girls grow bigger.
2. True — Occurs when a late spawning male pike fertilizes a female muskies eggs.
3. True — It's been well documented that muskies may spawn twice during a season.
4. False — It's the other way around. Pike spawn first then feed on the later hatching musky.
5. True — Maybe it's that kamikaze feeding attitude it inherited from the pike.
6. True — Yes sir! Get out those topwater baits.
7. True — Just like its dad, the pike.
8. True — It makes them great candidates for hatchery reproduction.
9. False — They're springtime lovers.
10. True — It's all work and no play.
11. False — It's actually shaped like a pear. Great way to determine the sex of a musky.
12. False — The male is shaped like a keyhole.
13. True — They may lay one batch of eggs, take a break and come back to lay a second batch.

Do You Know Your Musky Biology?

14. True — Don't confuse them with caviar.
15. False — She's good but not that good. Two is the norm.
16. False — In a word they are called "multiple" spawners.
17. True — Contrary to popular belief.
18. True — Apparently Ken O'Brien's Canadian record contained over 800,000 eggs.
19. True — So the experts say.
20. True — Maybe that's why they hit those four-inch Rapalas used by walleye fishermen.
21. True — That is why some lakes do not produce 50-pound muskies.

• • •

Larry's Lesson — Most top musky anglers modify lures with hooks that are directly wired to the bait. By attaching the lure with split rings, muskies are unable to use the bait for leverage to pull the hook out. Musky pros after big fish use double stainless steel split rings (i.e. a No. 5 inside a No. 7) to ensure a big fish doesn't straighten them out! Top grade Rosco stainless split rings can be obtained from suppliers such as Trophy Fishing, P. O. Box 2633, South Bend, Indiana, 46680, USA.

Estimated Weight Charts

What did that released musky really weigh?

By Larry Ramsell

For several years now, since the dramatic increase in the release of live muskies, anglers have been using the standard weight formula: Girth X Girth X Length/800 = Estimated Weight.

While this formula is adequate for fish under 30 pounds, it has been found wanting for larger fish, in that the standard formula "overstates" estimated weights in fish from 30-pounders to 40-pounders and even more so in fish over 40 pounds. While it is not seemingly harmful for the estimated weight of a released fish to be overstated, it is unfair to anglers who have caught legitimate large fish and hung them on a scale, to have them surpassed by an unweighed released fish. More importantly, these "overestimates" have resulted in the death of many fish that, had the anglers known the "true weight" was less than the desired target or goal, they would have been released!

Warren Wilkinson, past director of Muskies Canada, did an informal study comparing "live girth" vs "dead girth" on many muskies that, after quick calculation, estimated weight reached the magic number (goal) of the anglers involved. In many cases when this estimate was very close to the desired goal, the true weight of the fish hung on the scale came up short. After checking many fish, Warren learned that "live girth" was a 1/2-inch larger than "dead girth" on fish from 30 pounds to 40 pounds and 3/4-inch larger in fish over 40 pounds. In order to provide anglers with a more accurate "estimate" of "live" muskies, I have modified the standard formula to reflect the difference as applied to live released fish. This new release chart is "user friendly" in that "live girth" can be used to immediately estimate the weight of your released musky and will hopefully see many more "close calls" returned to the water instead

Length	Girth	Weight	Length	Girth	Weight	Length	Girth	Weight	Length	Girth	Weight
33.00	12.00	5.94	36.00	12.00	6.46	39.00	12.00	7.02	42.00	14.00	10.29
33.00	13.00	6.97	36.00	13.00	7.61	39.00	13.00	8.24	42.00	15.00	11.81
33.00	14.00	8.09	36.00	14.00	8.82	39.00	14.00	9.56	42.00	16.00	13.44
33.00	15.00	9.28	36.00	15.00	10.13	39.00	15.00	10.97	42.00	17.00	15.17
33.00	16.00	10.56	36.00	16.00	11.52	39.00	16.00	12.48	42.00	18.00	17.01
33.00	17.00	11.92	36.00	17.00	13.01	39.00	17.00	14.09	42.00	19.00	18.95
33.00	18.00	13.37	36.00	18.00	14.58	39.00	18.00	15.80	42.00	20.00	21.00
33.00	19.00	14.89	36.00	19.00	16.25	39.00	19.00	17.58	42.00	21.00	23.15
33.00	20.00	16.50	36.00	20.00	18.00	39.00	20.00	19.50	42.00	22.00	25.41
33.00	21.00	18.19	36.00	21.00	19.85	39.00	21.00	21.50	42.00	23.00	27.77
34.00	12.00	6.12	37.00	12.00	6.66	40.00	12.00	7.20	43.00	14.00	10.54
34.00	13.00	7.18	37.00	13.00	7.82	40.00	13.00	8.45	43.00	15.00	12.09
34.00	14.00	8.33	37.00	14.00	9.07	40.00	14.00	9.80	43.00	16.00	13.76
34.00	15.00	9.56	37.00	15.00	10.41	40.00	15.00	11.25	43.00	17.00	15.53
34.00	16.00	10.88	37.00	16.00	11.84	40.00	16.00	12.80	43.00	18.00	17.42
34.00	17.00	12.28	37.00	17.00	13.37	40.00	17.00	14.45	43.00	19.00	19.40
34.00	18.00	13.77	37.00	18.00	14.99	40.00	18.00	16.20	43.00	20.00	21.50
34.00	19.00	15.34	37.00	19.00	16.70	40.00	19.00	18.05	43.00	21.00	23.70
34.00	20.00	17.00	37.00	20.00	18.50	40.00	20.00	20.00	43.00	22.00	26.02
34.00	21.00	18.74	37.00	21.00	20.40	40.00	21.00	22.05	43.00	23.00	28.43
35.00	12.00	6.30	38.00	12.00	6.84	41.00	14.00	10.05	44.00	14.00	10.78
35.00	13.00	7.39	38.00	13.00	8.03	41.00	15.00	11.53	44.00	15.00	12.36
35.00	14.00	8.58	38.00	14.00	9.31	41.00	16.00	13.12	44.00	16.00	14.08
35.00	15.00	9.84	38.00	15.00	10.69	41.00	17.00	14.81	44.00	17.00	15.90
35.00	16.00	11.20	38.00	16.00	12.16	41.00	18.00	16.61	44.00	18.00	17.82
35.00	17.00	12.64	38.00	17.00	13.73	41.00	19.00	18.50	44.00	19.00	19.86
35.00	18.00	14.18	38.00	18.00	15.39	41.00	20.00	20.50	44.00	20.00	22.00
35.00	19.00	15.79	38.00	19.00	17.15	41.00	21.00	22.60	44.00	21.00	24.26
35.00	20.00	17.50	38.00	20.00	19.00	41.00	22.00	24.81	44.00	22.00	26.62
35.00	21.00	19.29	38.00	21.00	20.95	41.00	23.00	27.11	44.00	23.00	29.10

1996 Musky Hunter's Almanac

Length	Girth	Weight	Length	Girth	Weight	Length	Girth	Weight	Length	Girth	Weight
45.00	14.00	11.03	45.50	14.00	11.15	46.00	14.00	11.27	46.50	14.00	11.39
45.00	14.25	11.42	45.50	14.25	11.55	46.00	14.25	11.68	46.50	14.25	11.80
45.00	14.50	11.83	45.50	14.50	11.96	46.00	14.50	12.09	46.50	14.50	12.22
45.00	14.75	12.24	45.50	14.75	12.37	46.00	14.75	12.51	46.50	14.75	12.65
45.00	15.00	12.66	45.50	15.00	12.80	46.00	15.00	12.94	46.50	15.00	13.08
45.00	15.25	13.08	45.50	15.25	13.23	46.00	15.25	13.37	46.50	15.25	13.52
45.00	15.50	13.51	45.50	15.50	13.66	46.00	15.50	13.81	46.50	15.50	13.96
45.00	15.75	13.95	45.50	15.75	14.11	46.00	15.75	14.26	46.50	15.75	14.42
45.00	16.00	14.40	45.50	16.00	14.56	46.00	16.00	14.72	46.50	16.00	14.88
45.00	16.25	14.85	45.50	16.25	15.02	46.00	16.25	15.18	46.50	16.25	15.35
45.00	16.50	15.31	45.50	16.50	15.48	46.00	16.50	15.65	46.50	16.50	15.82
45.00	16.75	15.78	45.50	16.75	15.95	46.00	16.75	16.13	46.50	16.75	16.31
45.00	17.00	16.25	45.50	17.00	16.44	46.00	17.00	16.62	46.50	17.00	16.80
45.00	17.25	16.74	45.50	17.25	16.92	46.00	17.25	17.11	46.50	17.25	17.30
45.00	17.50	17.23	45.50	17.50	17.42	46.00	17.50	17.61	46.50	17.50	17.80
45.00	17.75	17.72	45.50	17.75	17.92	46.00	17.75	18.12	46.50	17.75	18.31
45.00	18.00	18.23	45.50	18.00	18.43	46.00	18.00	18.63	46.50	18.00	18.83
45.00	18.25	18.73	45.50	18.25	18.94	46.00	18.25	19.15	46.50	18.25	19.36
45.00	18.50	19.25	45.50	18.50	19.47	46.00	18.50	19.68	46.50	18.50	19.89
45.00	18.75	19.78	45.50	18.75	20.00	46.00	18.75	20.21	46.50	18.75	20.43
45.00	19.00	20.31	45.50	19.00	20.53	46.00	19.00	20.76	46.50	19.00	20.98
45.00	19.25	20.84	45.50	19.25	21.08	46.00	19.25	21.31	46.50	19.25	21.54
45.00	19.50	21.39	45.50	19.50	21.63	46.00	19.50	21.86	46.50	19.50	22.10
45.00	19.75	21.94	45.50	19.75	22.18	46.00	19.75	22.43	46.50	19.75	22.67
45.00	20.00	22.50	45.50	20.00	22.75	46.00	20.00	23.00	46.50	20.00	23.25
45.00	20.25	23.07	45.50	20.25	23.32	46.00	20.25	23.58	46.50	20.25	23.83
45.00	20.50	23.64	45.50	20.50	23.90	46.00	20.50	24.16	46.50	20.50	24.43
45.00	20.75	24.22	45.50	20.75	24.49	46.00	20.75	24.76	46.50	20.75	25.03
45.00	21.00	24.81	45.50	21.00	25.08	46.00	21.00	25.36	46.50	21.00	25.63
45.00	21.25	25.40	45.50	21.25	25.68	46.00	21.25	25.96	46.50	21.25	26.25
45.00	21.50	26.00	45.50	21.50	26.29	46.00	21.50	26.58	46.50	21.50	26.87
45.00	21.75	26.61	45.50	21.75	26.91	46.00	21.75	27.20	46.50	21.75	27.50
45.00	22.00	27.23	45.50	22.00	27.53	46.00	22.00	27.83	46.50	22.00	28.13
45.00	22.25	27.85	45.50	22.25	28.16	46.00	22.25	28.47	46.50	22.25	28.78
45.00	22.50	28.48	45.50	22.50	28.79	46.00	22.50	29.11	46.50	22.50	29.43

Length	Girth	Weight	Length	Girth	Weight	Length	Girth	Weight	Length	Girth	Weight
45.25	14.00	11.09	45.75	14.00	11.21	46.25	14.00	11.33	46.75	14.00	11.45
45.25	14.25	11.49	45.75	14.25	11.61	46.25	14.25	11.74	46.75	14.25	11.87
45.25	14.50	11.89	45.75	14.50	12.02	46.25	14.50	12.16	46.75	14.50	12.29
45.25	14.75	12.31	45.75	14.75	12.44	46.25	14.75	12.58	46.75	14.75	12.71
45.25	15.00	12.73	45.75	15.00	12.87	46.25	15.00	13.01	46.75	15.00	13.15
45.25	15.25	13.16	45.75	15.25	13.30	46.25	15.25	13.45	46.75	15.25	13.59
45.25	15.50	13.59	45.75	15.50	13.74	46.25	15.50	13.89	46.75	15.50	14.04
45.25	15.75	14.03	45.75	15.75	14.19	46.25	15.75	14.34	46.75	15.75	14.50
45.25	16.00	14.48	45.75	16.00	14.64	46.25	16.00	14.80	46.75	16.00	14.96
45.25	16.25	14.94	45.75	16.25	15.10	46.25	16.25	15.27	46.75	16.25	15.43
45.25	16.50	15.40	45.75	16.50	15.57	46.25	16.50	15.74	46.75	16.50	15.91
45.25	16.75	15.87	45.75	16.75	16.04	46.25	16.75	16.22	46.75	16.75	16.40
45.25	17.00	16.35	45.75	17.00	16.53	46.25	17.00	16.71	46.75	17.00	16.89
45.25	17.25	16.83	45.75	17.25	17.02	46.25	17.25	17.20	46.75	17.25	17.39
45.25	17.50	17.32	45.75	17.50	17.51	46.25	17.50	17.71	46.75	17.50	17.90
45.25	17.75	17.82	45.75	17.75	18.02	46.25	17.75	18.21	46.75	17.75	18.41
45.25	18.00	18.33	45.75	18.00	18.53	46.25	18.00	18.73	46.75	18.00	18.93
45.25	18.25	18.84	45.75	18.25	19.05	46.25	18.25	19.26	46.75	18.25	19.46
45.25	18.50	19.36	45.75	18.50	19.57	46.25	18.50	19.79	46.75	18.50	20.00
45.25	18.75	19.89	45.75	18.75	20.10	46.25	18.75	20.32	46.75	18.75	20.54
45.25	19.00	20.42	45.75	19.00	20.64	46.25	19.00	20.87	46.75	19.00	21.10
45.25	19.25	20.96	45.75	19.25	21.19	46.25	19.25	21.42	46.75	19.25	21.65
45.25	19.50	21.51	45.75	19.50	21.75	46.25	19.50	21.98	46.75	19.50	22.22
45.25	19.75	22.06	45.75	19.75	22.31	46.25	19.75	22.55	46.75	19.75	22.79
45.25	20.00	22.63	45.75	20.00	22.88	46.25	20.00	23.13	46.75	20.00	23.38
45.25	20.25	23.19	45.75	20.25	23.45	46.25	20.25	23.71	46.75	20.25	23.96
45.25	20.50	23.77	45.75	20.50	24.03	46.25	20.50	24.30	46.75	20.50	24.56
45.25	20.75	24.35	45.75	20.75	24.62	46.25	20.75	24.89	46.75	20.75	25.16
45.25	21.00	24.94	45.75	21.00	25.22	46.25	21.00	25.50	46.75	21.00	25.77
45.25	21.25	25.54	45.75	21.25	25.82	46.25	21.25	26.11	46.75	21.25	26.39
45.25	21.50	26.15	45.75	21.50	26.43	46.25	21.50	26.72	46.75	21.50	27.01
45.25	21.75	26.76	45.75	21.75	27.05	46.25	21.75	27.35	46.75	21.75	27.64
45.25	22.00	27.38	45.75	22.00	27.68	46.25	22.00	27.98	46.75	22.00	28.28
45.25	22.25	28.00	45.75	22.25	28.31	46.25	22.25	28.62	46.75	22.25	28.93
45.25	22.50	28.63	45.75	22.50	28.95	46.25	22.50	29.27	46.75	22.50	29.58

Estimated Weight Charts

Length	Girth	Weight	Length	Girth	Weight	Length	Girth	Weight	Length	Girth	Weight
47.00	20.00	23.50	47.50	20.00	23.75	48.00	20.00	24.00	48.50	20.00	24.25
47.00	20.25	24.09	47.50	20.25	24.35	48.00	20.25	24.60	48.50	20.25	24.86
47.00	20.50	24.69	47.50	20.50	24.95	48.00	20.50	25.22	48.50	20.50	25.48
47.00	20.75	25.30	47.50	20.75	25.56	48.00	20.75	25.83	48.50	20.75	26.10
47.00	21.00	25.91	47.50	21.00	26.18	48.00	21.00	26.46	48.50	21.00	26.74
47.00	21.25	26.53	47.50	21.25	26.81	48.00	21.25	27.09	48.50	21.25	27.38
47.00	21.50	27.16	47.50	21.50	27.45	48.00	21.50	27.74	48.50	21.50	28.02
47.00	21.75	27.79	47.50	21.75	28.09	48.00	21.75	28.38	48.50	21.75	28.68
47.00	22.00	28.44	47.50	22.00	28.74	48.00	22.00	29.04	48.50	22.00	29.34
47.00	22.25	29.08	47.50	22.25	29.39	48.00	22.25	29.70	48.50	22.25	30.01
47.00	22.50	29.74	47.50	22.50	30.06	48.00	22.50	30.38	48.50	22.50	30.69
47.00	22.75	30.41	47.50	22.75	30.73	48.00	22.75	31.05	48.50	22.75	31.38
47.00	23.00	31.08	47.50	23.00	31.41	48.00	23.00	31.74	48.50	23.00	32.07
47.00	23.25	31.76	47.50	23.25	32.10	48.00	23.25	32.43	48.50	23.25	32.77
47.00	23.50	32.44	47.50	23.50	32.79	48.00	23.50	33.14	48.50	23.50	33.48
47.00	23.75	33.14	47.50	23.75	33.49	48.00	23.75	33.84	48.50	23.75	34.20
47.00	24.00	33.84	47.50	24.00	34.20	48.00	24.00	34.56	48.50	24.00	34.92
47.00	24.25	34.55	47.50	24.25	34.92	48.00	24.25	35.28	48.50	24.25	35.65
47.00	24.50	35.26	47.50	24.50	35.64	48.00	24.50	36.02	48.50	24.50	36.39
47.00	24.75	35.99	47.50	24.75	36.37	48.00	24.75	36.76	48.50	24.75	37.14
47.00	25.00	36.72	47.50	25.00	37.11	48.00	25.00	37.50	48.50	25.00	37.89
47.00	25.25	37.46	47.50	25.25	37.86	48.00	25.25	38.25	48.50	25.25	38.65
47.00	25.50	38.20	47.50	25.50	38.61	48.00	25.50	39.02	48.50	25.50	39.42
47.00	25.75	38.95	47.50	25.75	39.37	48.00	25.75	39.78	48.50	25.75	40.20
47.00	26.00	39.72	47.50	26.00	40.14	48.00	26.00	40.56	48.50	26.00	40.98
47.00	26.25	40.48	47.50	26.25	40.91	48.00	26.25	41.34	48.50	26.25	41.77
47.00	26.50	41.26	47.50	26.50	41.70	48.00	26.50	42.14	48.50	26.50	42.57
47.00	26.75	42.04	47.50	26.75	42.49	48.00	26.75	42.93	48.50	26.75	43.38
47.00	27.00	42.83	47.50	27.00	43.28	48.00	27.00	43.74	48.50	27.00	44.20
47.00	27.25	43.63	47.50	27.25	44.09	48.00	27.25	44.55	48.50	27.25	45.02
47.00	27.50	44.43	47.50	27.50	44.90	48.00	27.50	45.38	48.50	27.50	45.85
47.00	27.75	45.24	47.50	27.75	45.72	48.00	27.75	46.20	48.50	27.75	46.69
47.00	28.00	46.06	47.50	28.00	46.55	48.00	28.00	47.04	48.50	28.00	47.53
47.00	28.25	46.89	47.50	28.25	47.38	48.00	28.25	47.88	48.50	28.25	48.38
47.00	28.50	47.72	47.50	28.50	48.23	48.00	28.50	48.74	48.50	28.50	49.24

Length	Girth	Weight	Length	Girth	Weight	Length	Girth	Weight	Length	Girth	Weight
47.25	20.00	23.63	47.75	20.00	23.88	48.25	20.00	24.13	48.75	20.00	24.38
47.25	20.25	24.22	47.75	20.25	24.48	48.25	20.25	24.73	48.75	20.25	24.99
47.25	20.50	24.82	47.75	20.50	25.08	48.25	20.50	25.35	48.75	20.50	25.61
47.25	20.75	25.43	47.75	20.75	25.70	48.25	20.75	25.97	48.75	20.75	26.24
47.25	21.00	26.05	47.75	21.00	26.32	48.25	21.00	26.60	48.75	21.00	26.87
47.25	21.25	26.67	47.75	21.25	26.95	48.25	21.25	27.23	48.75	21.25	27.52
47.25	21.50	27.30	47.75	21.50	27.59	48.25	21.50	27.88	48.75	21.50	28.17
47.25	21.75	27.94	47.75	21.75	28.24	48.25	21.75	28.53	48.75	21.75	28.83
47.25	22.00	28.59	47.75	22.00	28.89	48.25	22.00	29.19	48.75	22.00	29.49
47.25	22.25	29.24	47.75	22.25	29.55	48.26	22.25	29.86	48.75	22.25	30.17
47.25	22.50	29.90	47.75	22.50	30.22	48.25	22.50	30.53	48.75	22.50	30.85
47.25	22.75	30.57	47.75	22.75	30.89	48.25	22.75	31.22	48.75	22.75	31.54
47.25	23.00	31.24	47.75	23.00	31.57	48.25	23.00	31.91	48.75	23.00	32.24
47.25	23.25	31.93	47.75	23.25	32.26	48.25	23.25	32.60	48.75	23.25	32.94
47.25	23.50	32.62	47.75	23.50	32.96	48.25	23.50	33.31	48.75	23.50	33.65
47.25	23.75	33.31	47.75	23.75	33.67	48.25	23.75	34.02	48.75	23.75	34.37
47.25	24.00	34.02	47.75	24.00	34.38	48.25	24.00	34.74	48.75	24.00	35.10
47.25	24.25	34.73	47.75	24.25	35.10	48.25	24.25	35.47	48.75	24.25	35.84
47.25	24.50	35.45	47.75	24.50	35.83	48.25	24.50	36.20	48.75	24.50	36.58
47.25	24.75	36.18	47.75	24.75	36.56	48.25	24.75	36.95	48.75	24.75	37.33
47.25	25.00	36.91	47.75	25.00	37.30	48.25	25.00	37.70	48.75	25.00	38.09
47.25	25.25	37.66	47.75	25.25	38.05	48.25	25.25	38.45	48.75	25.25	38.85
47.25	25.50	38.41	47.75	25.50	38.81	48.25	25.50	39.22	48.75	25.50	39.62
47.25	25.75	39.16	47.75	25.75	39.58	48.25	25.75	39.99	48.75	25.75	40.41
47.25	26.00	39.93	47.75	26.00	40.35	48.25	26.00	40.77	48.75	26.00	41.19
47.25	26.25	40.70	47.75	26.25	41.13	48.25	26.25	41.56	48.75	26.25	41.99
47.25	26.50	41.48	47.75	26.50	41.92	48.25	26.50	42.35	48.75	26.50	42.79
47.25	26.75	42.26	47.75	26.75	42.71	48.25	26.75	43.16	48.75	26.75	43.60
47.25	27.00	43.06	47.75	27.00	43.51	48.25	27.00	43.97	48.75	27.00	44.42
47.25	27.25	43.86	47.75	27.25	44.32	48.25	27.25	44.79	48.75	27.25	45.25
47.25	27.50	44.67	47.75	27.50	45.14	48.25	27.50	45.61	48.75	27.50	46.08
47.25	27.75	45.48	47.75	27.75	45.96	48.25	27.75	46.44	48.75	27.75	46.93
47.25	28.00	46.31	47.75	28.00	46.80	48.25	28.00	47.29	48.75	28.00	47.78
47.25	28.25	47.14	47.75	28.25	47.63	48.25	28.25	48.13	48.75	28.25	48.63
47.25	28.50	47.97	47.75	28.50	48.48	48.25	28.50	48.99	48.75	28.50	49.50

1996 Musky Hunter's Almanac

Length	Girth	Weight	Length	Girth	Weight	Length	Girth	Weight	Length	Girth	Weight
49.00	21.00	27.01	49.50	21.00	27.29	50.00	21.00	27.56	50.50	21.00	27.84
49.00	21.25	27.66	49.50	21.25	27.94	50.00	21.25	28.22	50.50	21.25	28.50
49.00	21.50	28.31	49.50	21.50	28.60	50.00	21.50	28.89	50.50	21.50	29.18
49.00	21.75	28.98	49.50	21.75	29.27	50.00	21.75	29.57	50.50	21.75	29.86
49.00	22.00	29.65	49.50	22.00	29.95	50.00	22.00	30.25	50.50	22.00	30.55
49.00	22.25	30.32	49.50	22.25	30.63	50.00	22.25	30.94	50.50	22.25	31.25
49.00	22.50	31.01	49.50	22.50	31.32	50.00	22.50	31.64	50.50	22.50	31.96
49.00	22.75	31.70	49.50	22.75	32.02	50.00	22.75	32.35	50.50	22.75	32.67
49.00	23.00	32.40	49.50	23.00	32.73	50.00	23.00	33.06	50.50	23.00	33.39
49.00	23.25	33.11	49.50	23.25	33.45	50.00	23.25	33.79	50.50	23.25	34.12
49.00	23.50	33.83	49.50	23.50	34.17	50.00	23.50	34.52	50.50	23.50	34.86
49.00	23.75	34.55	49.50	23.75	34.90	50.00	23.75	35.25	50.50	23.75	35.61
49.00	24.00	35.28	49.50	24.00	35.64	50.00	24.00	36.00	50.50	24.00	36.36
49.00	24.25	36.02	49.50	24.25	36.39	50.00	24.25	36.75	50.50	24.25	37.12
49.00	24.50	36.77	49.50	24.50	37.14	50.00	24.50	37.52	50.50	24.50	37.89
49.00	24.75	37.52	49.50	24.75	37.90	50.00	24.75	38.29	50.50	24.75	38.67
49.00	25.00	38.28	49.50	25.00	38.67	50.00	25.00	39.06	50.50	25.00	39.45
49.00	25.25	39.05	49.50	25.25	39.45	50.00	25.25	39.85	50.50	25.25	40.25
49.00	25.50	39.83	49.50	25.50	40.23	50.00	25.50	40.64	50.50	25.50	41.05
49.00	25.75	40.61	49.50	25.75	41.03	50.00	25.75	41.44	50.50	25.75	41.86
49.00	26.00	41.41	49.50	26.00	41.83	50.00	26.00	42.25	50.50	26.00	42.67
49.00	26.25	42.21	49.50	26.25	42.64	50.00	26.25	43.07	50.50	26.25	43.50
49.00	26.50	43.01	49.50	26.50	43.45	50.00	26.50	43.89	50.50	26.50	44.33
49.00	26.75	43.83	49.50	26.75	44.28	50.00	26.75	44.72	50.50	26.75	45.17
49.00	27.00	44.65	49.50	27.00	45.11	50.00	27.00	45.56	50.50	27.00	46.02
49.00	27.25	45.48	49.50	27.25	45.95	50.00	27.25	46.41	50.50	27.25	46.87
49.00	27.50	46.32	49.50	27.50	46.79	50.00	27.50	47.27	50.50	27.50	47.74
49.00	27.75	47.17	49.50	27.75	47.65	50.00	27.75	48.13	50.50	27.75	48.61
49.00	28.00	48.02	49.50	28.00	48.51	50.00	28.00	49.00	50.50	28.00	49.49
49.00	28.25	48.88	49.50	28.25	49.38	50.00	28.25	49.88	50.50	28.25	50.38
49.00	28.50	49.75	49.50	28.50	50.26	50.00	28.50	50.77	50.50	28.50	51.27
49.00	28.75	50.63	49.50	28.75	51.14	50.00	28.75	51.66	50.50	28.75	52.18
49.00	29.00	51.51	49.50	29.00	52.04	50.00	29.00	52.56	50.50	29.00	53.09
49.00	29.25	52.40	49.50	29.25	52.94	50.00	29.25	53.47	50.50	29.25	54.01
49.00	29.50	53.30	49.50	29.50	53.85	50.00	29.50	54.39	50.50	29.50	54.93

Length	Girth	Weight	Length	Girth	Weight	Length	Girth	Weight	Length	Girth	Weight
49.25	21.00	27.15	49.75	21.00	27.42	50.25	21.00	27.70	50.75	21.00	27.98
49.25	21.25	27.80	49.75	21.25	28.08	50.25	21.25	28.36	50.75	21.25	28.65
49.25	21.50	28.46	49.75	21.50	28.75	50.25	21.50	29.04	50.75	21.50	29.32
49.25	21.75	29.12	49.75	21.75	29.42	50.25	21.75	29.71	50.75	21.75	30.01
49.25	22.00	29.80	49.75	22.00	30.10	50.25	22.00	30.40	50.75	22.00	30.70
49.25	22.25	30.48	49.75	22.25	30.79	50.25	22.25	31.10	50.75	22.25	31.41
49.25	22.50	31.17	49.75	22.50	31.48	50.25	22.50	31.80	50.75	22.50	32.12
49.25	22.75	31.86	49.75	22.75	32.19	50.25	22.75	32.51	50.75	22.75	32.83
49.25	23.00	32.57	49.75	23.00	32.90	50.25	23.00	33.23	50.75	23.00	33.56
49.25	23.25	33.28	49.75	23.25	33.62	50.25	23.25	33.95	50.75	23.25	34.29
49.25	23.50	34.00	49.75	23.50	34.34	50.25	23.50	34.69	50.75	23.50	35.03
49.25	23.75	34.73	49.75	23.75	35.08	50.25	23.75	35.43	50.75	23.75	35.78
49.25	24.00	35.46	49.75	24.00	35.82	50.25	24.00	36.18	50.75	24.00	36.54
49.25	24.25	36.20	49.75	24.25	36.57	50.25	24.25	36.94	50.75	24.25	37.31
49.25	24.50	36.95	49.75	24.50	37.33	50.25	24.50	37.70	50.75	24.50	38.08
49.25	24.75	37.71	49.75	24.75	38.09	50.25	24.75	38.48	50.75	24.75	38.86
49.25	25.00	38.48	49.75	25.00	38.87	50.25	25.00	39.26	50.75	25.00	39.65
49.25	25.25	39.25	49.75	25.25	39.66	50.25	25.25	40.05	50.75	25.25	40.45
49.25	25.50	40.03	49.75	25.50	40.44	50.25	25.50	40.84	50.75	25.50	41.25
49.25	25.75	40.82	49.75	25.75	41.23	50.25	25.75	41.65	50.75	25.75	42.06
49.25	26.00	41.62	49.75	26.00	42.04	50.25	26.00	42.46	50.75	26.00	42.88
49.25	26.25	42.42	49.75	26.25	42.85	50.25	26.25	43.28	50.75	26.25	43.71
49.25	26.50	43.23	49.75	26.50	43.67	50.25	26.50	44.11	50.75	26.50	44.55
49.25	26.75	44.05	49.75	26.75	44.50	50.25	26.75	44.95	50.75	26.75	45.39
49.25	27.00	44.88	49.75	27.00	45.33	50.25	27.00	45.79	50.75	27.00	46.25
49.25	27.25	45.71	49.75	27.25	46.18	50.25	27.25	46.64	50.75	27.25	47.11
49.25	27.50	46.56	49.75	27.50	47.03	50.25	27.50	47.50	50.75	27.50	47.97
49.25	27.75	47.41	49.75	27.75	47.89	50.25	27.75	48.37	50.75	27.75	48.85
49.25	28.00	48.27	49.75	28.00	48.76	50.25	28.00	49.25	50.75	28.00	49.74
49.25	28.25	49.13	49.75	28.25	49.63	50.25	28.25	50.13	50.75	28.25	50.63
49.25	28.50	50.00	49.75	28.50	50.51	50.25	28.50	51.02	50.75	28.50	51.53
49.25	28.75	50.89	49.75	28.75	51.40	50.25	28.75	51.92	50.75	28.75	52.44
49.25	29.00	51.77	49.75	29.00	52.30	50.25	29.00	52.83	50.75	29.00	53.35
49.25	29.25	52.67	49.75	29.25	53.21	50.25	29.25	53.74	50.75	29.25	54.27
49.25	29.50	53.57	49.75	29.50	54.12	50.25	29.50	54.66	50.75	29.50	55.21

Estimated Weight Charts

Length	Girth	Weight	Length	Girth	Weight	Length	Girth	Weight	Length	Girth	Weight
51.00	21.00	28.11	51.50	21.00	28.39	52.00	21.00	28.67	52.50	21.00	28.94
51.00	21.25	28.79	51.50	21.25	29.07	52.00	21.25	29.35	52.50	21.25	29.63
51.00	21.50	29.47	51.50	21.50	29.76	52.00	21.50	30.05	52.50	21.50	30.34
51.00	21.75	30.16	51.50	21.75	30.45	52.00	21.75	30.75	52.50	21.75	31.04
51.00	22.00	30.86	51.50	22.00	31.16	52.00	22.00	31.46	52.50	22.00	31.76
51.00	22.25	31.56	51.50	22.25	31.87	52.00	22.25	32.18	52.50	22.25	32.49
51.00	22.50	32.27	51.50	22.50	32.59	52.00	22.50	32.91	52.50	22.50	33.22
51.00	22.75	32.99	51.50	22.75	33.32	52.00	22.75	33.64	52.50	22.75	33.97
51.00	23.00	33.72	51.50	23.00	34.05	52.00	23.00	34.39	52.50	23.00	34.72
51.00	23.25	34.46	51.50	23.25	34.80	52.00	23.25	35.14	52.50	23.25	35.47
51.00	23.50	35.21	51.50	23.50	35.55	52.00	23.50	35.90	52.50	23.50	36.24
51.00	23.75	35.96	51.50	23.75	36.31	52.00	23.75	36.66	52.50	23.75	37.02
51.00	24.00	36.72	51.50	24.00	37.08	52.00	24.00	37.44	52.50	24.00	37.80
51.00	24.25	37.49	51.50	24.25	37.86	52.00	24.25	38.22	52.50	24.25	38.59
51.00	24.50	38.27	51.50	24.50	38.64	52.00	24.50	39.02	52.50	24.50	39.39
51.00	24.75	39.05	51.50	24.75	39.43	52.00	24.75	39.82	52.50	24.75	40.20
51.00	25.00	39.84	51.50	25.00	40.23	52.00	25.00	40.63	52.50	25.00	41.02
51.00	25.25	40.64	51.50	25.25	41.04	52.00	25.25	41.44	52.50	25.25	41.84
51.00	25.50	41.45	51.50	25.50	41.86	52.00	25.50	42.27	52.50	25.50	42.67
51.00	25.75	42.27	51.50	25.75	42.68	52.00	25.75	43.10	52.50	25.75	43.51
51.00	26.00	43.10	51.50	26.00	43.52	52.00	26.00	43.94	52.50	26.00	44.36
51.00	26.25	43.93	51.50	26.25	44.36	52.00	26.25	44.79	52.50	26.25	45.22
51.00	26.50	44.77	51.50	26.50	45.21	52.00	26.50	45.65	52.50	26.50	46.09
51.00	26.75	45.62	51.50	26.75	46.06	52.00	26.75	46.51	52.50	26.75	46.96
51.00	27.00	46.47	51.50	27.00	46.93	52.00	27.00	47.39	52.50	27.00	47.84
51.00	27.25	47.34	51.50	27.25	47.80	52.00	27.25	48.27	52.50	27.25	48.73
51.00	27.50	48.21	51.50	27.50	48.68	52.00	27.50	49.16	52.50	27.50	49.63
51.00	27.75	49.09	51.50	27.75	49.57	52.00	27.75	50.05	52.50	27.75	50.54
51.00	28.00	49.98	51.50	28.00	50.47	52.00	28.00	50.96	52.50	28.00	51.45
51.00	28.25	50.88	51.50	28.25	51.38	52.00	28.25	51.87	52.50	28.25	52.37
51.00	28.50	51.78	51.50	28.50	52.29	52.00	28.50	52.80	52.50	28.50	53.30
51.00	28.75	52.69	51.50	28.75	53.21	52.00	28.75	53.73	52.50	28.75	54.24
51.00	29.00	53.61	51.50	29.00	54.14	52.00	29.00	54.67	52.50	29.00	55.19
51.00	29.25	54.54	51.50	29.25	55.08	52.00	29.25	55.61	52.50	29.25	56.15
51.00	29.50	55.48	51.50	29.50	56.02	52.00	29.50	56.57	52.50	29.50	57.11
51.25	21.00	28.25	51.75	21.00	28.53	52.25	21.00	28.80	52.75	21.00	29.08
51.25	21.25	28.93	51.75	21.25	29.21	52.25	21.25	29.49	52.75	21.25	29.77
51.25	21.50	29.61	51.75	21.50	29.90	52.25	21.50	30.19	52.75	21.50	30.48
51.25	21.75	30.31	51.75	21.75	30.60	52.25	21.75	30.90	52.75	21.75	31.19
51.25	22.00	31.01	51.75	22.00	31.31	52.25	22.00	31.61	52.75	22.00	31.91
51.25	22.25	31.71	51.75	22.25	32.02	52.25	22.25	32.33	52.75	22.25	32.64
51.25	22.50	32.43	51.75	22.50	32.75	52.25	22.50	33.06	52.75	22.50	33.38
51.25	22.75	33.16	51.75	22.75	33.48	52.25	22.75	33.80	52.75	22.75	34.13
51.25	23.00	33.89	51.75	23.00	34.22	52.25	23.00	34.55	52.75	23.00	34.88
51.25	23.25	34.63	51.75	23.25	34.97	52.25	23.25	35.31	52.75	23.25	35.64
51.25	23.50	35.38	51.75	23.50	35.72	52.25	23.50	36.07	52.75	23.50	36.41
51.25	23.75	36.14	51.75	23.75	36.49	52.25	23.75	36.84	52.75	23.75	37.19
51.25	24.00	36.90	51.75	24.00	37.26	52.25	24.00	37.62	52.75	24.00	37.98
51.25	24.25	37.67	51.75	24.25	38.04	52.25	24.25	38.41	52.75	24.25	38.78
51.25	24.50	38.45	51.75	24.50	38.83	52.25	24.50	39.20	52.75	24.50	39.58
51.25	24.75	39.24	51.75	24.75	39.63	52.25	24.75	40.01	52.75	24.75	40.39
51.25	25.00	40.04	51.75	25.00	40.43	52.25	25.00	40.82	52.75	25.00	41.21
51.25	25.25	40.84	51.75	25.25	41.24	52.25	25.25	41.64	52.75	25.25	42.04
51.25	25.50	41.66	51.75	25.50	42.06	52.25	25.50	42.47	52.75	25.50	42.88
51.25	25.75	42.48	51.75	25.75	42.89	52.25	25.75	43.31	52.75	25.75	43.72
51.25	26.00	43.31	51.75	26.00	43.73	52.25	26.00	44.15	52.75	26.00	44.57
51.25	26.25	44.14	51.75	26.25	44.57	52.25	26.25	45.00	52.75	26.25	45.44
51.25	26.50	44.99	51.75	26.50	45.43	52.25	26.50	45.87	52.75	26.50	46.30
51.25	26.75	45.84	51.75	26.75	46.29	52.25	26.75	46.74	52.75	26.75	47.18
51.25	27.00	46.70	51.75	27.00	47.16	52.25	27.00	47.61	52.75	27.00	48.07
51.25	27.25	47.57	51.75	27.25	48.03	52.25	27.25	48.50	52.75	27.25	48.96
51.25	27.50	48.45	51.75	27.50	48.92	52.25	27.50	49.39	52.75	27.50	49.87
51.25	27.75	49.33	51.75	27.75	49.81	52.25	27.75	50.29	52.75	27.75	50.78
51.25	28.00	50.23	51.75	28.00	50.72	52.25	28.00	51.21	52.75	28.00	51.70
51.25	28.25	51.13	51.75	28.25	51.63	52.25	28.25	52.12	52.75	28.25	52.62
51.25	28.50	52.03	51.75	28.50	52.54	52.25	28.50	53.05	52.75	28.50	53.56
51.25	28.75	52.95	51.75	28.75	53.47	52.25	28.75	53.98	52.75	28.75	54.50
51.25	29.00	53.88	51.75	29.00	54.40	52.25	29.00	54.93	52.75	29.00	55.45
51.25	29.25	54.81	51.75	29.25	55.34	52.25	29.25	55.88	52.75	29.25	56.41
51.25	29.50	55.75	51.75	29.50	56.29	52.25	29.50	56.84	52.75	29.50	57.38

1996 Musky Hunter's Almanac

Length	Girth	Weight	Length	Girth	Weight	Length	Girth	Weight	Length	Girth	Weight
53.00	21.00	29.22	53.50	21.00	29.49	54.00	22.00	32.67	54.50	22.00	32.97
53.00	21.25	29.92	53.50	21.25	30.20	54.00	22.25	33.42	54.50	22.25	33.73
53.00	21.50	30.62	53.50	21.50	30.91	54.00	22.50	34.17	54.50	22.50	34.49
53.00	21.75	31.34	53.50	21.75	31.64	54.00	22.75	34.94	54.50	22.75	35.26
53.00	22.00	32.07	53.50	22.00	32.37	54.00	23.00	35.71	54.50	23.00	36.04
53.00	22.25	32.80	53.50	22.25	33.11	54.00	23.25	36.49	54.50	23.25	36.83
53.00	22.50	33.54	53.50	22.50	33.86	54.00	23.50	37.28	54.50	23.50	37.62
53.00	22.75	34.29	53.50	22.75	34.61	54.00	23.75	38.07	54.50	23.75	38.43
53.00	23.00	35.05	53.50	23.00	35.38	54.00	24.00	38.88	54.50	24.00	39.24
53.00	23.25	35.81	53.50	23.25	36.15	54.00	24.25	39.69	54.50	24.25	40.06
53.00	23.50	36.59	53.50	23.50	36.93	54.00	24.50	40.52	54.50	24.50	40.89
53.00	23.75	37.37	53.50	23.75	37.72	54.00	24.75	41.35	54.50	24.75	41.73
53.00	24.00	38.16	53.50	24.00	38.52	54.00	25.00	42.19	54.50	25.00	42.58
53.00	24.25	38.96	53.50	24.25	39.33	54.00	25.25	43.04	54.50	25.25	43.43
53.00	24.50	39.77	53.50	24.50	40.14	54.00	25.50	43.89	54.50	25.50	44.30
53.00	24.75	40.58	53.50	24.75	40.97	54.00	25.75	44.76	54.50	25.75	45.17
53.00	25.00	41.41	53.50	25.00	41.80	54.00	26.00	45.63	54.50	26.00	46.05
53.00	25.25	42.24	53.50	25.25	42.64	54.00	26.25	46.51	54.50	26.25	46.94
53.00	25.50	43.08	53.50	25.50	43.49	54.00	26.50	47.40	54.50	26.50	47.84
53.00	25.75	43.93	53.50	25.75	44.34	54.00	26.75	48.30	54.50	26.75	48.75
53.00	26.00	44.79	53.50	26.00	45.21	54.00	27.00	49.21	54.50	27.00	49.66
53.00	26.25	45.65	53.50	26.25	46.08	54.00	27.25	50.12	54.50	27.25	50.59
53.00	26.50	46.52	53.50	26.50	46.96	54.00	27.50	51.05	54.50	27.50	51.52
53.00	26.75	47.41	53.50	26.75	47.85	54.00	27.75	51.98	54.50	27.75	52.46
53.00	27.00	48.30	53.50	27.00	48.75	54.00	28.00	52.92	54.50	28.00	53.41
53.00	27.25	49.19	53.50	27.25	49.66	54.00	28.25	53.87	54.50	28.25	54.37
53.00	27.50	50.10	53.50	27.50	50.57	54.00	28.50	54.83	54.50	28.50	55.33
53.00	27.75	51.02	53.50	27.75	51.50	54.00	28.75	55.79	54.50	28.75	56.31
53.00	28.00	51.94	53.50	28.00	52.43	54.00	29.00	56.77	54.50	29.00	57.29
53.00	28.25	52.87	53.50	28.25	53.37	54.00	29.25	57.75	54.50	29.25	58.29
53.00	28.50	53.81	53.50	28.50	54.32	54.00	29.50	58.74	54.50	29.50	59.29
53.00	28.75	54.76	53.50	28.75	55.28	54.00	29.75	59.74	54.50	29.75	60.29
53.00	29.00	55.72	53.50	29.00	56.24	54.00	30.00	60.75	54.50	30.00	61.31
53.00	29.25	56.68	53.50	29.25	57.22	54.00	30.25	61.77	54.50	30.25	62.34
53.00	29.50	57.65	53.50	29.50	58.20	54.00	30.50	62.79	54.50	30.50	63.37

Length	Girth	Weight	Length	Girth	Weight	Length	Girth	Weight	Length	Girth	Weight
53.25	22.00	32.22	53.75	22.00	32.52	54.25	22.00	32.82	54.75	22.00	33.12
53.25	22.25	32.95	53.75	22.25	33.26	54.25	22.25	33.57	54.75	22.25	33.88
53.25	22.50	33.70	53.75	22.50	34.01	54.25	22.50	34.33	54.75	22.50	34.65
53.25	22.75	34.45	53.75	22.75	34.77	54.25	22.75	35.10	54.75	22.75	35.42
53.25	23.00	35.21	53.75	23.00	35.54	54.25	23.00	35.87	54.75	23.00	36.20
53.25	23.25	35.98	53.75	23.25	36.32	54.25	23.25	36.65	54.75	23.25	36.99
53.25	23.50	36.76	53.75	23.50	37.10	54.25	23.50	37.45	54.75	23.50	37.79
53.25	23.75	37.55	53.75	23.75	37.90	54.25	23.75	38.25	54.75	23.75	38.60
53.25	24.00	38.34	53.75	24.00	38.70	54.25	24.00	39.06	54.75	24.00	39.42
53.25	24.25	39.14	53.75	24.25	39.51	54.25	24.25	39.88	54.75	24.25	40.25
53.25	24.50	39.95	53.75	24.50	40.33	54.25	24.50	40.70	54.75	24.50	41.08
53.25	24.75	40.77	53.75	24.75	41.16	54.25	24.75	41.54	54.75	24.75	41.92
53.25	25.00	41.60	53.75	25.00	41.99	54.25	25.00	42.38	54.75	25.00	42.77
53.25	25.25	42.44	53.75	25.25	42.84	54.25	25.25	43.23	54.75	25.25	43.63
53.25	25.50	43.28	53.75	25.50	43.69	54.25	25.50	44.10	54.75	25.50	44.50
53.25	25.75	44.14	53.75	25.75	44.55	54.25	25.75	44.96	54.75	25.75	45.38
53.25	26.00	45.00	53.75	26.00	45.42	54.25	26.00	45.84	54.75	26.00	46.26
53.25	26.25	45.87	53.75	26.25	46.30	54.25	26.25	46.73	54.75	26.25	47.16
53.25	26.50	46.74	53.75	26.50	47.18	54.25	26.50	47.62	54.75	26.50	48.06
53.25	26.75	47.63	53.75	26.75	48.06	54.25	26.75	48.52	54.75	26.75	48.97
53.25	27.00	48.52	53.75	27.00	48.98	54.25	27.00	49.44	54.75	27.00	49.89
53.25	27.25	49.43	53.75	27.25	49.89	54.25	27.25	50.36	54.75	27.25	50.82
53.25	27.50	50.34	53.75	27.50	50.81	54.25	27.50	51.28	54.75	27.50	51.76
53.25	27.75	51.26	53.75	27.75	51.74	54.25	27.75	52.22	54.75	27.75	52.70
53.25	28.00	52.19	53.75	28.00	52.68	54.25	28.00	53.17	54.75	28.00	53.66
53.25	28.25	53.12	53.75	28.25	53.62	54.25	28.25	54.12	54.75	28.25	54.62
53.25	28.50	54.07	53.75	28.50	54.57	54.25	28.50	55.08	54.75	28.50	55.59
53.25	28.75	55.02	53.75	28.75	55.53	54.25	28.75	56.05	54.75	28.75	56.57
53.25	29.00	55.98	53.75	29.00	56.50	54.25	29.00	57.03	54.75	29.00	57.56
53.25	29.25	56.95	53.75	29.25	57.48	54.25	29.25	58.02	54.75	29.25	58.55
53.25	29.50	57.93	53.75	29.50	58.47	54.25	29.50	59.01	54.75	29.50	59.56
53.25	29.75	58.91	53.75	29.75	59.47	54.25	29.75	60.02	54.75	29.75	60.57
53.25	30.00	59.91	53.75	30.00	60.47	54.25	30.00	61.03	54.75	30.00	61.59
53.25	30.25	60.91	53.75	30.25	61.48	54.25	30.25	62.05	54.75	30.25	62.62
53.25	30.50	61.92	53.75	30.50	62.50	54.25	30.50	63.08	54.75	30.50	63.66

Estimated Weight Charts

Length	Girth	Weight	Length	Girth	Weight	Length	Girth	Weight	Length	Girth	Weight
55.00	22.00	33.28	55.50	22.00	33.58	56.00	22.00	33.88	56.50	22.00	34.18
55.00	22.25	34.04	55.50	22.25	34.34	56.00	22.25	34.65	56.50	22.25	34.96
55.00	22.50	34.80	55.50	22.50	35.12	56.00	22.50	35.44	56.50	22.50	35.75
55.00	22.75	35.58	55.50	22.75	35.91	56.00	22.75	36.23	56.50	22.75	36.55
55.00	23.00	36.37	55.50	23.00	36.70	56.00	23.00	37.03	56.50	23.00	37.36
55.00	23.25	37.16	55.50	23.25	37.50	56.00	23.25	37.84	56.50	23.25	38.18
55.00	23.50	37.97	55.50	23.50	38.31	56.00	23.50	38.66	56.50	23.50	39.00
55.00	23.75	38.78	55.50	23.75	39.13	56.00	23.75	39.48	56.50	23.75	39.84
55.00	24.00	39.60	55.50	24.00	39.96	56.00	24.00	40.32	56.50	24.00	40.68
55.00	24.25	40.43	55.50	24.25	40.80	56.00	24.25	41.16	56.50	24.25	41.53
55.00	24.50	41.27	55.50	24.50	41.64	56.00	24.50	42.02	56.50	24.50	42.39
55.00	24.75	42.11	55.50	24.75	42.50	56.00	24.75	42.88	56.50	24.75	43.26
55.00	25.00	42.97	55.50	25.00	43.36	56.00	25.00	43.75	56.50	25.00	44.14
55.00	25.25	43.83	55.50	25.25	44.23	56.00	25.25	44.63	56.50	25.25	45.03
55.00	25.50	44.70	55.50	25.50	45.11	56.00	25.50	45.52	56.50	25.50	45.92
55.00	25.75	45.59	55.50	25.75	46.00	56.00	25.75	46.41	56.50	25.75	46.83
55.00	26.00	46.48	55.50	26.00	46.90	56.00	26.00	47.32	56.50	26.00	47.74
55.00	26.25	47.37	55.50	26.25	47.80	56.00	26.25	48.23	56.50	26.25	48.67
55.00	26.50	48.28	55.50	26.50	48.72	56.00	26.50	49.16	56.50	26.50	49.60
55.00	26.75	49.19	55.50	26.75	49.64	56.00	26.75	50.09	56.50	26.75	50.54
55.00	27.00	50.12	55.50	27.00	50.57	56.00	27.00	51.03	56.50	27.00	51.49
55.00	27.25	51.05	55.50	27.25	51.52	56.00	27.25	51.98	56.50	27.25	52.44
55.00	27.50	51.99	55.50	27.50	52.46	56.00	27.50	52.94	56.50	27.50	53.41
55.00	27.75	52.94	55.50	27.75	53.42	56.00	27.75	53.90	56.50	27.75	54.39
55.00	28.00	53.90	55.50	28.00	54.39	56.00	28.00	54.88	56.50	28.00	55.37
55.00	28.25	54.87	55.50	28.25	55.37	56.00	28.25	55.86	56.50	28.25	56.36
55.00	28.50	55.84	55.50	28.50	56.35	56.00	28.50	56.86	56.50	28.50	57.37
55.00	28.75	56.83	55.50	28.75	57.34	56.00	28.75	57.86	56.50	28.75	58.38
55.00	29.00	57.82	55.50	29.00	58.34	56.00	29.00	58.87	56.50	29.00	59.40
55.00	29.25	58.82	55.50	29.25	59.35	56.00	29.25	59.89	56.50	29.25	60.42
55.00	29.50	59.83	55.50	29.50	60.37	56.00	29.50	60.92	56.50	29.50	61.46
55.00	29.75	60.85	55.50	29.75	61.40	56.00	29.75	61.95	56.50	29.75	62.51
55.00	30.00	61.88	55.50	30.00	62.44	56.00	30.00	63.00	56.50	30.00	63.56
55.00	30.25	62.91	55.50	30.25	63.48	56.00	30.25	64.05	56.50	30.25	64.63
55.00	30.50	63.95	55.50	30.50	64.54	56.00	30.50	65.12	56.50	30.50	65.70

Length	Girth	Weight	Length	Girth	Weight	Length	Girth	Weight	Length	Girth	Weight
55.25	23.00	36.53	55.75	23.00	36.86	56.25	23.00	37.20	56.75	23.00	37.53
55.25	23.25	37.33	55.75	23.25	37.67	56.25	23.25	38.01	56.75	23.25	38.35
55.25	23.50	38.14	55.75	23.50	38.48	56.25	23.50	38.83	56.75	23.50	39.18
55.25	23.75	38.96	55.75	23.75	39.31	56.25	23.75	39.66	56.75	23.75	40.01
55.25	24.00	39.78	55.75	24.00	40.14	56.25	24.00	40.50	56.75	24.00	40.86
55.25	24.25	40.61	55.75	24.25	40.98	56.25	24.25	41.35	56.75	24.25	41.72
55.25	24.50	41.45	55.75	24.50	41.83	56.25	24.50	42.21	56.75	24.50	42.58
55.25	24.75	42.31	55.75	24.75	42.69	56.25	24.75	43.07	56.75	24.75	43.45
55.25	25.00	43.16	55.75	25.00	43.55	56.25	25.00	43.95	56.75	25.00	44.34
55.25	25.25	44.03	55.75	25.25	44.43	56.25	25.25	44.83	56.75	25.25	45.23
55.25	25.50	44.91	55.75	25.50	45.31	56.25	25.50	45.72	56.75	25.50	46.13
55.25	25.75	45.79	55.75	25.75	46.21	56.25	25.75	46.62	56.75	25.75	47.04
55.25	26.00	46.69	55.75	26.00	47.11	56.25	26.00	47.53	56.75	26.00	47.95
55.25	26.25	47.59	55.75	26.25	48.02	56.25	26.25	48.45	56.75	26.25	48.88
55.25	26.50	48.50	55.75	26.50	48.94	56.25	26.50	49.38	56.75	26.50	49.82
55.25	26.75	49.42	55.75	26.75	49.87	56.25	26.75	50.31	56.75	26.75	50.76
55.25	27.00	50.35	55.75	27.00	50.80	56.25	27.00	51.26	56.75	27.00	51.71
55.25	27.25	51.28	55.75	27.25	51.75	56.25	27.25	52.21	56.75	27.25	52.68
55.25	27.50	52.23	55.75	27.50	52.70	56.25	27.50	53.17	56.75	27.50	53.65
55.25	27.75	53.18	55.75	27.75	53.66	56.25	27.75	54.15	56.75	27.75	54.63
55.25	28.00	54.15	55.75	28.00	54.64	56.25	28.00	55.13	56.75	28.00	55.62
55.25	28.25	55.12	55.75	28.25	55.61	56.25	28.25	56.11	56.75	28.25	56.61
55.25	28.50	56.10	55.75	28.50	56.60	56.25	28.50	57.11	56.75	28.50	57.62
55.25	28.75	57.08	55.75	28.75	57.60	56.25	28.75	58.12	56.75	28.75	58.63
55.25	29.00	58.08	55.75	29.00	58.61	56.25	29.00	59.13	56.75	29.00	59.66
55.25	29.25	59.09	55.75	29.25	59.62	56.25	29.25	60.16	56.75	29.25	60.69
55.25	29.50	60.10	55.75	29.50	60.65	56.25	29.50	61.19	56.75	29.50	61.73
55.25	29.75	61.12	55.75	29.75	61.68	56.25	29.75	62.23	56.75	29.75	62.78
55.25	30.00	62.16	55.75	30.00	62.72	56.25	30.00	63.28	56.75	30.00	63.84
55.25	30.25	63.20	55.75	30.25	63.77	56.25	30.25	64.34	56.75	30.25	64.91
55.25	30.50	64.25	55.75	30.50	64.83	56.25	30.50	65.41	56.75	30.50	65.99
55.25	30.75	65.30	55.75	30.75	65.89	56.25	30.75	66.48	56.75	30.75	67.08
55.25	31.00	66.37	55.75	31.00	66.97	56.25	31.00	67.57	56.75	31.00	68.17
55.25	31.25	67.44	55.75	31.25	68.05	56.25	31.25	68.66	56.75	31.25	69.27
55.25	31.50	68.53	55.75	31.50	69.15	56.25	31.50	69.77	56.75	31.50	70.39

1996 Musky Hunter's Almanac

Length	Girth	Weight	Length	Girth	Weight	Length	Girth	Weight	Length	Girth	Weight
57.00	23.00	37.69	57.50	23.00	38.02	58.00	23.00	38.35	58.50	23.00	38.68
57.00	23.25	38.52	57.50	23.25	38.85	58.00	23.25	39.19	58.50	23.25	39.53
57.00	23.50	39.35	57.50	23.50	39.69	58.00	23.50	40.04	58.50	23.50	40.38
57.00	23.75	40.19	57.50	23.75	40.54	58.00	23.75	40.89	58.50	23.75	41.25
57.00	24.00	41.04	57.50	24.00	41.40	58.00	24.00	41.76	58.50	24.00	42.12
57.00	24.25	41.90	57.50	24.25	42.27	58.00	24.25	42.63	58.50	24.25	43.00
57.00	24.50	42.77	57.50	24.50	43.14	58.00	24.50	43.52	58.50	24.50	43.89
57.00	24.75	43.65	57.50	24.75	44.03	58.00	24.75	44.41	58.50	24.75	44.79
57.00	25.00	44.53	57.50	25.00	44.92	58.00	25.00	45.31	58.50	25.00	45.70
57.00	25.25	45.43	57.50	25.25	45.82	58.00	25.25	46.22	58.50	25.25	46.62
57.00	25.50	46.33	57.50	25.50	46.74	58.00	25.50	47.14	58.50	25.50	47.55
57.00	25.75	47.24	57.50	25.75	47.66	58.00	25.75	48.07	58.50	25.75	48.49
57.00	26.00	48.17	57.50	26.00	48.59	58.00	26.00	49.01	58.50	26.00	49.43
57.00	26.25	49.10	57.50	26.25	49.53	58.00	26.25	49.96	58.50	26.25	50.39
57.00	26.50	50.04	57.50	26.50	50.47	58.00	26.50	50.91	58.50	26.50	51.35
57.00	26.75	50.98	57.50	26.75	51.43	58.00	26.75	51.88	58.50	26.75	52.33
57.00	27.00	51.94	57.50	27.00	52.40	58.00	27.00	52.85	58.50	27.00	53.31
57.00	27.25	52.91	57.50	27.25	53.37	58.00	27.25	53.84	58.50	27.25	54.30
57.00	27.50	53.88	57.50	27.50	54.36	58.00	27.50	54.83	58.50	27.50	55.30
57.00	27.75	54.87	57.50	27.75	55.35	58.00	27.75	55.83	58.50	27.75	56.31
57.00	28.00	55.86	57.50	28.00	56.35	58.00	28.00	56.84	58.50	28.00	57.33
57.00	28.25	56.86	57.50	28.25	57.36	58.00	28.25	57.86	58.50	28.25	58.36
57.00	28.50	57.87	57.50	28.50	58.38	58.00	28.50	58.89	58.50	28.50	59.40
57.00	28.75	58.89	57.50	28.75	59.41	58.00	28.75	59.93	58.50	28.75	60.44
57.00	29.00	59.92	57.50	29.00	60.45	58.00	29.00	60.97	58.50	29.00	61.50
57.00	29.25	60.96	57.50	29.25	61.49	58.00	29.25	62.03	58.50	29.25	62.56
57.00	29.50	62.01	57.50	29.50	62.55	58.00	29.50	63.09	58.50	29.50	63.64
57.00	29.75	63.06	57.50	29.75	63.61	58.00	29.75	64.17	58.50	29.75	64.72
57.00	30.00	64.13	57.50	30.00	64.69	58.00	30.00	65.26	58.50	30.00	65.81
57.00	30.25	65.20	57.50	30.25	65.77	58.00	30.25	66.34	58.50	30.25	66.91
57.00	30.50	66.28	57.50	30.50	66.86	58.00	30.50	67.44	58.50	30.50	68.02
57.00	30.75	67.37	57.50	30.75	67.96	58.00	30.75	68.55	58.50	30.75	69.14
57.00	31.00	68.47	57.50	31.00	69.07	58.00	31.00	69.67	58.50	31.00	70.27
57.00	31.25	69.58	57.50	31.25	70.19	58.00	31.25	70.80	58.50	31.25	71.41
57.00	31.50	70.70	57.50	31.50	71.32	58.00	31.50	71.94	58.50	31.50	72.56
Length	Girth	Weight	Length	Girth	Weight	Length	Girth	Weight	Length	Girth	Weight
57.25	24.00	41.22	57.75	24.00	41.58	58.25	24.00	41.94	58.75	24.00	42.30
57.25	24.25	42.08	57.75	24.25	42.45	58.25	24.25	42.82	58.75	24.25	43.19
57.25	24.50	42.96	57.75	24.50	43.33	58.25	24.50	43.71	58.75	24.50	44.08
57.25	24.75	43.84	57.75	24.75	44.22	58.25	24.75	44.60	58.75	24.75	44.99
57.25	25.00	44.73	57.75	25.00	45.12	58.25	25.00	45.51	58.75	25.00	45.90
57.25	25.25	45.63	57.75	25.25	46.02	58.25	25.25	46.42	58.75	25.25	46.82
57.25	25.50	46.53	57.75	25.50	46.94	58.25	25.50	47.35	58.75	25.50	47.75
57.25	25.75	47.45	57.75	25.75	47.86	58.25	25.75	48.28	58.75	25.75	48.69
57.25	26.00	48.38	57.75	26.00	48.80	58.25	26.00	49.22	58.75	26.00	49.64
57.25	26.25	49.31	57.75	26.25	49.74	58.25	26.25	50.17	58.75	26.25	50.60
57.25	26.50	50.25	57.75	26.50	50.69	58.25	26.50	51.13	58.75	26.50	51.57
57.25	26.75	51.21	57.75	26.75	51.65	58.25	26.75	52.10	58.75	26.75	52.55
57.25	27.00	52.17	57.75	27.00	52.62	58.25	27.00	53.08	58.75	27.00	53.54
57.25	27.25	53.14	57.75	27.25	53.60	58.25	27.25	54.07	58.75	27.25	54.53
57.25	27.50	54.12	57.75	27.50	54.59	58.25	27.50	55.06	58.75	27.50	55.54
57.25	27.75	55.11	57.75	27.75	55.59	58.25	27.75	56.07	58.75	27.75	56.55
57.25	28.00	56.11	57.75	28.00	56.60	58.25	28.00	57.09	58.75	28.00	57.58
57.25	28.25	57.11	57.75	28.25	57.61	58.25	28.25	58.11	58.75	28.25	58.61
57.25	28.50	58.13	57.75	28.50	58.63	58.25	28.50	59.14	58.75	28.50	59.65
57.25	28.75	59.15	57.75	28.75	59.67	58.25	28.75	60.18	58.75	28.75	60.70
57.25	29.00	60.18	57.75	29.00	60.71	58.25	29.00	61.24	58.75	29.00	61.76
57.25	29.25	61.23	57.75	29.25	61.76	58.25	29.25	62.30	58.75	29.25	62.83
57.25	29.50	62.28	57.75	29.50	62.82	58.25	29.50	63.37	58.75	29.50	63.91
57.25	29.75	63.34	57.75	29.75	63.89	58.25	29.75	64.44	58.75	29.75	65.00
57.25	30.00	64.41	57.75	30.00	64.97	58.25	30.00	65.53	58.75	30.00	66.09
57.25	30.25	65.48	57.75	30.25	66.06	58.25	30.25	66.63	58.75	30.25	67.20
57.25	30.50	66.57	57.75	30.50	67.15	58.25	30.50	67.73	58.75	30.50	68.32
57.25	30.75	67.67	57.75	30.75	68.25	58.25	30.75	68.85	58.75	30.75	69.44
57.25	31.00	68.77	57.75	31.00	69.37	58.25	31.00	69.97	58.75	31.00	70.57
57.25	31.25	69.89	57.75	31.25	70.50	58.25	31.25	71.11	58.75	31.25	71.72
57.25	31.50	71.01	57.75	31.50	71.63	58.25	31.50	72.25	58.75	31.50	72.87
57.25	31.75	72.14	57.75	31.75	72.77	58.25	31.75	73.40	58.75	31.75	74.03
57.25	32.00	73.28	57.75	32.00	73.92	58.25	32.00	74.56	58.75	32.00	75.20
57.25	32.25	74.43	57.75	32.25	75.08	58.25	32.25	75.73	58.75	32.25	76.38
57.25	32.50	75.59	57.75	32.50	76.25	58.25	32.50	76.91	58.75	32.50	77.57

Estimated Weight Charts

Length	Girth	Weight	Length	Girth	Weight	Length	Girth	Weight	Length	Girth	Weight
59.00	24.00	42.48	59.50	24.00	42.84	60.00	24.00	43.20	60.50	24.00	43.56
59.00	24.25	43.37	59.50	24.25	43.74	60.00	24.25	44.10	60.50	24.25	44.47
59.00	24.50	44.27	59.50	24.50	44.64	60.00	24.50	45.02	60.50	24.50	45.39
59.00	24.75	45.18	59.50	24.75	45.56	60.00	24.75	45.94	60.50	24.75	46.33
59.00	25.00	46.09	59.50	25.00	46.48	60.00	25.00	46.88	60.50	25.00	47.27
59.00	25.25	47.02	59.50	25.25	47.42	60.00	25.25	47.82	60.50	25.25	48.22
59.00	25.50	47.96	59.50	25.50	48.36	60.00	25.50	48.77	60.50	25.50	49.18
59.00	25.75	48.90	59.50	25.75	49.32	60.00	25.75	49.73	60.50	25.75	50.14
59.00	26.00	49.86	59.50	26.00	50.28	60.00	26.00	50.70	60.50	26.00	51.12
59.00	26.25	50.82	59.50	26.25	51.25	60.00	26.25	51.68	60.50	26.25	52.11
59.00	26.50	51.79	59.50	26.50	52.23	60.00	26.50	52.67	60.50	26.50	53.11
59.00	26.75	52.77	59.50	26.75	53.22	60.00	26.75	53.67	60.50	26.75	54.11
59.00	27.00	53.76	59.50	27.00	54.22	60.00	27.00	54.68	60.50	27.00	55.13
59.00	27.25	54.76	59.50	27.25	55.23	60.00	27.25	55.69	60.50	27.25	56.16
59.00	27.50	55.77	59.50	27.50	56.25	60.00	27.50	56.72	60.50	27.50	57.19
59.00	27.75	56.79	59.50	27.75	57.27	60.00	27.75	57.75	60.50	27.75	58.24
59.00	28.00	57.82	59.50	28.00	58.31	60.00	28.00	58.80	60.50	28.00	59.29
59.00	28.25	58.86	59.50	28.25	59.36	60.00	28.25	59.86	60.50	28.25	60.35
59.00	28.50	59.90	59.50	28.50	60.41	60.00	28.50	60.92	60.50	28.50	61.43
59.00	28.75	60.96	59.50	28.75	61.48	60.00	28.75	61.99	60.50	28.75	62.51
59.00	29.00	62.02	59.50	29.00	62.55	60.00	29.00	63.08	60.50	29.00	63.60
59.00	29.25	63.10	59.50	29.25	63.63	60.00	29.25	64.17	60.50	29.25	64.70
59.00	29.50	64.18	59.50	29.50	64.72	60.00	29.50	65.27	60.50	29.50	65.81
59.00	29.75	65.27	59.50	29.75	65.83	60.00	29.75	66.38	60.50	29.75	66.93
59.00	30.00	66.38	59.50	30.00	66.94	60.00	30.00	67.50	60.50	30.00	68.06
59.00	30.25	67.49	59.50	30.25	68.06	60.00	30.25	68.63	60.50	30.25	69.20
59.00	30.50	68.61	59.50	30.50	69.19	60.00	30.50	69.77	60.50	30.50	70.35
59.00	30.75	69.74	59.50	30.75	70.33	60.00	30.75	70.92	60.50	30.75	71.51
59.00	31.00	70.87	59.50	31.00	71.47	60.00	31.00	72.08	60.50	31.00	72.68
59.00	31.25	72.02	59.50	31.25	72.63	60.00	31.25	73.24	60.50	31.25	73.85
59.00	31.50	73.18	59.50	31.50	73.80	60.00	31.50	74.42	60.50	31.50	75.04
59.00	31.75	74.34	59.50	31.75	74.97	60.00	31.75	75.60	60.50	31.75	76.23
59.00	32.00	75.52	59.50	32.00	76.16	60.00	32.00	76.80	60.50	32.00	77.44
59.00	32.25	76.70	59.50	32.25	77.35	60.00	32.25	78.00	60.50	32.25	78.65
59.00	32.50	77.90	59.50	32.50	78.56	60.00	32.50	79.22	60.50	32.50	79.88

Length	Girth	Weight	Length	Girth	Weight	Length	Girth	Weight	Length	Girth	Weight
59.25	24.00	42.66	59.75	24.00	43.02	60.25	24.00	43.38	60.75	24.00	43.74
59.25	24.25	43.55	59.75	24.25	43.92	60.25	24.25	44.29	60.75	24.25	44.66
59.25	24.50	44.46	59.75	24.50	44.83	60.25	24.50	45.21	60.75	24.50	45.58
59.25	24.75	45.37	59.75	24.75	45.75	60.25	24.75	46.13	60.75	24.75	46.52
59.25	25.00	46.29	59.75	25.00	46.68	60.25	25.00	47.07	60.75	25.00	47.46
59.25	25.25	47.22	59.75	25.25	47.62	60.25	25.25	48.02	60.75	25.25	48.41
59.25	25.50	48.16	59.75	25.50	48.57	60.25	25.50	48.97	60.75	25.50	49.38
59.25	25.75	49.11	59.75	25.75	49.52	60.25	25.75	49.94	60.75	25.75	50.35
59.25	26.00	50.07	59.75	26.00	50.49	60.25	26.00	50.91	60.75	26.00	51.33
59.25	26.25	51.03	59.75	26.25	51.46	60.25	26.25	51.90	60.75	26.25	52.33
59.25	26.50	52.01	59.75	26.50	52.45	60.25	26.50	52.89	60.75	26.50	53.33
59.25	26.75	53.00	59.75	26.75	53.44	60.25	26.75	53.89	60.75	26.75	54.34
59.25	27.00	53.99	59.75	27.00	54.45	60.25	27.00	54.90	60.75	27.00	55.36
59.25	27.25	55.00	59.75	27.25	55.46	60.25	27.25	55.92	60.75	27.25	56.39
59.25	27.50	56.01	59.75	27.50	56.48	60.25	27.50	56.96	60.75	27.50	57.43
59.25	27.75	57.03	59.75	27.75	57.51	60.25	27.75	58.00	60.75	27.75	58.48
59.25	28.00	58.07	59.75	28.00	58.56	60.25	28.00	59.05	60.75	28.00	59.54
59.25	28.25	59.11	59.75	28.25	59.61	60.25	28.25	60.10	60.75	28.25	60.60
59.25	28.50	60.16	59.75	28.50	60.66	60.25	28.50	61.17	60.75	28.50	61.68
59.25	28.75	61.22	59.75	28.75	61.73	60.25	28.75	62.25	60.75	28.75	62.77
59.25	29.00	62.29	59.75	29.00	62.81	60.25	29.00	63.34	60.75	29.00	63.86
59.25	29.25	63.37	59.75	29.25	63.90	60.25	29.25	64.43	60.75	29.25	64.97
59.25	29.50	64.45	59.75	29.50	65.00	60.25	29.50	65.54	60.75	29.50	66.08
59.25	29.75	65.55	59.75	29.75	66.10	60.25	29.75	66.66	60.75	29.75	67.21
59.25	30.00	66.66	59.75	30.00	67.22	60.25	30.00	67.78	60.75	30.00	68.34
59.25	30.25	67.77	59.75	30.25	68.34	60.25	30.25	68.92	60.75	30.25	69.49
59.25	30.50	68.90	59.75	30.50	69.48	60.25	30.50	70.06	60.75	30.50	70.64
59.25	30.75	70.03	59.75	30.75	70.62	60.25	30.75	71.21	60.75	30.75	71.80
59.25	31.00	71.17	59.75	31.00	71.77	60.25	31.00	72.38	60.75	31.00	72.98
59.25	31.25	72.33	59.75	31.25	72.94	60.25	31.25	73.55	60.75	31.25	74.16
59.25	31.50	73.49	59.75	31.50	74.11	60.25	31.50	74.73	60.75	31.50	75.35
59.25	31.75	74.66	59.75	31.75	75.29	60.25	31.75	75.92	60.75	31.75	76.55
59.25	32.00	75.84	59.75	32.00	76.48	60.25	32.00	77.12	60.75	32.00	77.76
59.25	32.25	77.03	59.75	32.25	77.68	60.25	32.25	78.33	60.75	32.25	78.98
59.25	32.50	78.23	59.75	32.50	78.89	60.25	32.50	79.55	60.75	32.50	80.21

1996 Musky Hunter's Almanac

Length	Girth	Weight	Length	Girth	Weight	Length	Girth	Weight	Length	Girth	Weight
61.00	24.00	43.92	61.50	24.00	44.28	62.00	24.00	44.64	62.50	24.00	45.00
61.00	24.25	44.84	61.50	24.25	45.21	62.00	24.25	45.57	62.50	24.25	45.94
61.00	24.50	45.77	61.50	24.50	46.14	62.00	24.50	46.52	62.50	24.50	46.89
61.00	24.75	46.71	61.50	24.75	47.09	62.00	24.75	47.47	62.50	24.75	47.86
61.00	25.00	47.66	61.50	25.00	48.05	62.00	25.00	48.44	62.50	25.00	48.83
61.00	25.25	48.61	61.50	25.25	49.01	62.00	25.25	49.41	62.50	25.25	49.81
61.00	25.50	49.58	61.50	25.50	49.99	62.00	25.50	50.39	62.50	25.50	50.80
61.00	25.75	50.56	61.50	25.75	50.97	62.00	25.75	51.39	62.50	25.75	51.80
61.00	26.00	51.55	61.50	26.00	51.97	62.00	26.00	52.39	62.50	26.00	52.81
61.00	26.25	52.54	61.50	26.25	52.97	62.00	26.25	53.40	62.50	26.25	53.83
61.00	26.50	53.55	61.50	26.50	53.99	62.00	26.50	54.42	62.50	26.50	54.86
61.00	26.75	54.56	61.50	26.75	55.01	62.00	26.75	55.46	62.50	26.75	55.90
61.00	27.00	55.59	61.50	27.00	56.04	62.00	27.00	56.50	62.50	27.00	56.95
61.00	27.25	56.62	61.50	27.25	57.08	62.00	27.25	57.55	62.50	27.25	58.01
61.00	27.50	57.66	61.50	27.50	58.14	62.00	27.50	58.61	62.50	27.50	59.08
61.00	27.75	58.72	61.50	27.75	59.20	62.00	27.75	59.68	62.50	27.75	60.16
61.00	28.00	59.78	61.50	28.00	60.27	62.00	28.00	60.76	62.50	28.00	61.25
61.00	28.25	60.85	61.50	28.25	61.35	62.00	28.25	61.85	62.50	28.25	62.35
61.00	28.50	61.93	61.50	28.50	62.44	62.00	28.50	62.95	62.50	28.50	63.46
61.00	28.75	63.03	61.50	28.75	63.54	62.00	28.75	64.06	62.50	28.75	64.58
61.00	29.00	64.13	61.50	29.00	64.65	62.00	29.00	65.18	62.50	29.00	65.70
61.00	29.25	65.24	61.50	29.25	65.77	62.00	29.25	66.31	62.50	29.25	66.84
61.00	29.50	66.36	61.50	29.50	66.90	62.00	29.50	67.44	62.50	29.50	67.99
61.00	29.75	67.49	61.50	29.75	68.04	62.00	29.75	68.59	62.50	29.75	69.15
61.00	30.00	68.63	61.50	30.00	69.19	62.00	30.00	69.75	62.50	30.00	70.31
61.00	30.25	69.77	61.50	30.25	70.35	62.00	30.25	70.92	62.50	30.25	71.49
61.00	30.50	70.93	61.50	30.50	71.51	62.00	30.50	72.09	62.50	30.50	72.68
61.00	30.75	72.10	61.50	30.75	72.69	62.00	30.75	73.28	62.50	30.75	73.87
61.00	31.00	73.28	61.50	31.00	73.88	62.00	31.00	74.48	62.50	31.00	75.08
61.00	31.25	74.46	61.50	31.25	75.07	62.00	31.25	75.68	62.50	31.25	76.29
61.00	31.50	75.66	61.50	31.50	76.28	62.00	31.50	76.90	62.50	31.50	77.52
61.00	31.75	76.86	61.50	31.75	77.49	62.00	31.75	78.12	62.50	31.75	78.75
61.00	32.00	78.08	61.50	32.00	78.72	62.00	32.00	79.36	62.50	32.00	80.00
61.00	32.25	79.30	61.50	32.25	79.95	62.00	32.25	80.60	62.50	32.25	81.25
61.00	32.50	80.54	61.50	32.50	81.20	62.00	32.50	81.86	62.50	32.50	82.52

Length	Girth	Weight	Length	Girth	Weight	Length	Girth	Weight	Length	Girth	Weight
61.25	24.00	44.10	61.75	24.00	44.46	62.25	24.00	44.82	62.75	24.00	45.18
61.25	24.25	45.02	61.75	24.25	45.39	62.25	24.25	45.76	62.75	24.25	46.13
61.25	24.50	45.96	61.75	24.50	46.33	62.25	24.50	46.71	62.75	24.50	47.08
61.25	24.75	46.90	61.75	24.75	47.28	62.25	24.75	47.67	62.75	24.75	48.05
61.25	25.00	47.85	61.75	25.00	48.24	62.25	25.00	48.63	62.75	25.00	49.02
61.25	25.25	48.81	61.75	25.25	49.21	62.25	25.25	49.61	62.75	25.25	50.01
61.25	25.50	49.78	61.75	25.50	50.19	62.25	25.50	50.60	62.75	25.50	51.00
61.25	25.75	50.77	61.75	25.75	51.18	62.25	25.75	51.59	62.75	25.75	52.01
61.25	26.00	51.76	61.75	26.00	52.18	62.25	26.00	52.60	62.75	26.00	53.02
61.25	26.25	52.76	61.75	26.25	53.19	62.25	26.25	53.62	62.75	26.25	54.05
61.25	26.50	53.77	61.75	26.50	54.20	62.25	26.50	54.64	62.75	26.50	55.08
61.25	26.75	54.79	61.75	26.75	55.23	62.25	26.75	55.68	62.75	26.75	56.13
61.25	27.00	55.81	61.75	27.00	56.27	62.25	27.00	56.73	62.75	27.00	57.18
61.25	27.25	56.85	61.75	27.25	57.32	62.25	27.25	57.78	62.75	27.25	58.24
61.25	27.50	57.90	61.75	27.50	58.37	62.25	27.50	58.85	62.75	27.50	59.32
61.25	27.75	58.96	61.75	27.75	59.44	62.25	27.75	59.92	62.75	27.75	60.40
61.25	28.00	60.03	61.75	28.00	60.52	62.25	28.00	61.01	62.75	28.00	61.50
61.25	28.25	61.10	61.75	28.25	61.60	62.25	28.25	62.10	62.75	28.25	62.60
61.25	28.50	62.19	61.75	28.50	62.70	62.25	28.50	63.20	62.75	28.50	63.71
61.25	28.75	63.28	61.75	28.75	63.80	62.25	28.75	64.32	62.75	28.75	64.83
61.25	29.00	64.39	61.75	29.00	64.91	62.25	29.00	65.44	62.75	29.00	65.97
61.25	29.25	65.50	61.75	29.25	66.04	62.25	29.25	66.57	62.75	29.25	67.11
61.25	29.50	66.63	61.75	29.50	67.17	62.25	29.50	67.72	62.75	29.50	68.26
61.25	29.75	67.76	61.75	29.75	68.32	62.25	29.75	68.87	62.75	29.75	69.42
61.25	30.00	68.91	61.75	30.00	69.47	62.25	30.00	70.03	62.75	30.00	70.59
61.25	30.25	70.06	61.75	30.25	70.63	62.25	30.25	71.20	62.75	30.25	71.78
61.25	30.50	71.22	61.75	30.50	71.80	62.25	30.50	72.39	62.75	30.50	72.97
61.25	30.75	72.39	61.75	30.75	72.99	62.25	30.75	73.58	62.75	30.75	74.17
61.25	31.00	73.58	61.75	31.00	74.18	62.25	31.00	74.78	62.75	31.00	75.38
61.25	31.25	74.77	61.75	31.25	75.38	62.25	31.25	75.99	62.75	31.25	76.60
61.25	31.50	75.97	61.75	31.50	76.59	62.25	31.50	77.21	62.75	31.50	77.83
61.25	31.75	77.18	61.75	31.75	77.81	62.25	31.75	78.44	62.75	31.75	79.07
61.25	32.00	78.40	61.75	32.00	79.04	62.25	32.00	79.68	62.75	32.00	80.32
61.25	32.25	79.63	61.75	32.25	80.28	62.25	32.25	80.93	62.75	32.25	81.58
61.25	32.50	80.87	61.75	32.50	81.53	62.25	32.50	82.19	62.75	32.50	82.85

Good Advice

We asked some of North America's top musky fishermen, "If you were to give a novice musky angler one piece of advice, what would it be?" This is what they had to say.

"Turn back now! — before you really get hooked on it. If that doesn't work, my advice from that point would be: a strong back and an open mind are key; use information available, but remember there are no rules; just stick with it — personal time on the water is the best teacher."

Pete Maina, musky guide and lure maker
Hayward, Wisconsin, (715) 462-3431

"With 60 years of musky fishing experience I can honestly say that musky fishing is really hunting. Fish all the different waters you can. Fish the waters up to the 15-foot depths for action fishing. For record musky fishing I caught most of my catches trolling the 25- to 35-foot depths. Fish the most unfished waters. Here is where the big muskies are usually found. To become an expert musky fisherman: THINK LIKE A MUSKY!"

Len Hartman, The Fish'n Fool
Westchester, Illinois

1996 Musky Hunter's Almanac

"Obtain a hydrographic map of the lake you intend to fish and look for areas of shoreline, island points and flats dropping off to deeper water. Muskies like to hang around those areas and ambush forage fish moving up from deeper water to feed in the shallows."
Paul Gasbarino, past president of Muskies Canada Inc.
54 Peach, Willoway, Willowdale, Ontario, (416) 493-1912

"Buy good equipment ... hire a competent guide who is a good teacher ... fish hard and often ... photograph your muskies and then carefully release them to upgrade future fishing."
Marv Heeler, guide
7885 Lost Lake Drive, St. Germain, Wisconsin, 54558

"Get as much knowledge about musky fishing as you can, get good equipment and keep your bait in the water!"
Joe Jasek, guide, manufacturer of Joe's Bucktails
Rt. 1, Couderay, Wisconsin, 54828-9811, (715) 945-2549

"This is the largest oxymoron in fishing, for the novice musky angler is usually a highly skilled sport fisherman in transition. If this is the case, as it usually is, remember that the only two muskies you will ever catch will be significant: 1.) your personal best, and 2.) the world record."
Mike Lazarus, guide
5791 Victoria, Montreal, Quebec, H3W 2R3

"Don't look for the "magic lake" where big fish are easy to catch — there are none. Rather, pick a body of water you can fish often and has numbers of fish so your action is steady. Learn that body of water and work on your fishing basics. Casting, synchronizing your

Good Advice

lure hitting the water and engaging the reel. Work on figure-8s, backing off on the drag (if needed) when a big fish hits or on a boat-side hit. Learn the basics well, everything you do will become second nature to you and you'll put more and bigger fish in your boat during your musky career."

Al Denninger, lure maker
10251 West Leon Terrace, Milwaukee, WI, 53224, (414) 353-5760

"Muskies will often suspend off a structure due to forage availability, wind or fishing pressure. So when casting to a weedbed, point, hump, edge of flat, etc., make four to five casts to the structure then fire one out in the opposite direction over deep water to check for suspended fish."

Spence Petros, former editor, Fishing Facts Magazine
P.O. Box 331, Milwaukee, Wisconsin, 53201-0331, (414) 287-4309

"You need to gain an understanding of, and have the want, to capture and release the greatest of all freshwater predators but, most of all you need to have the patience and persistence to achieve your own personal fishing goal."

Don Pursch, guide and proprietor, Nielsen's Fly-In Lodge
Rowan Lake, Box 6, Nestor Falls, Ontario, P0X 1K0, (807) 226-1234

"Put as much effort into the "release" as is put into the "pursuit" of this rare and surprisingly fragile creature. Over the years I've witnessed the good, bad, and ugly attempts at releasing these fish and have come to a very basic conclusion. Unless you are able to easily unhook the fish in the water use a cradle! Forget the net or that paralyzing jaw hold; both can harm a thrashing musky. Leave your ego

1996 Musky Hunter's Almanac

at the dock, don't forget the cradle, and above all enjoy the sport!
Gordon Bastable, guide and proprietor
Vermilion Bay Lodge, Eagle Lake,
General Delivery, Vermilion Bay, Ontario, P0V 2V0, (807) 755-2436

"Find a good partner. Carefully release all muskies. Above all have fun!"
Betsy Pearson, St. Cloud, Minnesota

"Read. Watch videos. Try a good guide. If possible, start out on water with numbers of muskies in it. Remember — there is no substitute for time on the water."
Dick Pearson, St. Cloud, Minnesota

"Learn as much about the fish as possible. You can do this by reading the various musky books and magazines that are available. You can also learn a great deal from watching the different musky videos that are on the market today. You should also consider joining a local musky club in your area, like Muskies, Inc. or Muskies Canada, Inc. One of the fastest ways to learn about musky fishing is to hire a professional musky guide. He can show you hands-on techniques, tackle and location for the muskies in your area. A good musky guide is well worth the money, and can help you out tremendously when you are just getting started. The two most important ingredients for successful musky fishing is patience and perseverance.

Shawn McCarthy, McCarthy's Tackle & Guide Service
24 Merrylynn Drive, Richmond Hill, ONT L4C 5A9
(905) 884-0615

"Gweedo" The Guide Sez!

For fishing in flowages, carry a long forked stick to get plugs loose from snags. If they move set the hook!

- A piece of indoor-outdoor carpet helps keep aluminum boats quiet.

- Keep your tackle box closed at all times when fishing for muskies.

- Putting your hand in the mouth of a musky (dead or alive), is asking for sucker's blood on your fingers.

- When clubbing a musky, be sure the plug is out of the way first, to prevent busting it or knocking it loose.

- He who puts his hand in a muskies' mouth might wish he had shaken hands with a porcupine instead.

- No musky grows faster than the one that got away!

- He who ventures out on new waters without a guide best beware of prop-eating rocks and stumps.

1996 Musky Hunter's Almanac

• Casting light bucktails into the wind is asking for a backlash.

• He who casts an Eddie Bait with a strong wind at his back should have a stout rod, strong grip and 100 yards of line.

• When clubbing a musky, make sure the other hand is out of the way to prevent "fat" knuckles.

• If you stand up in a moving boat you should know how to walk on water.

• Tip your motor up while playing a large musky.

• Figure-8 or make a 90 degree turn at the end of your cast; it will greatly increase your chances of catching a musky.

• To venture out onto a large body of water with a small boat and/or motor is asking for a dangerous bath.

• A man or woman who catches many muskies keeps the bait in the water.

• A fish is a fish is a fish, until you catch a musky!

• Epoxy glue on bucktail threads make them last much longer.

• Waxing your rod helps prevent the varnish from cracking and peeling off.

Gweedo The Guide Sez!

Gweedo to his client — "I know that you believe that you understood what you think I said, BUT, I am not sure you realize that what you heard is not what I meant!

• • •

Hambug's Hint — High walls are thought of as prime fall musky magnets. Actually they will hold some of the biggest fish in the system all season long. Don't overlook them during the summer months. You may get the surprise of your life.

• • •

Did You Know — Stanley S. Zack, in his publication "The Muskellunge — A Bibliography", comments that during the course of his research he found 66 different spellings of the word muskellunge — or is that muscalinga — no, maybe masquallongee — or should it be mascanongy! Anyhow, some of the stranger ones would include maskenosha, maskenozha, modkalonge, muskige and musk-a-lone. — BH*

• • •

Quotable Notable — 'The charm of fishing is that it is the pursuit of what is elusive but attainable, a perpetual series of occasions for hope."
— John Buchan*

Hedrik Wachelka Is The Armchair Musky Angler

Hedrik is editor of the Muskies Canada Release Journal. The Journal is published ten times a year.

"The bait struggles for a bare yard when dreamily, you note a quickly widening "V" darting from the pocket — right toward the lure. You freeze to the handle in the exact instant that a huge eruption engulfs the bait, leaving a hole in the surface as big as a washtub. Your reflexes jab the rod tip back and you feel the great, dead weight of an immovable object. Then there's a pulsing jerk or two and a long brown and silver body smashes up through the surface, wide cruel jaws agape, head thrashing furiously from side to side. Your little eight-pound line snaps back toward your rod tip, you let go of your breath in a big whoosh, and you nervously wind the remaining gossamer stuff back on the reel."

— *Larry Koller*

No matter the descriptive power, words sometimes tend to be inadequate when depicting the microcosm of muskellunge fishing. Nevertheless, today we come to praise him, not to hunt him. After a long season it's sometimes nice just to sit down in an old armchair and for this we give thanks. For musky fishermen, this occurs sometime after November 30, the date most musky seasons come to a close. Around that date we're usually busy doing our thing. Some of us may have had great years, others may only have had a couple of passing shots at a musky, but we all learned a little bit more, experienced moments of fulfillment and have been richly rewarded in ways that can't be measured by monetary value.

We chase the noble creature, a majestic fish — old King Musky; master of his waters suddenly appearing and disappearing to and from his mysterious domain. A body designed exquisitely for a rapacious life. Whether shaded in turquoise or tinted in copper, it has the magnetic lure of gold in the eyes of an addicted musky chaser.

Musky fishing is a work of anticipation, meditation, and sweat. In general, fishing is usually classified as a blood sport; in our case, sometimes the blood of the musky and sometimes the blood of the angler. However, the musky fishing experience is usually not concluded in some death ritual, some meat for the table, but more properly an affirmation of life with the sight of a beautiful animal slowly sliding from your hands back into harmony with nature.

We know there is a certain tragedy in the needless death of a muskellunge for it will not reach its natural potential, but more importantly, the tragedy arises from the hunter's respect for his quarry and his understanding of its place in the world, a place not much different from his own albeit in a different element. It should always be remembered that both partners have their own pressing needs for survival.

For me the delight of musky fishing is the moment of the strike; its sharp edge of excitement flashing through my limbs and striking some primal chord in my brain. Before and after this moment, it's the long hunt and short battle with both protagonists employing all their evolved instincts and skills in a ritualistic cycle of survival, the proverbial cat and mouse game.

The live careful release of this elegant animal after capture is a justifiable crowning achievement of an angling day, and for this we give thanks.

The angling environment with a plenitude of peaceful moments, clean waters, big sky and rugged shoreline cannot be underappreciated, and for this we give thanks.

The companionship of good friends, whether they be skilled anglers or questioning novices, with their jokes, their stories, their helpfulness, their silent understanding — all in pursuit of a common dream, and for this we give thanks.

The presence of organizations to lobby for the interests of the muskellunge, to promote catch and release, to advocate an egoless approach to the sport and to provide a vehicle into the world of fishing wisdom, and for this we give thanks.

Let's close by letting flow a few words from people who have encountered the muskellunge and wrote to tell, and for this we give thanks.

"Musky fishing offers an attractive niche in the world of freshwater angling, ideally situated between the imposed gentility of fly-fishing and the commonness of bass fishing."
— C.H. Shook

"Casters prospect for muskellunge somewhat as hunters roam the woods trying to outguess deer."
— Joseph Bates Jr.

Hedrik Wachelka Is The Armchair Musky Angler

"Don't ignore the muskellunge, but on the other hand don't stand in awe of him."

— Bob Turnbull

"No other freshwater sportfish is quite like a musky; none other has the combined gift of strength, wolfishness and dazzle. None is more difficult to find and capture on a hook — a major reason in itself why the fish is revered and obsessively pursued. A dedicated musky fisherman doesn't simply fish for muskies; he quests for them. What begins as a pleasant sport may culminate in a burning obsession."

— Tony Acerrano

"The musky's moody, unpredictable nature has fascinated generations of anglers. Musky fishing has become an obsession for many, even though they catch very few."

— Dick Sternberg

"Fishing for muskies gets into people's blood."

— Silvio Calabi

"This is a challenge fish. The challenge is in obtaining the strike."

— James Westman

"Great fish often attract great men."

— Burton Myers

"There lies the musky, hidden quiet and when it takes the swift-

1996 Musky Hunter's Almanac

ly-reeled lure, it is with a suddenness and fury that defies description."

— B.A. Bensley

"This is the musky — the peerless gamefish of inland waters. This is the big, heavy-bodied fighter of Ontario's northern lakes; the behemoth of the fish world."

— Dave Reddick

"Muscallongitis is a progressive malady, characterized by certain bilious and unappreciative observers as a harmless form of mania, for the taxaemia of which there is no known antidote. It terminates only with life, and but one single remedy has ever been found effectual in temporarily reducing its most violent manifestation, and that is for the victim of the disease to take as often as opportunity permits a hair of the dog that bit him."

— Dr. F. Whiting

"There are a couple easy ways to get muskies ... just as there are to get a million dollars."

— Geoffery Norman

"Thanks to the muskellunge's velleity, muskellunge fishermen have the peculiar need to communicate a frequently fishless experience."

— A.J. McClane

• • •

Hambug's Hint — Visualization is a technique used by people in sport such as gymnasts, golfers and skiers whereby they mentally visualize their routines and mechanics to enhance performance. This technique can also be used effectively to sharpen your casting skills. Mentally projecting each cast you will find yourself in control of the subtleties in presentation that will set you apart from the average fisherman. It will also help you reduce backlashes.

A converted "trout" net barely holds this 1936 musky. Note to musky picture takers — "cutting off" the angler's head is not recommended.

HOW TO DETERMINE THE SEX OF A MUSKY

Bernard Lebeau and Gerard Pageau, in their paper, "Comparative urogenital morphology and external sex determination in muskellunge, *Esox masquinongy Mitchill*," identify a simple but effective and reliable way of sexing muskellunge.

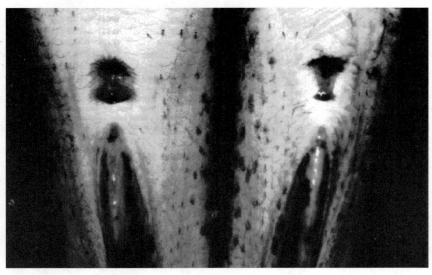

Pictured are the urogenital regions of muskellunge captured at Lake Wabigoon, northwestern Ontario, May 23, 1985. On the left is a female fish. On the right a male fish.

Without getting all scientific and going into a lot of detail, the method is based on a visual check of the muskellunge's urogenital region (anal cavity). A region that is shaped like a pear, as illustrated on the left in the photo, is a female musky. A region that is shaped like a keyhole, as illustrated on the right, is a male musky.

This method of sexing muskellunge is effective for the catch and release angler who likes to maintain a statistical record of such details. Muskies may be sexed quickly without removing them from the water by gently turning them on their back.

Picture and study results courtesy Bernard Lebeau, Department of Zoology, University of Toronto, Ramsay Wright Zoological Laboratories, 25 Harbord Street, Toronto, Ont., Canada M5S 1A1

• • •

Hambug's Hint — Where I come from on Georgian Bay the term "figure-8," as it applies to musky fishing, is actually a figure of speech. If you have a big musky follow your bait to the boat the best tactic is to bury your rod into the water up to the last guide and do a large, sweeping circle, bringing the lure to the surface as it moves to the top of the circle. Big fish can turn on a large circle more easily than a tight figure-8 and will hit the bait more frequently. Watch for them to make their move as the bait rises near the surface. They will often completely clear the water in their attack on the bait. I hope you have a good heart — you'll need it!

How To Make Your Own Secchi Disk

*M*ore and more musky fishermen are learning the importance of determining water clarity before deciding on the type, size, and color of lure to use. The universal method for measuring water clarity, that is, distinguishing between dark, murky, stained and clear water, is a secchi disk. Making your own disk is very simple and inexpensive but the knowledge to be gained in its use is priceless.

The Parts You Will Need
1   6-inch square piece of plywood
1   eyebolt
2   washers
2   nuts
1   1-inch to 1/2-inch galvanized reducer coupling or similar weight.
1   10-foot piece of rope or line
small amounts of black and white paint

To Assemble Your Secchi Disk
1. Cut the plywood into a 6-inch diameter disk and paint it in the black and white patterns shown. Drill a hole in the center of the disk slightly larger than your eyebolt.

2. Thread one nut on the full length of the eyebolt.
3. In the prescribed order, place the following onto the eyebolt: a washer, the secchi disk, the galvanized coupling, and the last washer.
4. Thread on the remaining bolt and tighten.
5. Tie the line onto the eyebolt, marking it in one foot intervals with a magic marker.

To Use The Secchi Disk
Drop the disk over the shaded side of your boat. Lower it until the black and white pattern becomes indistinguishable. Record the depth on the graduated line and compare it to the universal scale for measuring water clarity.

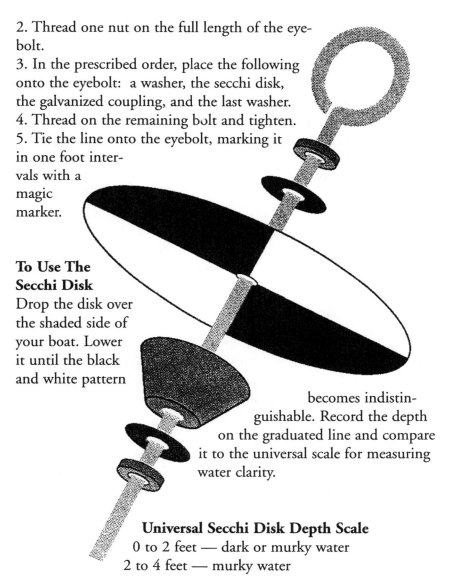

Universal Secchi Disk Depth Scale
0 to 2 feet — dark or murky water
2 to 4 feet — murky water

1996 Musky Hunter's Almanac

4 to 6 feet — stained water
6 to 8 feet — clear water

There you have it. The same method used by scientists and biologists to determine water clarity on the lakes you fish. Use it to compare the water clarity of different bodies of water or to gauge the changes in clarity that take place on a single body as you progress through the seasons. Adjust your lure choices accordingly and your catch rate will undoubtedly improve.

• • •

Did You Know — *The musky is considered by* In-Fisherman *magazine to be one of the world's 20 toughest freshwater fish ... "huge muskies remain one of the most difficult of all fish to catch, and the battle, while short lived, can be among the most spectacular in freshwater fishing!"* — *LR*

• • •

Humor — *I caught a world record size musky once. I put it on the floor of my camper, but I never got to weigh it. the bears ate it. Well, not all of it; just the part that hung out the door!*

• • •

Quotable Notable — *"So if escapism is a reason for angling — then the escape is to reality. The sense of freedom that we enjoy in the outdoors is, after all, a normal reaction to a more rational environment."*
— *A. J. McClane*

Interview

BILL HAMBLIN TALKS WITH JOHN PARRY, CREATOR OF PARRYWINKLE LURES

John Parry has been actively fishing for muskies since 1982. Although he has many large fish to his credit and is a strong advocate of catch and release fishing, he is most noted for the baits which he designs and manufactures. They are appropriately named the Parrywinkles. With reports of many large Georgian Bay fish appearing in the Muskies Inc. magazine over the years a great deal of interest has developed in John's baits, yet for many, knowledge of the man and his creations has remained a mystery. John has very kindly agreed to an interview to share his expertise and put to rest those questions that keep so many of us up at night dreaming of lunker 'lunge.

Bill: John how did you get started building lures?

John: Al Jessop of Muskies Canada actually got me started making musky baits although I have been tinkering with baits since I was nine years old. My grandfather was instrumental in getting me interested in lure construction when I was young.

Bill: But it was the musky fishing that got you involved in a big way?

1996 Musky Hunter's Almanac

John: Oh yeah! I started by making reproductions of baits I saw in catalogs.

Bill: Did you start making your own because you couldn't buy what you wanted or because you enjoyed creating your own baits?

John: It really started just as a hobby. I got a great deal of satisfaction out of making my own baits and catching fish with them. Then as friends and others started to use them I'd get a real charge out of seeing them do well with them as well. To this day this is the greatest enjoyment I get.

Bill: How did you come up with the name, "Parrywinkle"?

John: Actually Paul Gasbarino of Muskies Canada came up with the name. I really didn't know what to call them. I showed one to Paul at a Muskies Canada event. He laughed but came up with the idea of a Parrywinkle. I could think of 10,000 names I'd rather call them but that is the name that stuck.

Bill: A lot of the fisherman I talk to ask me what a Parrywinkle is, not realizing that you make a number of different baits. What types of baits do you make?

John: The one that most people have heard about is a large, 10-inch, large-lipped diving bait I call the Ohio Shad. It was originally fashioned after Bagley's DB08. I made a prototype and it seemed to work real good. I could never really figure out the action. It had a real squirrely type of action, often jumping out of the water, so I put a lot of lead on the underside of it. This kept it down.

Interview With John Parry

I remember being at a Muskies Canada derby on Balsam Lake with one of the early versions. My partner, Jim Hutchings, and I were fishing when we heard over the radio that John Damman had a big fish, a 48-incher. We saw John out on the water and thought we'd go over to talk to him. Jim put the throttle down — we were doing about ten miles an hour when my rod took off — it just screamed out. On the end of it was a 51-inch musky. The fish won the derby. (laughing) I don't think John talked to me for a month.

This was the first real indication the lure would catch big fish. It has gone through many changes since then to evolve into what today is a lure most noted for its catches of 40-plus-pound fish on Georgian Bay.

Bill: What other baits do you make?

John: I have experimented with many but the more popular are a shallower running version of the deep diver and another bait that most closely resembles a Wades Wobbler — the Wades is a fantastic bait. I also make a bucktail called a Parrytail.

I like to take an existing bait and find ways to improve upon it. An example would be baits that use brass wire in their construction. Muskies will break the tail loops as it flexes back and forth. I first tried galvanized wire but I have found that very acidic lakes can eat at this wire and weaken it, so I now use stainless steel wire exclusively in all my baits.

Bill: Do you make the crankbaits in both solid and jointed versions?

John: I don't make the jointed as much any more. Jointed baits always seem to have a problem when they really get hammered. They can break at the joint.

Bill: Let's talk for a moment about construction of your baits. What types of materials do you use, specifically for bodies and lips?

John: All my bait bodies are made from cedar. I have experimented with many different types of wood and at one time used mostly Douglas fir. It has tremendous, water-resistant qualities, but I found the cedar makes for a much lighter bait and doesn't crack once it gets wet. The fir was also much harder to work with. I carve all the bodies and drill the baits by hand. It's not uncommon for the hardwood to deflect the drill bit off line as much as a half-inch. This is not so much of a problem with the cedar.

Bill: What about your lips?

John: I use both lexan and aluminum. The lexan is very tough but I find the aluminum stands up better on the larger deep-diving lips. On Georgian Bay you can break the lexan on the rocks.

Bill: Generally speaking, you use the lexan on your shallower running baits and the aluminum on the deeper divers.

John: That's right.

Bill: Tell us about how the lures are actually constructed.

John: All my lures are made with through-wire construction. That is, the same piece of wire forms the eyelet in the lip at the front of the bait and the eyelet at the end of the bait to which the split rings are

Interview With John Parry

connected for the tail hook. In the event that the lure should break, through-wire construction ensures that you will remain connected to the fish. The front and center treble hooks are also connected directly to the wire using cotter pins.

Bill: Do you groove the bait and lay the wire in it?

John: No, I drill through the bait by hand.

Bill: Perhaps a trademark of the Parrywinkle bait is the lead around the front eyelet.

John: The lead I use is actually buckshot I melt down in a pan. Using a small mold I make from pegboard and plasticine I pour the lead from the back of the lip through the hole in the lip that the wire for the eyelet passes. That serves two purposes. It not only secures the eyelet to the lip but it's soft enough to permit tuning the bait if necessary.

Bill: I notice that the bait has very big and prominent eyes. Do you get these from a taxidermist?

John: No, they are actually doll's eyes. I get them from a hobby and crafts store. I like to buy clear eyes so that I can paint them to suit my own color preferences.

Bill: Your lures have a beautiful finish on them. Can you tell us what goes into finishing the final product?

John: I start with two coats of an epoxy to seal the wood. Then

1996 Musky Hunter's Almanac

depending upon the pattern and color combination I intend to use, I may add as many as four or five different coats of paint. This is then covered with two final coats of epoxy. To ensure an even finish I will coat the bait in epoxy and hang it until dry, say from the tail hook.. For the second coat I will hang it from the lip.

Bill: John, if you were to give the novice lure builder one piece of advice, what would it be?

John: To make use of the advice offered by those like myself who have learned from their mistakes and their experience. As much as 10 hours of labor goes into each one of these big baits. The novice may save himself a lot of time by accepting the advice of others who have been there. So many times I have people tell me "I should have listened to your advice." I often just chuckle but deep inside I can't resist the old 'I told you so!'"

Bill: John, your baits have gained quite a reputation for catching big fish from the depths of Georgian Bay. Can you tell us what type of presentation is typical on this type of water with your deep-diving Parrywinkle?

John: Most people troll them on single strand wire line. I prefer about 35-pound test. The wire enables you to present the bait over a wide range of depths but the 25- to 35-foot range has proven to be best.

Bill: Are you working a suspended baitfish pattern or a rock structure type of pattern?

Interview With John Parry

John: Actually it's a combination of the two. We look for the rock structure first and then the schools of baitfish that relate to it. Once we have contacted the baitfish we can troll the area for the big fish that follow these schools.

Bill: What type of equipment do you use?

John: I prefer the Ambassadeur 7000 reel for the wire line and a heavy-action, spring-tipped trolling rod. However, we are experimenting more with the use of downrigger sticks with conventional carboloy tips. The rod's action compensates for the lack of stretch in the line and makes it easier to fight the fish. Surprisingly, the rod tips have held up quite well and do not crimp the wire.

Bill: Do you use a leader?

John: Not normally. Most often I just tie the wire directly to a snap. If I expect to be contacting bottom a fair bit, sometimes I will also use a ball bearing swivel. If these big baits foul they will often go into a spin and that can create havoc on your line. The swivel will save that wear and tear.

Bill: Everyone likes to hear big fish stories. What is your most memorable experience using your own baits?

John: Oddly enough, one of my most memorable experiences involves a trip in August 1993 to the Challunge Cup on Lake Chautauqua in New York. Once again I was fishing with Jim Hutchings. *(Editor's Note: Jim is an accomplished bait manufacturer himself.)* We had come to the end of the day and Jim said, "It's time to bring in the lines."

Just as I was to remove the rod from its holder the line began to scream off the reel. Picking up the rod I felt more weight than I've ever felt on a fish before. Surprisingly, the fish came to the side of the boat with relative ease. By our estimates the fish was well over 50 inches and by virtue of its enormous girth in the 50-pound range. Typically, as the case seems to be, every time you hook a big fish the net was tangled in the boat controls. As the fish lay quietly at the side of the boat Jim tried frantically to free the net. As it came loose Jim raised it over his head to position it for the netting. Unfortunately, this seemed to startle the fish. She went frantic, opened her huge mouth and dove. The big bait that she held crosswise in her mouth came free. To this day she remains the largest fish I have ever seen.

Bill: I guess at the very least that would prove that the Parrywinkle is not just a bait for Georgian Bay.

John, now for the question that I know our readers have been waiting for me to ask. I know because inevitably either at sports shows or when I'm out guiding it's the one that ultimately comes up. Are these lures available to the public and how can someone get their own Parrywinkle?

John: Presently the lures are not available in stores. In truth, with each lure taking as much as 10 hours to complete it's all I can do to keep up with my own needs and those of the people and friends I fish with. I am happy to discuss baits with anyone who would like to contact me, but availability of baits will depend largely on how much time I've had to devote to construction. At this time it remains just a hobby and there are no plans to make baits on a larger scale.

Interview With John Parry

Bill: John, I would like to thank you for taking time out to talk with me. I'm sure our talk will go a long way to solving the many mysteries that seem to have surrounded the man and the bait in recent years.

John: You're welcome.

John Parry and his Parrywinkle crankbait.

John Parry, 58 Pluto Drive, Brampton, Ontario, Canada, L6V 3W5, 1-905-455-3270

Larry Ramsell's Chronological Listing Of World Records

Date	Angler	Location	Weight	Length	Girth	Lure
August 1883	Annie Lee	St. Lawrence River, NY	36-2	54	NA	No. 3 Gold Spoon (spinner)

From history's archives. Picture Exists. No weight verification exists. Listed for information only.

| August 1883 | H.K. Greene | Indian River, NY | 49-8 | 54 | 28 | Chapman's No. 3 |

From history's archives. No weight verification exists. Listed for information only.

| 1887 | Mr. Saunders | Planting Ground, WI | 55-0 | 59 | 28 | NA |

Very limited information is available. No weight verification exists. Listed for information only.

| 1908 | A.J. Van Sise | Lake LeBouf, Pennsylvania | 44-2 | NA | NA | NA |

From history's archives. Picture exists. No weight verification exists. Listed for information only.

| 9/3/11 | Dr. Fred Whiting | St. Lawrence R., NY/ONT | 48-0 | 59 | 25 | No. 9 Corbett Spoon (spinner) |

Field & Stream contest winner.

Date	Angler	Location	Weight	Length	Girth	Lure
9/13/16	F. J. Swint	Chief Lake, Wisconsin	51-0	55	24	No. 8 Skinner Spoon (spinner) & frog

Field & Stream contest winner.

7/16/19	John A. Knobla	Lac Vieux Desert. WI/MI	51-3	54	25 1/4	Unknown (preferred Skinner's)

Listed originally as a world record musky. It is now the hybrid musky world record.
Field & Stream contest winner.

1917	William Fulton	French River, Ontario	57-10	59	30	Unknown

From history's archives. Mount exists. No weight verification exists.
Listed for information only.

1923	John J. Hoogan	Shishebogama, WI	52-0	NA	NA	Unknown

From history's archives. No weight verification exists.
Listed for information only.

9/30/24	Lewis Walker Jr.	Conneaut Lake, PA	54-3	57	NA	Dead 8" Red Chub

Verified but never before listed because it was not entered in the Field & Stream contest.

7/1/29	E. A. Oberland	Pokegama Lake, WI	52-12	52	29	Pflueger Spoon

Superseded by Walker fish but listed here because of its recognition as the world record for 66 years.
Field & Stream contest fish.

1996 Musky Hunter's Almanac

Date	Angler	Location	Weight	Length	Girth	Lure
8/25/29	Gordon Curtis	Lake of the Woods, ONT	53-12	57	25 1/4	No. 7 Skinner Spoon (spinner)

Superseded by Walker fish but listed here because of its recognition as the world record for 66 years. Field & Stream contest winner.

| 7/24/31 | Jack W. Collin | Lake of the Woods, ONT | 56-7 | 55 | 29 5/8 | Pflueger Muskill |

Field & Stream contest winner.

| 9/24/32 | George Neimuth | Lake of the Woods, ONT | 58-4 | 59 | 34 1/2 | Creek Chub Pikie |

Field & Stream contest winner.

| 7/27/39 | Louie Spray | Grindstone Lake, WI | 59-8 | 58 1/4 | 32 1/2 | Marathon Musky Houn |

Field & Stream contest winner. Verified beyond any shadow of a doubt.

| 10/3/39 | John J. Coleman | Eagle Lake, Ontario | 60-8 | 58 1/2 | 31 1/2 | Creek Chub Pikie |

Field & Stream contest winner. Verified beyond any shadow of a doubt.

| 8/19/40 | Louie Spray | Lac Courte Oreilles, WI | 61-13 | 59 1/4 | 32 1/2 | True Temper Bass Pop |

Field & Stream contest winner. Verified beyond any shadow of a doubt.

Chronological Listing Of World Records

Date	Angler	Location	Weight	Length	Girth	Lure
7/24/49	Cal Johnson	Lac Courte Oreilles, WI	67-8	60 1/4	33 1/2	South Bend Pike-O-Reno

Field & Stream contest fish. Verified beyond any shadow of a doubt.

10/20/49	Louie Spray	Chippewa Flowage, WI	69-11	63 1/2	31 1/4	Spray Sucker Harness/Sucker

Field & Stream contest winner. Verified beyond any shadow of a doubt.

6/6/54	Robert Malo	Middle Eau Claire L., WI	70-0	55	32	Sucker

Verified in my mind but not presently accepted by the National Fresh Water Fishing Hall of Fame.

Pro's Pointers

The boat-side rise! "While working minnow baits and jerk baits try stopping your retrieve 10 to 12 feet away from the boat and allow the bait to slowly rise towards the surface. Then crank the bait back to boatside and finish with a figure-8. Oftentimes this slight pause will trigger some of the most awesome strikes."

Bill Schwartz, Slammer Bait Company, (414) 476-0307

"Everyone knows that the early fall period is dynamite for shallow water big fish action. What a lot of people don't realize is that 'fall' can start anytime after mid August in northern Wisconsin — two weeks either side of Labor Day are usually prime — don't wait till the leaves start falling."

Bruce Shumway, musky guide, lure designer, Route 1, Box 82 Drummond, WI, 54832, (715) 798-3441

"When it comes down to fishing 'dog days' summer musky, head for a river. My first choice would be to fish an incoming creek into the main river. In midsummer an incoming creek means cooler water. The lower water temperature attracts baitfish and in turn muskies. Also look for any deep hole adjacent to the creek to hold the largest fish."

Mike Mladenik, guide, smallmouth expert, custom smallmouth baits, Rt. 2, Crivitz, WI, 54114, (715) 854-2055

"When fishing in the fall you will be confronted with many fishing conditions. It's like fishing an entire season in itself. The most important thing to remember is to keep an open mind about fish location and having confidence, using your tools at hand to catch them"

Bill "Fuzzy" Shumway, guide, manufacturer of Fuzzy Duzzit Lures, Route 3, Box 3384A, Hayward, WI, 54843, (715) 634-3204

"One of the most important things in musky fishing is to be a proficient caster. If you are a proficient caster the muskies will come."

Tony Rizzo, guide, author and lure maker, Box 154, Star Lake, Wisconsin, 54561, (715) 542-3420

"When you know where the fish is, we're talking a pocket in the weeds, underwater point, whatever it may be and you can't get the fish to hit, I take the blade (back blade if it is a tandem) off my spinnerbait and replace it with a No. 6 walleye hook and put a twister on it. I cut the hair short to the back hook and put another twister on it. Now you have three twisters (one original on front single hook). All these fingers then 'boil up' the water and will trigger a non-hitting 'hot' fish 90% of the time."

Marv Kiley, guide and lure maker, Route #2, Box 2880, Palisade, Minnesota, 56469, (218) 927-2544

"Pay attention to your bait. Don't take your eyes off it!"

Ray Kirby, guide, Chippewa Flowage, Route #9, Twin Bay Road, Hayward, Wisconsin, 54843, Winter (708) 395-2587, Summer (708) 395 — 0524

1996 Musky Hunter's Almanac

"For the big ones — after 18 years of owning a camp on Eagle Lake and plugging for muskies nearly every evening, I've found that when baby ducks are hatching, use black surface plugs, make somewhat of a disturbance and make your retrieval slow. The fact of the matter is, just like us the bigger and older we get the slower we move and the less we want to!"
Ron Both, Eagle Lake Island Lodge, Eagle River, Ontario,
Winter (605) 676-2492, Summer (807) 755-5522

"Stay away from the 'magic bait' syndrome. Spend more time and energy learning intimately the patterns and movements of the musky in the system you fish. The proper presentation will follow. You can't catch them if you're not where they are!"
Steve Herbeck, former Boulder Junction/Vilas County guide,
Now operator/guide Andy Myer's Lodge, Eagle Lake, Ontario,
Nov. to April — Box 572, Boulder Junction, Wisconsin, 54512,
(715) 385-2813
April to Nov. — Box 58, Vermilion Bay, Ontario P0V 2V0,
(807) 227-2610

"Superlines. One of the greatest advancements in recent years for dedicated musky hunters are the new braided superlines. Under trade names like Spectra, Spiderwire and Iron Thread, their ultra-thin diameter and near-zero stretch give a whole new dimension to musky fishing. A tip to remember when using these lines is to have your reel drag set lighter than when using mono or dacron. The near-zero stretch dictates a lighter drag setting to prevent possible rod, line or leader breakage when setting the hook.
Dick Gries, guide and lure maker, 118 Buckhorn Circle,
Arbor Vitae, Wisconsin, 54568, (715) 356-2503

Pros' Pointers

"Lighter tackle; lighter lures; removing the tail hook on all lures; very slow retrieves for big fish. If you want the same results as everyone else ... do the same things ... If not — get different."
Craig Engebretson, guide and lure maker, 3608 N. 94th Street, Milwaukee, Wisconsin, 53222, (414) 536-0889

"In September, as the water cools, numbers of muskies seem 'maybe' to be a few less, but the "BIG ONES" wake up and move from the weeds as the weeds begin to decay and go out to the rocks for their pre-winter 'pigout' feeding session."
Jim Weinkauf, owner, South Shore Lodge, Eagle Lake, Ontario, Winter (612) 493-2555, Summer (807) 227-5553

"When fishing is tough on a hot, calm day try twitching a Suick or Fooler over a weedbed so that it flops back and forth on top of the water."
Ty Sennett, guide, Chippewa Flowage, Wisconsin, R. R. #9, Box 9396B, Hayward, Wisconsin, 54843, Summer Cabin (715) 462-9403, Home (815) 653-2837

"When your glider jerk baits start losing some paint, don't toss them aside or even repaint because you may have even a better lure than when you purchased it new! For some super fall fishing soak them overnight in a bucket of water. This added water weight provides for an evenly dispersed, natural weighting system. Fish then deep and very slow for some deadly cold water action."
Mark Zeak, Trophy Fishing Musky Tackle Catalog, P.O. Box 2633, South Bend, Indiana, 46680, (800) 445-7205

1996 Musky Hunter's Almanac

"Make sure all of your equipment is in top shape. Good line; keep it retied, good split rings, sharp hooks, real greased and everything ready. There is nothing worse than losing a big fish because of equipment failure."

Dave Dorazio, guide and lure manufacturer, Rt. 9, Hayward, Wisconsin, 54843, (715) 462-3885

"If you're frustrated by the 'dog days' during a summer vacation, enjoy the warm, hot days with your family. After dark, sneak off to a clear water lake and fish parallel to the weed edges with a crankbait. Be sure to hang onto your rod!"

Steve Heiting, managing editor of Musky Hunter *magazine, book author and Vilas County guide, 8148 Lost Lake Drive S., St. Germain, WI 54558, (715) 542-3941*

"Never give up! When you are tired, keep going. If you are in and tired, go back out. There is no substitute for persistence. The next cast may be the one! Never give up!"

George Wahl, Eagle Tail Lures

• • •

Did You Know — During the 1930s and 1940s, 30% to 40% of the largest muskies caught and entered in the annual Field & Stream contest, were taken on surface baits! — LR

• • •

Humor — I stopped by the bait shop near the end of the season. A guy there said "take all the suckers you want for $1." I said, "Give me $2 worth!"

Allison Drake caught this huge musky from the West Fork of the Chippewa River in the early 1920s.

Profile of a Legend

HOMER LEBLANC

By Larry Ramsell

*I*f big muskies had known the day that Homer LeBlanc invented the Swim Whizz it would mean the future "demise" of many of their large sisters and brothers they would have declared an annual day of mourning and tried to figure out a way to sink his ever-present boat on Lake St. Clair! I have been tracking big musky catches for over 40 years and one of the most prominent and prolific musky catchers throughout the North American musky range has been Homer's lure, bar none!

Homer also developed "prop-wash" trolling and taught it in seminars throughout muskyland. He was considered by many to be the father of modern day musky fishing.

Homer was born in Stoney Point, Ontario, in 1901 and spent a major portion of his life in St. Clair Shores, Michigan, on the shore of his beloved Lake St. Clair. Homer brought this lake and its "musky factory" to national prominence.

Homer passed away in 1993 after a musky fishing career of 88 years (he caught his first musky when he was 5), at the age of 92.

For over 40 years Homer earned his living as Lake St. Clair's top musky guide. He and his clients caught well over 3,000 muskies, the largest one weighing over 56 pounds. Homer didn't specialize in big fish, Homer specialized in fun!! Before I fished with Homer in the 1970s, I had read his book, *Musky Fishing: Fact and Fancy, Lore And Lures.* Our day on the water was deja vu, as I anticipated every sequence and was not disappointed. I cannot remember a more fun day on the water.

Homer, with good friend and photographer Joe Lepage, formed the Michigan-Ontario Musky Club in the early 1950s.

Some of the most treasured lures in my collection are prototype lures that Homer sent me home with after my visit with him.

He will be missed by all.

From Homer's Pen

Big Thriller

"My first big thrill was in my early days of musky fishing. I was

Captain Homer on his lifelong water, Lake St. Clair, circa 1975.

1996 Musky Hunter's Almanac

trolling with a spinner and bucktail lure. The tip of my rod bent back and it felt like I had hit some weeds. I quickly reeled in my lure to check it. As the lure neared the boat, the spinner blade broke water by two feet and a huge musky grabbed it in mid air. I hadn't seen him and it must have come from nowhere to grab that lure. Needless to say, it scared the heck out of me, and I jerked back and luckily hooked it. The battle lasted for about an hour in a pouring rain. It rained for two days. I had to go to work; the result was that it never got weighed. One of my neighbors had cleaned it. Estimated at about 55 pounds."

The Big One That Got Away

"The biggest musky I ever had grab a lure gave me a sickening kind of thrill. That day, I was fishing for charter with four fishermen. We caught two muskies. They had to be back at the dock by two p.m., as they had to catch a train back to New York.

After they left, I decided to go out and try to catch a musky, since company was coming for dinner and they had never eaten any.

I had trolled only a few minutes and this monster musky grabbed my lure. It held its ground and I kept losing line. I put the motor out of gear to stop the forward motion. The lake was fairly rough and the boat kept drifting away and I kept losing more line. The musky wouldn't give ground, so I decided to put the motor in gear and turn the boat around, back to the musky. To make headway, I had to accelerate the motor. I gave it just a little too much acceleration. The result was that I wound up with a slack line for a few seconds. I got a tight line again and was gaining most of my line back. The musky was about 40 feet away and definitely was a world record. He violently shook his head and threw the lure a good 40 feet. An observer in a rowboat saw the action and the musky. He

Profile Of A Legend — Homer LeBlanc

came over to console me and said, 'he was as big and as long as a railroad tie.' The musky gave me several thrills, one was a very disheartening one. I felt like crying."

Biggest Thrill

"Late one afternoon, I invited a neighbor to go musky fishing with me. We were trolling an area that had several heavy cabbage beds.

I hooked a giant musky with a casting size lure, and with a light flexible rod. All hell broke loose; the musky charged the boat and came flying out of the water by three feet and only about four feet back of the boat. There was nothing I could do to get him away from the boat and the weedbed. This musky made seven jumps in all, each time he would head for bottom. The musky hooked the lure into the base of a big stalk of cabbage weed and tore himself loose. The lure was well embedded into the weeds and I pulled it up roots and all. We estimated that it would weigh close to 50 pounds.

I can still see that huge head, shaking back and forth, trying to throw the lure. Sure would have made the greatest moving pictures ever. Oh well! Those pictures are in my head forever and will never fade."

Homer's Daily Prayer

After Homer would point out several churches of different denominations at different places around the shore of Lake St. Clair he would utter the following:

"*Dear Lord, may we catch fish so big we will never have to lie about them. Bring us safely back with our limit so we will never have to lie again.*"

The Cleithrum Project

NEW FACTS FROM OLD BONES

How old was my muskellunge?
How fast was it growing?
How long do muskellunge live?

By E.J. Crossman

Those questions, so often posed by anglers, were set out at the top of the first page of an information package which Dr. John Casselman and I used to introduce the Cleithrum Project in 1979. The project is an activity associated with the interpretation of various kinds of life history information for individual muskellunge and other species in the group to which the muskellunge belongs. The package included instructions for the removal, cleaning, documentation and submission of these bones, and it was sent originally to a list of Ontario taxidermists. Taxidermists were asked to participate by obtaining permission to remove the cleithrum from one side of muskellunge and large northern pike brought in for mounting. In return they were told they would receive information, as precise as possible, on the age of the fish. In turn they could offer this information to their customers as a service.

John and I felt the increase in angler pressure on the muskellunge made it imperative that we develop additional information on growth, age-class strength, and true life expectancy for the muskellunge across the whole of its distribution. The very effective concept of catch and release, which we had encouraged, had been wholeheartedly adopted by organized muskellunge anglers. One of the consequences of that, however, was far fewer large specimens available for data. Most of the specimens killed were to be mounted. As a result, it was necessary to suggest to anglers that fish should not necessarily be killed for data but that every fish killed should yield as much information as possible. The submission of cleithral bones from fish killed for any purpose was a way to achieve this. A further point about that time was the encouraging willingness of resource agencies to reconsider minimum size regulations on the basis of the life history of populations in single lakes or groups of lakes, as opposed to one minimum size statewide and provincewide. If this biologically-based concept was to work, more information on more populations would be required. On the whole, anglers as a group come in contact with more muskellunge than a research or management biologist could ever hope to. Angler involvement in this project can be considered an appropriate component of a "user pay" philosophy in regard to natural resource management.

Anglers who catch large fishes are always interested in how old the animal was. In the past, age of fishes was derived mainly from scales, and to a lesser extent from calcareous structures in the middle ear (otoliths), from bones such as the gill cover, and for fishes without scales from thin cross-sections of bony finrays. The best opportunity to interpret the passage of time (i.e. age) is on as large and flat a structure as possible. In temperate regions like our own, the marks on the bony structures and scales result largely from changes in the growth of the animal, and of each of its parts, in response to annual cycles of warmer and colder water temperatures. Research on pike by Dr. Casselman revealed that as the animal grew larger, especially after becoming sexually mature, ages derived from scales become steadily more unreliable. In contrast the cleithrum bone of this group was ideal. It is large, mostly flat, easily removed from fresh individuals, and once cleaned can be stored dry, and needs no further preparation prior to interpretation. Reliability of the interpretation of growth and terminal age is not lowered significantly with advancing years.

The cleithrum is a long, crescent shaped bone. It is the longest in a vertical series of bones attached to the skull immediately behind the gill chamber, and it is visible externally. This series of bones supports the girdle of the pectoral fin. Another advantage of this bone in this group of fishes is that Dr. Casselman was able to demonstrate that the bone grew at a rate approximately one-tenth that of the body. One need only measure, in millimeters, to the mark representing each year of life, and convert those to centimeters for an approximation of the length of the animal at each of those past anniversaries. The distance between annual marks can be used to determine the growth of the fish in each year. Since males and females grow at different rates, and

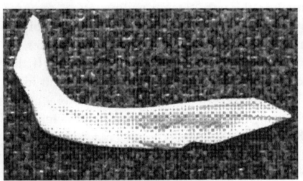

A cleithrum bone.

New Facts From Old Bones

for different numbers of years, it is sometimes possible to determine the sex of the animal from the record of the bone. Another interesting point is that the shape of the bone differs in the muskellunge, the pike, and in the "tiger muskellunge" the hybrid between the two species. As a result, it is possible to detect errors in the identification provided with the bones submitted to the project.

Over the years the existence of the project became more widely known with the help of the notes in publications of Muskies, Inc., Muskies Canada, Inc., in *Studio North,* a North American taxidermy magazine, and by word of mouth. As a result, cleithra arrived from research biologists, resource managers, individual anglers and taxidermists. The single largest contributor is Ron Lax, a taxidermist in Conover, Wisconsin. Lax has contributed more samples than the total for all taxidermists in Ontario. In the period covered by the Project Report for 1993-1994, Lax contributed 249 of the total of 279 samples received from the United States. The rates of contributions waxes and wanes. The reasons for this appear to be: 1.) contributors claim to have thought that only a fixed number of bones was wanted and discontinue their contributions, 2.) discouragement arising from a long interval between submission of cleithra and the return of results, and 3.) potential contributors indicating that taxidermists claim that it is impossible to make a first class mount if the cleithrum is removed. The fallacy of the last is obvious in the praise received from customers by Ron Lax, our major contributor. Significant work on the project has been possible only when I manage to receive an outside grant to support a salary for an assistant. Grants for technical assistance in the past have been made available by the Environmental Youth Corps program of the Ontario Ministry of Natural Resources. Funds for various project supplies have been provided most recently by the Ontario Federation of Anglers and

1996 Musky Hunter's Almanac

Hunters.

The project is presently in one of its down periods; that is, without an assistant and with very few contributions arriving. The last progress report indicated that the present totals of cleithra are as follows:

All species	4,656
Muskellunge	3,518
Muskellunge captured in Canada	1,372
Muskellunge captured in the U.S.	2,146
"Tiger Muskellunge" (all sources)	281
Northern pike (all sources)	857

Almost all hybrids originate in the U.S., and almost all northern pike are from Canada.

Information derived from the collection has regularly been provided to individual contributors, to Muskies, Inc. and to Muskies Canada. At times, series of bones from individual research projects are interpreted and the results published by the researcher in agency reports or scientific journals. Regular requests are made by natural resource agencies for information useful in developing management strategies for specific populations. The latest request was for Lac Seul but very few samples for that body of water have been received. The first summary of detailed results from the project appeared in 1986, the published contributions to the International Symposium held in LaCrosse, Wisconsin, in a book entitled *Managing Muskies*, published by the American Fisheries Society. That paper by Casselman and Crossman, was entitled "Size, age, and growth of trophy muskellunge and muskellunge-northern pike hybrids — The Cleithrum Project 1979-1983." Although the project is presently in

New Facts From Old Bones

a low period of contributions the entire collection of muskellunge cleithra is being subjected to very intensive analysis for another publication. This includes an extensive examination of the reliability of age interpretations which involves repeated, blind interpretations of large subsamples. Results for all cleithra are now inserted directly from the measuring device into an interesting computer program called CSAGES, developed in the Ontario Ministry of Natural Resources by Dr. Casselman and Kenn Scott. The information on length, weight, age and growth for individual fish will be compared with latitude of capture, and fluctuation in daily temperature over a period of 50 years, from three locations north to south. By this means it will be possible to test for good and bad years which have contributed to the variable growth of muskellunge across the range of the species.

The computer program in use provides a wealth of information about individual muskellunge and also generates some very interesting graphic interpretations of that information. In 1988, Ken O'Brien caught a muskellunge which weighed 65 pounds. It was taken in the Moon River, a tributary to the Georgian Bay portion of Lake Huron. We had the fish at the Royal Ontario Museum in order to make a mold for the preparation of models of this record fish. That enabled us to acquire the cleithrum and "read on it" parts of the life story of the fish. It revealed that the fish was between 28 and 30 years of age when captured. It had hatched in 1959. Between its sixth and seventh growing seasons (ages five and six) there was a decrease in the rate of growth per year which probably coincided with the first development of eggs and spawning. Toward the end of its life it was adding less than 0.5 inches of length per year. It is probable that at that point in the life of O'Brien's fish the conversion of food energy was concentrated in maintenance, development of eggs, and whatever was left over went into increase in weight.

I hope the above will indicate that the Cleithrum Project is an opportunity for individuals to make a significant contribution to the increase in our knowledge of the muskellunge. The Cleithrum Project is not dead — send us your old bones. The next step I contemplate is an attempt to stimulate participation from Quebec by preparing a French language version of the information package and distributing it in that province. I have been concerned in the past about doing that when there is no technical assistance, for fear of a flood of bones which would have to wait some time for analysis and reply. Does anybody know of an individual (retired?), without fear of a simple computer interaction, who would like to commit some volunteer time to the project at the ROM?

E. J. Crossman, Department of Ichthyology and Herpetology, Royal Ontario Museum, 100 Queen's Park, Toronto, Ontario, M5S 2C6, (416) 586-5549.

• • •

Hambug's Hint — If you're a musky fanatic and spend most of your free time on the water hunting for muskies, try converting your livewell into a tackle box. Line it with plastic tubing that you've joined together with electrician's tape (6 to 8 tubes to a bundle). You can often hang 2 to 3 lures in each tube and most livewells will accommodate all your baits. Your boat will be a much neater, more efficient and safer fishing machine. At the end of the season or on those days you'd just like to dabble for bluegills the tubes can be quickly removed complete with lures for easy storage.

THE 50-POUND CLUB
Revised

Compiled by Larry Ramsell as of March 3, 1995

*T*he following list includes muskies that were caught and kept that were 50 pounds or larger that — to date — have either supporting documentation; pictures that support the weight; or have no doubt cast upon them at this time. Others of questionable value or proven to be falsified have been left off the list. Any anglers with multiple catches over 50 pounds who have had one or more of their fish disqualified due to falsification have had all of their fish removed from this list until such time as absolute verification of any of their possible legitimate catches can be made.

No.	Weight	Angler	Date	Lure	Water
1.	70-0	Robert Malo	6/6/54	Live Sucker	Middle Eau Claire, WI
2.	69-11	Louie Spray	10/20/49	Spray Harness Sucker	Chippewa Flowage, WI
3.	67-8	Cal Johnson	7/24/49	South Bend Pike-Oreno	Lac Courte Oreilles, WI
4.	65-0	Ken O'Brien	10/16/88	Countdown Rapala	Moon River, ON
5.*	62-0	Gary Ishii	10/11/81	LeBlanc Swim Whizz	Moon River, ON

1996 Musky Hunter's Almanac

No.	Weight	Angler	Date	Lure	Water
6.	61-13	Louie Spray	8/19/40	True Temper Bass Pop	Lac Courte Oreilles, WI
7.	61-9	Edward Walden	10/8/40	#12 Pflueger Muskill	Eagle Lake, ON
8.	60-8	John Coleman	10/3/39	Creek Chub Pikie Minnow	Eagle Lake, ON
9.	59-11	Art Barefoot	6/5/89	Cisco Kid Diver	French River, ON
10.	59-8	Louie Spray	7/27/39	Marathon Musky Houn	Grindstone Lake, WI
11.	58-8	Ruben Green	7/25/45	Ottertail Spinner	McGregor Bay-Georgian Bay, ON
12.	58-4	George E. Neimuth	9/24/32	Creek Chub Pikie	Lake of the Woods, ON
13.	57-10	William Fulton	1917	Unknown	French River, ON
14.	56-11	Gene Borucki	8/30/84	Rapala	Manitou Lake, ON
15.	56-8	Jack W. Collins	7/24/31	Pflueger Muskill	Lake of the Woods, ON
Tie	56-8	R.D. Shawvan	9/4/41	Heddon Giant Vamp	Lake of the Woods, ON
17.	56-0	Fred Reinhart	9/12/44	Rinehart Jinx	Lake of the Woods, ON
18.	55-11	Sam Finsky	6/20/63	#3 Mepps Gold Spinner	Lake Kakagi, ON
19.	55-2	Dr. Neal Crawford	9/13/46	Marathon Musky Houn	Lake of the Woods, ON
Tie	55-2	Joe Lykins	4/1/72	Creek Chub Pikie Minnow	Piedmont Lake, OH
21.	55-0	Arthur J. Ross	9/28/42	Marathon Musky Houn	Chippewa Flowage, WI
Tie	55-0	Herman Reber	10/4/42	Heddon Vamp Spook	Pipestone Lake, ON
Tie	55-0	Stanley Baker	9/16/49	Big Spoon (spinner)	St. Lawrence River

The 50-Pound Club

No.	Weight	Angler	Date	Lure	Water
Tie	55-0	Charles Fawcett	10/2/54	Heddon River Runt	English River, ON
Tie	55-0	Steve Albers	9/22/85	Whopper Stopper Hell Cat	Eagle Lake, ON
Tie	55-0	John P. Ryan	8/25/92	Radke Pike Minnow	English River, ON
27.	54-8.5	Mark Kontianen	10/15/77	LeBlanc Swim Whizz	Moon River, ON
28.	54-3	Lewis Walker Jr.	9/30/24	Dead 8" Red Chub	Conneaut Lake, PA
Tie	54-3	Jim Carrol	7/16/87	Lindy Rig & Worm	Restoule Lake, ON
30.	54-0	William Walshe	8/22/43	Willow Spinner	St. Lawrence River
Tie	54-0	C.W. Frale	9/8/50	Johnson Silver Minnow	Lake of the Woods, ON
Tie	54-0	Karl Ghaster	9/21/54	Marathon Musky Houn	Eagle Lake, ON
Tie	54-0	Michael Pederson	10/21/55	Cisco Kid	Honey Harbour-Georgian Bay, ON
Tie	54-0	Art Lyons	8/28/57	Dardevle	Big Winnibigoshish, MN
35.	53-12	Gordon M. Curtis	8/25/29	#7 Skinner Spoon (spinner)	Lake of the Woods, ON
Tie	53-12	Myrl McFaul	9/22/53	Worth Musky Fin	North Twin Lake, WI
37.	53-8	W.L. Kirkpatrick	9/8/32	Creek Chub Pike Minnow	Lake of the Woods, ON
Tie.	53-8	Adolph Bockus	9/16/40	Marathon Musky Houn	Lake of the Woods, ON
Tie	53-8	Lew Morgan	9/27/44	Marathon Musky Houn	Big Vermilion Lake, ON
40.	53-0	Dr. George Collins	7/10/46	Johnson Spoon	Lake of the Woods, ON

1996 Musky Hunter's Almanac

No.	Weight	Angler	Date	Lure	Water
Tie	53-0	E.W. Flint	8/29/46	Marathon Musky Houn	St. Lawrence River
42.	52-12	Emanuel A. Oberland	7/1/29	Pflueger Spoon (spinner)	Pokegama Lake, WI
43.	52-8.75	Rita Hillenbrand	11/11/69	Live Sucker	Flambeau Flowage, WI
44.	52-8	Gerry Winteregg	9/22/41	Roberts Mud Puppy	Lake of the Woods, ON
45.	52-8	Harry Faulkerson	6/24/50	Unknown	Lac Courte Oreilles, WI
46.	52-4	Harry Gardner	8/16/49	Roberts Mud Puppy	Eagle Lake, ON
Tie	52-4	George McQuillen	11/12/94	Kwikfish	Lake of Two Mountains, PQ
48.	52-0	Gust Peterson	10/10/35	Pflueger Spoon (spinner)	White Sand Lake, WI
Tie	52-0	William Dashley	10/9/42	Creek Chub Pikie Minnow	St. Lawrence River
Tie	52-0	Charles Rothermal	8/18/45	Heddon Plug	Trout Lake, WI
Tie	52-0	Harold Ferguson	10/1/54	Creek Chub Pikie Minnow	St. Lawrence River
52.	51-12	Joseph Mathis Jr.	7/22/48	Casco Slo-jo	Lake Winnebago, WI
Tie	51-12	Eugene Avrill	10/12/64	South Bend Bass-Oreno	Lake of the Woods, ON
54	51-11	George Moore	8/5/37	Marathon Musky Houn	Lake of the Woods, ON
55	51-8	Lewis Hilfer	10/10/38	South Bend Musk-Oreno	Eagle Lake, ON
Tie	51-8	Robert Geister	9/23/75	Creek Chub Giant Pikie	Pipestone Lake, ON
57.	51-8	Don Reed	7/23/82	Lindy Musky Tandem	Wabigoon Lake, ON

The 50-Pound Club

No.	Weight	Angler	Date	Lure	Water
58.	51-6	Eugene Eggert	10/19/63	Bucktail Spinner	Manitou Lake, ON
59.	51-4	Dennis Kestner	9/18/53	Heddon River Runt	Lake of the Woods, ON
Tie	51-4	Joseph Bertoncini	10/1/57	Marathon Musky Hawk	Eagle Lake, ON
61.**	51-3	John Knobla	7/16/19	Skinner Spinner	Lac Vieux Desert, WI-MI
62.	51-1	Mike Kelner	5/19/73	Fathead Minnow	Leech Lake, MN
63.	51-0	F.J. Swint	9/13/16	#8 Skinner Trolling Spoon & Frog	Chief Lake, WI
Tie	51-0	Ed J. Smith	9/30/63	Creek Chub Pikie Minnow	Moon River, ON
Tie	51-0	Gene Allen	9/21/75	Bobbie Bait	Lac du Flambeau, WI
66.	50-14	Henry J. Bianco	8/21/46	Heddon Vamp	Lake of the Woods, ON
67.	50-12	Dr. H.C. Remele	9/25/46	Creek Chub	Woman Lake, MN
Tie	50-12	Stewart Levere	1968	Unknown	St. Lawrence River
69.	50-8	Melvin Westlake	7/21/37	Marathon Musky Houn	Lake of the Woods, ON
Tie	50-8	Lee Handley	10/10/37	South Bend Flash-Oreno	Dryberry Lake, ON
Tie	50-8	Russel Baker	9/3/51	Marathon Musky Houn	Eagle Lake, ON
Tie	50-8	Dennis Denman	10/1/81	Unknown	Mille Illes River, PQ
73.	50-7	Gordon Lawton	9/1/51	#9 Buffalo Spoon (spinner)	St. Lawrence River
74.	50-4	J.C. Nichols	8/12/25	11" Sucker	Columbus Lake, WI
Tie**	50-4	Delores Lapp	6/28/51	Marathon Musky Houn	Lac Vieux Desert, WI-MI

1996 Musky Hunter's Almanac

No.	Weight	Angler	Date	Lure	Water
Tie	50-4	Emmett Ostlund	9/11/51	Imitation Frog	Lake of the Woods, ON
Tie	50-4	Robert Grutt	6/10/89	Buchertail Willow Buck	Big Round Lake, WI
78.	50-3	John Vaughn	6/5/90	Mepps Aglia & Twister	St. Lawrence River
79.	50-2	Dominic Tasone	1/2/64	Creek Chub Pikie Minnow	St. Lawrence River
80.	50-1	Mrs. E. Reinardy	10/27/62	Live Sucker	Flambeau Flowage, WI
81.	50-0	Herbert Kerr	8/23/36	Pfleuger Bearcat Spinner	St. Lawrence River
Tie	50-0	Theodore Meisner	8/30/41	Marathon Musky Houn	Grindstone Lake, WI
Tie	50-0	Nicholas Dire	7/22/42	Spinner	Lac Du Flambeau, WI
Tie	50-0	Alfred Adolphsen	8/28/42	Unknown	Lake of the Woods, ON
Tie	50-0	Joseph Blazis	6/20/48	Heddon Queen	Rowan Lake, ON
Tie	50-0	Stanley Kroll	8/22/51	Creek Chub Pikie Minnow	Little Winnibigoshish, MN
Tie	50-0	Ray Kennedy	8/6/56	Marathon Musky Houn	Minocqua, WI
Tie	50-0	H. Marcus	8/4/57	AL & W Creek Chub Pikie	St. Lawrence River
Tie	50-0	Terry Bachman	9/21/83	Dardevle	Lake Nosbonsing, ON
Tie	50-0	Robert LaMay	10/18/83	Crane Bait	High Falls Flowage, WI

The first weighing of this fish was 62 pounds on a scale not thought at the time to be accurate and was weighed hours later on a second scale

The 50-Pound Club

after much handling and transportation. Upon subsequent checking of both scales by a Canadian Weights and Measures Inspector, both scales were found to be accurate. I am therefore upgrading it on the list to the original weight.

** *Hybrid*

Where Were They Caught (by province/state)?
Ontario, 54.7%; Wisconsin, 25.6%; New York/Ontario 12.8%; Minnesota 4.7%; Wisconsin/Michigan, 2.3%.

Where Were They Caught (by water)?
Lake of the Woods, 28.6%; St. Lawrence River, 17.5%; Eagle Lake, 11.1%; Georgian Bay, 11.1%; Chippewa Flowage, 3.2%; Others, 28.6%.

What Bait Did They Eat?
Spinner, 40.6%; Crankbait, 31.3%; Live Bait, 10.9%; Jerkbait, 9.4%; Spoon, 7.8%.

What Month Were They Caught In?
January, 0; February, 0; March, 0; April, 1; May, 1; June, 6; July, 11; August, 12; September, 22; October, 18; November, 1; December, 0.

• • •

Hambug's Hint — Having trouble reading your hydrographic charts? Try coloring the areas between contour lines with different colored pencil crayons. It will give you a good overview of the lake and its structural makeup.

THE 45-POUND RELEASE CLUB

Compiled by Larry Ramsell as of April 30, 1995

*I*t would be redundant to say that the live "release" program has been a resounding success. The record speaks for itself, and it is no accident that larger average size fish are being caught each year. This, coupled with new frontiers being found and explored, has resulted in muskies — that in years past were considered trophies for the wall — being released. These facts, I believe, are bringing us closer to the day when a new world record would be hung on the scale. While some "zealots" claim they would release even a world record fish, I think the "moment of truth" would find otherwise. What, I ask, would be the point? To release a fish of that caliber would deny the musky world what it has been waiting for; proof that such a fish is possible and does exist! With the "clouds of doubt" that surrounded every record musky since 1939, I can't believe anyone would release such a creature and then try to claim it! Nor can I believe anyone would release such a creature and keep quiet about it.

The purpose of this "club" is to acknowledge those anglers who have released super trophy fish, one of which could ultimately be recaught as a world record.

While I will be relying on angler honesty for fish placed in this club's listing, a few criteria will need to be met:

1. A picture will be required.

2. Length and girth measurement (To nearest 1/4") required.
3. A witness to the release and measurement is required.

"Estimated" weight for each fish listed is calculated using the "revised" estimated weight formula: (Girth - .75") X (Girth - .75") X Length / 800 = Estimated Weight. (See the estimated weight chart in the *Musky Hunter's Almanac* for a complete explanation of this formula.)

No.	Angler	Date	Length	Adj. Girth	Live Girth	Weight
1.	Ed Barbosa	10/20/94	58	27.75	28.5	55.83
2.	John Wozny	12/4/94	57.5	27.25	28	53.37
3.	Dave Johnson	9/29/85	55	27.25	28	51.05
4.	Rich Wren	11/13/94	54	26.75	27.5	48.30
5.	Mike Langhammer	10/7/94	55.5	25.75	26.5	46.0
6.	Shawn McCarthy	8/16/92	57	25.25	26	45.43

• • •

Humor — A sign seen hanging over Louie Spray's 1940, 61-pound 13-ounce world record. "The Lord was with me when I caught this fish so for further information contact him."

THE 40-HYBRID MUSKY CLUB

Compiled by Larry Ramsell as of June 1, 1995

The hybrid cross between a true muskellunge and a (northern) pike is one of nature's beautiful creatures. Hybrids over 40 pounds (18.144 kilos) are extremely rare and only two have ever exceeded 50 pounds (22.68 kilos) "officially," with one other near 50 that wasn't weighed for three days. The list of hybrids over 40 pounds is relatively short compared to the length of recorded musky history; it wasn't until the late 1920s that hybrids were even written about. Even today, many anglers are unaware of the fish's lineage when they catch one. I am sure that in the past 100 years there have been several others caught over 40 pounds (18.144 kilos) and not known or reported as such. Interestingly, nearly all fish on the list were "natural" hybrids, rather than "hatchery" hybrids.

No.	Weight	Angler	Date	Length	Girth	Lure	Water
1.	51-3	John Knobla	7/16/19	54	25 1/4	Skinner Spinner	Lac Vieux Desert, WI/MI
2.	50-4	Delores Lapp	6/28/51	56	26 1/2	Marathon Musky Houn	Lac Vieux Desert, WI/MI
3.	49-0	George Barber	1935	NA	NA	Heddon Vamp	Pelican Lake, WI
4.	48-8	Unknown	1943	52 3/4	NA	NA	Pickerel Lake, WI

No.	Weight	Angler	Date	Length	Girth	Lure	Water
5.	47-0	Elmer Caskey	1947	NA	NA	NA	Lac Vieux Desert, WI/MI
6.	44-9 1/2	Thomas Isaac	10/1/94	57 3/4	23 5/8	12" Rapala	Georgian Bay, ONT
7.	44-6	Wally Heinrich	7/11/46	NA	NA	Heddon Vamp	Planting Ground Lake, WI
8.	43-11	Red Degroot	1948	49	NA	NA	Lac Courte Oreilles, WI
9.	43-0	Tony Kerscher	late '40s	NA	NA	NA	Lac Vieux Desert, WI/MI
10.	43-0	Dick Lapp	1940s	NA	NA	NA	Lac Vieux Desert, WI/MI
11.	42-6	Allen F. Praefke	6/17/48	54	26	8" Sucker	Palmer Lake, WI
12.	42-0	George Tally	1950s	NA	NA	NA	Big Round Lake, WI
13.	41-0	Charles Casey	July 1920	NA	NA	So. Bend Bucktail Gang	Kawaguesaga Lake, WI
14.	40-2	Jason Potter	7/24/94	53	23 7/8	Burt Jerk	Quincy Reservoir, CO
15.	40-0	Dr. C. I. Pershbacker	1945	54	NA	NA	Big Sand Lake, WI
16.	40-0	M. Haroldson	1966	51	NA	NA	Riley Lake, WI
17.	40-0	Marvin Lee	1975	NA	NA	NA	Gravel Lake, ND
18.	40-0	Len Kubicki	NA	NA	NA	NA	St. Lawrence River

• • •

Quotable Notable — "While here, why not concentrate our individual efforts to try to make fishing on Earth as Heavenly as possible?"
— Ray Bergman

The Great Debate

The best way to net trophy muskies
or
"Tails I win — Heads you lose"

By Bill Hamblin

Considering the many hundreds of hours often required to track down a musky, it's to no one's surprise that the vast majority of published material is devoted to educating the angler where to find this magnificent fish, and of the techniques and methods required to hook one. Conversely, lit-

---

The Great Debate

Counter point

By Larry Ramsell

I am sure by now Bill's article has you thinking. I would like to offer the other perspective ... netting head-first. Any net can be a problem, especially in the hands of an inexperienced fisherman. There is a tendency to attempt to take the fish prematurely.

A net can be a very effective tool in the hands of an experienced person. If a trophy fish is hooked lightly, a large net can be the difference

tle is written suggesting how to properly play and land a musky, a task which may be infinitely more difficult than the former because most fishermen are unprepared for such an eventuality. This is not because they haven't taken the time to acquaint themselves with such skills, but rather due to the assumption that the general techniques employed in playing and landing one species of fish may be universally applied to all. As a rule of thumb, this is so, but it may be presumptuous to believe it applies to the musky, and in particular, trophy fish of lengthy proportions.

Popular convention has always maintained that a big musky should be netted head-first. Certainly this is the position most of the top guides and educators have upheld for years. And why not? The premise is simple. It's much easier to net a fish that is swimming into a net rather than one swimming away

See Tails I Win, Page 142

---

between a trophy mount on the wall or just another frustrating experience.

Personally I have netted muskies up to 44 pounds. One particular 32-pound fish, hooked by my fishing partner, was lightly hooked in the skin outside the jaw. Out of necessity, I netted this fish on its first pass by the boat only minutes after it hit. The instant the fish was in the net the hook came loose. Believe me, it is quite a job to lift a "green" 32-pound musky into the boat, even for two men. After the fish was in the boat it thrashed wildly and tried to destroy us, boat and contents! However, thanks to a king-size net, that fish is now hanging on the wall.

There are many "netting" methods employed by musky fishermen. Some tire the fish out, slip the net in the water, ease the fish over the net,

See Counter Point, Page 142

1996 Musky Hunter's Almanac

Tails I Win
Continued from Page 141

from a net. They will tell you it's simply a matter of common sense.

On the surface, the logic of this would seem to be undebatable and I would have to agree that on smaller fish the technique is — in a word — adequate. Well I don't know about you but when it really counts, when that fish of a life time is literally on the line, "adequate" just doesn't cut it. In the "few and far between" world of musky hunting it is vitally important that we tip the scales in our favor whenever possible and landing big fish is no exception. In my mind it's a major tactical error to try to net a big fish head-first. If 12 years of pursuing the giant fish of Georgian Bay has taught me anything it's that you net these "super" fish tail-first. And so begins The Great Debate.

Clearly in any situation, the better method is that which performs best under the worst possible conditions. Anything less would leave us unprepared. Typically, the worst case scenario has that once-in-a-lifetime trophy poorly hooked and spooking at boatside just as your partner Murphy (what can go wrong will go wrong) is about to net it. His choice is simple. Net the fish head-first or tail-first. Under the best conditions either method is adequate but under

---

Counter Point
Continued from Page 141

and raise it up. This method is fine for small fish or for the lone fisherman but leaves much to be desired. The main problem being if the fish is slightly longer than the size of the net hoop and if the attempt to net it is from underneath and if the lure catches on the hoop, the fish could escape merely by stiffening itself out and flipping forward out of the net.

Another method I have used is to put the net in the water with the handle perpendicular to the water and to lead the played fish into it. I dis-

The Great Debate

the worst conditions, the former could be disastrous. To illustrate my point, let's go fishing.

It's mid-October and prime lunker season. The moon is full, and the earth and the moon are in perigee. The water is cool but calm, and there is just enough sun to neutralize the nip in the air and warm your favorite shallow water structure. The time is ripe. You've paid your dues.

Suddenly you are startled by a massive strike. For a split second you're not sure it is for real or just another of those dreams you save for slow days on the water. You set the hook with the realization that this is no dream. You play her tirelessly, keeping the pressure on her, determined not to give the brute an opening. Finally, your opponent is showing signs of weakness — victory seems imminent. All that remains is the simple task of netting her. But then there is an instant of doubt. You've never netted one this big before. Can you count on your partner? What do you do? You quickly go over the options in your head. In anticipation of a head-first netting, the fish should be drawn in parallel to the boat, with the netter positioned on the opposite side of the angler, from which the fish will approach. It may then be guided past the angler and into

See Tails I Win, Page 144

like this method because it can easily cost a good fish. If the fish has any strength left it will usually dive under the hoop and either hook the lure on it or gain freedom with one last flurry.

My favorite and nearly foolproof method, if done correctly, is accomplished by two people. The person playing the fish heads it toward the man with the net at an angle slightly toward the boat, head-first. The person with the net is the "key" to success. They must remain calm and not swipe at the fish the moment it is in reach. They must let the fish get well

See Counter Point, Page 144

Tails I Win
Continued from Page 143

the net head-first. Hopefully! In the case of a tail-first attempt, the netter should position himself on the same side of the angler from which the musky will approach.

From the musky's point of view, it will experience one of two things. In the first instance all the action, movement etc., will take place in front of it. It will see the net come out and plunge into the water a foot or two in front of its nose, all before one inch of it has entered the net. The probability of spooking it on the first approach is very high, often resulting in either an aborted landing attempt or loss of the fish. In the second case the fish is drawn past the netter, so as to appear it is heading back into open water. This will have a calming influence on the fish, enabling you to quickly and quietly slip the net into the water, behind it and up the full length of its body, before it is aware of what is happening. Fewer fish will spook at boatside, giving you a higher success rate for the first landing attempt. You will recall, however, I stated earlier that the preferred method is that which works best under the worst possible conditions.

Counter Point
Continued from Page 143

within range, keep the net out of the water, and be poised and ready. When they are positive they can reach the fish the netter must make one fast "sweep" with the net, being sure to take the fish head-first. In this manner the netter can reach the fish even if it tries to dive away from the boat.

This method accomplishes several things: 1.) The fish is not spooked by the presence of the net in the water. 2.) There is no water resistance to

The Great Debate

Although tail-first netting will reduce the number of worst case scenarios you may face during the course of a season, it is under these more difficult circumstances that this method's true benefits become most evident. The angler's first instinct when a musky spooks is to apply more pressure on the line, to prevent slack and maintain control of the fish. An inexperienced netter's first instinct is to start scooping for the fish with the net. Both people are now working at odds with each other. The angler's tendency, by applying greater pressure, is to pull the musky's head out of the net and away from the netter. This often results in the fish entangling the hooks in the net, at which point the angler loses all control over the fish, and little more is required of the fish than to give one good yank and the hooks rip from its mouth. This hazard is compounded further when one considers the size of the plugs used in musky fishing. The chances of guiding even a docile fish of some 4 1/2 to 5 feet in length to the bottom of a net with that amount of hardware protruding from its mouth, without an entanglement, are not very good. Matters may be made even more difficult when you think of what happens to the actual netting

See Tails I Win, Page 146

---

slow up the "sweep" until the net is around the fish. 3.) By having the fish closer to the boat more leverage can be applied to lift the fish from the water and into the boat. 4.) When a large hoop is used and the fish centered in it, there will be no danger of catching a hook in the net until the fish hits the bottom. 5.) When the net is swished through the air, the netting opens up fully to the diameter of the hoop and makes it easy to encircle the fish.

The next time you see a large musky mounted on a wall, stop and

See Counter Point, Page 146

1996 Musky Hunter's Almanac

Tails I Win
Continued from Page 145

when put into the water. The frame itself may be guided accurately before the fish, however, the netting being lighter than water, will resist it upon impact and may actually block the opening of the net, requiring the fish to push the netting to fill out the bag. This situation may be overcome by inserting the net farther from the fish, enabling you to make a greater sweeping motion with the net, and allowing the water to fill out the bag. But then the farther from the fish the net enters the water, the greater the risks become. It is a Catch-22. Unless, you consider the advantages to a tail-first approach.

First, if the fish spooks, the angler and netter are working in unison. The added pressure applied by the angler actually pulls the fish back into the oncoming net. Second, any protruding hooks do not come in contact with the net until fully 90% of the fish is netted. Three, should it be decided that the best approach is to abort the netting attempt in favor of a second pass, the angler should never have lost control of the fish, and because it is swimming away from the netter into unobstructed open water, there is reduced risk of it

---

Counter Point
Continued from Page 145

think what a large part the "landing" must have played. You may have the best fishing equipment, excellent fishing techniques and luck, but these things can only get the fish to the boat. To hang that trophy on the wall it first must be landed! You should obtain or make the proper landing tools and study the proper landing techniques before the moment of truth arrives. Best of luck(?)!!!

Now, having said the above, I must admit to one and all that the

The Great Debate

fowling the net.

The advantages do not stop here. In the event that you appear to have the fish netted, be cautious not to become too complacent with your apparent success. The musky has one last tactic with which you must deal. Deep water represents ultimate security to a large fish. Hence, its natural instinct is to dive when in trouble. Given the power of these brutes and their naturally streamlined bodies, don't be at all surprised to see it swim right through the bottom of your net. I have personally had this happen to me on more than one occasion, and with nets I considered to be impenetrable. The head-first approach does nothing more than dare the musky to try it.

On the other hand, consider that a fish with its head on the surface has half the mobility and power of a submerged fish with its head down. When netting a musky tail-first, the natural sweeping action of the net frame will bring it up right under the fish's chin. This helps to keep the musky's head above water and prevents it from diving.

Another concern is the added pressure a sounding musky places on the

See Tails I Win, Page 148

---

points Bill makes have my attention. I intend to give his methods a try on my next big fish, especially if I'm fishing alone.

Bill and Larry welcome your comments and opinions concerning the issues discussed in "The Great Debate." Thoughtful responses will be published in the 1997 Musky Hunter's Almanac. We would also like to know what other issues you would like to see debated in almanacs to come. Please send your ideas to Bill Hamblin, 718 Dunbar Road, Kitchener, Ontario, N2M 2X6

1996 Musky Hunter's Almanac

Tails I Win

Continued from Page 147

net's frame. I have seen fishermen, in their eagerness to bring a fish into the boat, snap a net off at the hoop, only to see their prize catch unceremoniously dumped back into the lake. Just ask George Migas of Muskies Canada, Inc. His nickname, "Net Bender," was regrettably earned as a result of one such unfortunate incident. Netting a musky tail-first prevents it from using its body weight and speed to its own advantage. Bringing the hoop up under its chin will neutralize this last tactical maneuver, and it will fall gently to the bottom of your net.

Until now, the case for tails or heads has been limited to a discussion of the physical aspects of the netting procedure. There are philosophical factors of equal importance which should be considered.

Think of yourself as that person responsible for netting what could be a decade's or indeed a lifetime's dream. It could be argued that in any landing attempt the greatest pressure is on the netter — particularly, if the fish is of trophy proportions ... certainly, mixed emotions at best. Being all too human, we can easily rationalize our own mistakes which might have contributed to losing a fish, but may be less forgiving of others.

I don't think there is any self-respecting musky angler alive who wouldn't take 100% of the responsibility for landing his or her fish, if it were possible. But, aside from actually playing and boating the fish yourself, which in the case of a 40-plus-pound fish could be your biggest mistake, one must settle for the approach which places the greatest responsibility on the angler.

Once again, "tails" wins hands down. The reasons are simple. In a tail-first netting, the angler can maintain a tight line and consequently control the fish through the entire netting procedure. Neither the line nor lure should even come in contact with the net and at no time during the landing procedure does the onus of controlling the fish pass to the netter.

The Great Debate

To the contrary, when a musky enters head-first, the angler must reduce line pressure, resulting in a critical split second when the fish is not in the net and neither person has control. The onus for successful landing passes to the netter, and he must contend with line, lure and a determined musky which has just been handed the opportunity he's been waiting for. This is no simple task. The angler owes it to himself and to the netter to accept as much responsibility as is possible, because ultimately he will be given most of the credit.

There is one last point you may want to consider before choosing between the two methods. If you are a strong advocate of catch and release you will find it particularly appealing. Netting these fish tail-first will result in quicker, cleaner releases and a higher survival rate. Because the head ends up at the top of the bag near the hoop, fewer hooks are tangled in the net, the head is easily accessible for hook removal and you are able to extract the fish from the bag without setting it on the floor of the boat. Conversely, its almost impossible to free a head-netted fish from a net without laying it down. (Water release is preferable but often impossible.) Contact with the floor usually causes the fish to spook, resulting in a wild, tangled mess (if you haven't already got one) taking precious additional minutes to complete the release. Damage to the fish is often greater and mortality higher.

As with any theory applied to musky fishing, it is difficult to prove or disprove, based on one's own experiences. You may literally wait a lifetime to test a theory on a fish of true adversary proportions. This only serves to emphasize the importance of clubs where we may benefit from the fortunate, and yes, the unfortunate experiences of our fellow anglers. I have had the opportunity to successfully apply these techniques to numerous 40-pound fish. Your ability to do the same will be limited only by the degree of confidence you may have in your own techniques. Go with whatever landing method you personally feel confident with. But! I'd be willing to bet my last plug: "Tails I Win — Heads You Lose"!

THE STATE & PROVINCIAL RECORDS

as listed by the
National Fresh Water Fishing Hall of Fame
with additions by the Editors

With the ever growing popularity of sport fishing for musky and the consequential increased development of economically viable hatcheries, the muskellunge fishery, both natural and hybrid, has spread to include 34 of the United States and three Canadian Provinces. This has stimulated a growing interest in state and provincial as well as world records within the musky fishing community. The National Fresh Water Fishing Hall of Fame now recognizes 53 state records in the "catch and keep" category from 34 different states. Half of these records have been established since 1988.

Natural Musky

State	Weight	Angler	Location	Year
Alabama	19-8	Steve Leatherwood	Wilson Dam Tailwater	1972
Georgia	38-0	Rube Golden	Blue Ridge Lake	1957
Illinois	34-3	Charles Book	Lake Shabbona	1994
Indiana	35-8	George Webster	Lake Tippecanoe	1994

State	Weight	Angler	Location	Year
Iowa	40-5	Dennis Heidebrinke	West Okoboji Lake	1991
Kentucky	43-0	Peter Hash	Dale Hollow Lake	1978
Maine	22-12	Lance Geidel	Baker Lake	1988
Maryland	20-0	John Stepp	Conorvingo Dam	1978
Michigan*	62-8	Percy Haver	Lake St. Clair	1940
Michigan (inland)	45-0	William Pivar	Thousand Island Lake	1980
Minnesota	54-0	Art Lyons	Lake Winnebigoshish	1957
Missouri	41-2	Gene Snelling	Lake of the Ozarks	1981
Nebraska	41-8	Jared Haddix	Merritt Reservoir	1992
New Jersey	38-4	Dana Ross	Delaware Water Gap	1990
New York**	69-15	Art Lawton	St. Lawrence River	1957
N. Carolina	38-0	Dale J. Houge	Little Tennessee River	1957
N. Dakota	26-5	David A. Carlson	Spiritwood Lake	1989
Ohio	55-2	Joe D. Lykins	Piedmont Lake	1972
Ontario	65-0	Ken O'Brien	Moon River	1988
Pennsylvania	54-3	Lewis Walker Jr.	Conneaut Lake	1924
Quebec	52-4	George McQuillen	St. Lawrence River	1995
S. Carolina	19-1	Lee Ramsey	Broad River	1995
S. Dakota	40-0	Daniel B. Krueger	Amsden Dam	1991
Tennessee	42-8	Kyle F. Edwards	Norris Reservoir	1983
Vermont	29-8	Stephan Demar	Missisquoi River	1978
Virginia	45-0	Ronnie A. Underwood	New River	1989
W. Virginia	43-0	Lester Hayes	Elk River	1955
Wisconsin	69-11	Louis Spray	Chippewa Flowage	1949

*The Haver fish has been removed from the official listing of 60-pound muskies but the state of Michigan continues to recognize it as its state record.

**Although this fish has been disqualified by the world record keeping bodies, New York continues to recognize it as the state record.

State and Provincial Records for hybrid muskies can be found on Page 152

1996 Musky Hunter's Almanac

Hybrid or Tiger Musky

State	Weight	Angler	Location	Year
Arkansas	16-11	Larry Wyatt	Spring River	1993
Colorado	40-2	Jason Potter	Quincy Reservoir	1994
Idaho	7-13	Keith Millard	Hauser Lake Outlet	1993
Illinois	26-3	David Pan	Summerset Lake	1989
Indiana	22-0	John Adams	Blue Lake	1988
Iowa	27-2	Shannon Green	West Okoboji Lake	1990
Kentucky	13-12	James Mollett	Dervey Lake	1981
Maryland	26-12	Donald Stottler Jr.	Potomac River	1990
Massachusetts	19-4	Al Farland	Lake Quinsigamond	1987
Michigan	51-3	John Knobla	Lac Vieux Desert	1919
Minnesota	33-8	Christopher Sager	Lake Calhoun	1991
Missouri	22-0	Ned Posenki	Stockton Lake	1986
Montana	18-9	William Burdge	Lebo Lake	1993
Nebraska	24-8	P.B. Brewer Jr.	Oliver Reservoir	1993
N. Hampshire	11-12	Brian Patch	Connecticut River	1982
New Jersey	29-0	Larry Migliarese	Delaware River	1990
New York	35-8	Brett A. Gofgosky	Tioughnioga River	1990
North Carolina	33-8	Gary Dean Nanney	James Lake	1988
Ohio	26-8	James R. Prettyman	West Branch Reservoir	1984
Ontario	44-9 1/2	Thomas Isaac	Georgian Bay	1994
South Dakota	33-0	Kelly Whalen	Lake Francis Case	1992
Texas	9-1	Mike Gaines	Lake Nacona	1979
Utah	8-10	Eddie Walton	Pineview Reservoir	1993
Vermont	17-13	Daniel W. Magoon	Connecticut River	1987
Washington	14-2	Eric Mathis	Mayfield Lake	1993
West Virginia	28-2	Melvin Stotler	Sleepy Creek	1991
Wisconsin	51-3	John Knobla	Lac Vieux Desert	1919
Wyoming	29-6	Frank Rubrecht	Greyrocks Reservoir	1992

THE WORLD RECORDS

as recognized by the National Fresh Water Fishing Hall of Fame

With the advent of a resolute catch and release philosophy by the majority of musky hunters, new world records in both the "catch and keep" and "catch and release" categories are being established routinely. It is not unusual to see a new record set only to have it toppled by another catch a short time later. This is particularly true in the release divisions, a category that was established by the Hall of Fame a short time ago in response to the changing philosophy of conservation-minded fishermen. It is expected, in the near future, that many of the long-standing "kept" records will also fall, including Louis Spray's official all tackle world record of 69 pounds 11 ounces, as catch and release ushers in a new generation of super fish. For information about registering a potential world record fish you may contact the National Fresh Water Fishing Hall of Fame at Box 33, Hall of Fame Drive, Hayward, Wisconsin, 54843 or call (715) 634-4440.

The National Fresh Water Fishing Hall of Fame, Inc. is a non-profit museum and educational organization. Custodian of historical sport fishing artifacts/enshriner of persons for outstanding achievement and accomplishment, official qualifier and recorder of world record fresh

1996 Musky Hunter's Almanac

water sport-caught fish, librarian, educator and clearing house for contemporary and historical fishing facts.

Catch And Keep

Natural Musky, Conventional Angling

Line Test	Weight	Angler	Location	Date
All Tackle	69-11	Louis Spray	Chippewa Flowage, WI	10/20/49
2	19-4	Paul Gravunder	Chippewa Flowage, WI	6/26/90
4	31-15	Richard Strykowski	Cranberry Lake, WI	8/22/92
6	50-0	Robert W. La May	High Falls Flowage, WI	10/18/83
8	50-3	John M. Vaughn	St. Lawrence River, NY	6/5/90
10	45-0	Robert J. Krencisz	Middle Mckenzie L., WI	10/21/83
12	44-7	John Herman	Trout Lake, WI	6/14/89
14	37-0	David Nevinski	Wabigoon Lake, ONT	6/26/87
15	40-0	Robert Thompson	L. of the Woods, ONT	6/27/86
16	41-4	John Sparbel	Lake Wausau, WI	10/24/93
17	44-7	Rick Kaminski	Big Crawling Stone, WI	6/28/78
20	50-4	Robert G. Grutt	Big Round Lake, WI	6/10/89
25	55-0	Steven Albers	Eagle Lake, ONT	9/22/85
30	51-8	Donald J. Reed	Wabigoon Lake, ONT	7/23/82
36	51-0	Gene Allen	Flambeau Lake, WI	9/21/75
40	48-8	Jerry K. Nelson	Round Lake, WI	10/30/93
45	48-8	Marvin C. Bray	Big Sissabagama L., WI	7/23/77
50	44-4	Larry A. Ramsell	Eagle Lake, ONT	9/29/88
Unlimited	67-8	Cal Johnson	Lac Courte Oreilles, WI	7/24/49
* Unofficial	70-0	Robert Malo	M. Eau Claire L., WI	6/6/54

* Because of its probable record breaking size, the Malo fish is listed, but in an unofficial status due to the fact that discrepancies existed in the weigh-in process for record. Without such certification for absolute authenticity, we are obliged to list this catch as one of 70 pounds unofficial weight.

The World Records

Natural Musky, Power Trolling Division

Line Test	Weight	Angler	Location	Date
2	5-13	Jim Gamlin	Pincher Lake, ONT	8/14/84
4	42-3	Leonard Hartman	St. Lawrence River	9/7/63
6	47-1	Leonard Hartman	St. Lawrence River	9/2/62
8	59-13	Leonard Hartman	St. Lawrence River	8/6/60
10	67-15	Leonard Hartman	St. Lawrence River	8/10/61
12	65-0	Kenneth O'Brien	Georgian Bay, ONT	10/16/88
14	59-11	Arthur J. Barefoot	French R. Delta, ONT	6/5/89
15	47-12	Wendell O. Nichols	Clam Lake, MI	5/16/85
16	45-0	Dr. William Pivar	Thousand Island L., MI	7/26/80
17	47-11	Leonard Hartman	Eagle Lake, ONT	8/13/92
20	48-9	Joe Ehrhardt	Pewaukee Lake, WI	11/19/77
25	47-10	Steve White	Trout Lake, WI	11/9/92
30	37-0	Barbara Clemente	W. Branch Res., OH	6/9/84
36	56-11	Eugene Borucki	Manitou Lake, ONT	8/30/84
40	30-1	Roger McAuliffe	Thousand Island L., MI	7/17/85
45	55-0	Gary Ishii	Moon River, ONT	10/11/81
50	39-0	Richard Zebleckis	L. of the Woods, ONT	8/13/87
Unlimited	Open			

Natural Musky, Fly Fishing

Line Test	Weight	Angler	Location	Date
2	6-12	John Kavanaugh	Brunet River, WI	6/11/94
4	12-1	Jack Giles	M. Eau Claire L., WI	6/25/94
6	13-8	Gustav H. Johnson	M. McKenzie L., WI	7/16/92
8	19-8	Ronald P. Parks	N. Harper Lake, WI	5/27/85
10	18-9	Russell W. Fisher	Pike Lake, WI	6/28/89
12	Open			
14	Open			
16	Open			
Unlimited	Open			

1996 Musky Hunter's Almanac

Natural Musky, Pole/Line/No Reel

Line Test	Weight	Angler	Location	Date
Heaviest Only	25-4	Mark L. Dawson	Chippewa Flowage, WI	10/21/94

Natural Musky, Ice Fishing, Pole/Line

Line Test	Weight	Angler	Location	Date
Heaviest Only	44-13	Gary Frontino	Allegheny Reservoir, PA	2/8/80

Natural Musky, Ice Fishing, Tip-Up

Line Test	Weight	Angler	Location	Date
Heaviest	39-0	Gerald R. Vensel	Keystone Lake, PA	12/29/89

Hybrid Musky, Conventional Angling

Line Test	Weight	Angler	Location	Date
All Tackle	51-3	John A. Knobla	L. Vieux Desert, WI/MI	7/16/19
2	9-12	Randy Shields	Lake Monona, WI	7/17/82
4	25-9	Henry Weiten	Fence Lake, WI	7/4/91
6	29-11	Reen Korach	Iron Lake, MI	6/6/93
8	32-15	Thomas W. Krull	Quincy Reservoir, CO	6/25/93
10	36-8	Clyde E. Beckett	Mountwood Park Lake, WV	9/10/94
12	35-8	Brett A. Gofgosky	Tioughnioga River, NY	5/25/90
14	20-8	Lloyd Jackson	Clinton Lake, IL	8/30/85
15	20-12	Ray Pinter	Tenderfoot Lake, WI	7/6/86
16	28-0	Vernon Langholff	Apeekwa Lake, WI	7/15/84
17	25-14	Ray Pilmonas	Allequash Lake, WI	8/2/83
20	32-6	David Schnell	Trout Lake, WI	9/5/88
25	36-9	George Keller	Lake Finley, WI	8/3/84

The World Records

Hybrid Musky, Conventional Angling, *continued*

Line Test	Weight	Angler	Location	Date
30	34-4	Kenneth Mathwig	L. Vieux Desert, WI/MI	7/19/88
36	35-4	Jeff Hagemann	Big St. Germain L., WI	9/7/91
40	28-0	Mark Aaron Wright	Eagle Lake, ONT	8/2/82
45	34-9	Donald R. Simmons	Long Legged L., ONT	8/3/94
50	28-10	Juan Contreras	Lake Tomahawk, WI	9/17/94
Unlimited	50-4	Delores Ott-Lapp	L. Vieux Desert, WI/MI	6/28/51

Hybrid Musky, Power Trolling

Line Test	Weight	Angler	Location	Date
2	Open			
4	Open			
6	22-1	Charles A. Mistretta	Lake Mendota, WI	10/8/88
8	13-6	Joe Meyer	Lake George, IL	2/6/85
10	16-0	David K. Dunlop, Jr.	Quincy Reservoir, CO	9/8/91
12	27-0	Bryan Calvert	Bear Creek, CO	8/22/93
14	18-8	Jeffrey Ply	Austin Lake, MI	8/27/93
15	18-12	Charles A. Mistretta	Lake Mendota, WI	10/19/88
16	8-0	Jeffrey Ply	Austin Lake, MI	9/15/91
17	Open			
20	35-10	Paul R. Framsted	Quincy Reservoir, CO	7/10/94
25	26-8	James R. Prettyman	West Branch Res., OH	8/25/84
30	24-1	Bryan Steven	W. Lake Okoboji, IA	9/24/83
36	Open			
40	Open			
45	Open			
50	19-13	Louis Champa, Sr.	West Branch Res., OH	6/9/84
Unlimited	Open			

1996 Musky Hunter's Almanac

Hybrid Musky, Fly Fishing

Line Test	Weight	Angler	Location	Date
2	Open			
4	Open			
6	15-8	Barry Reynolds	Quincy Reservoir, CO	8/8/92
8	Open			
10	Open			
12	Open			
14	Open			
16	Open			
Unlimited	Open			

Hybrid Musky, Pole/Line/No Reel

Line Test	Weight	Angler	Location	Date
Heaviest Only	17-14	Ken Jackson	Little St. Germain, WI	10/19/92

Hybrid Musky, Ice Fishing, Pole/Line

Line Test	Weight	Angler	Location	Date
Heaviest Only	Open			

Hybrid Musky, Ice Fishing, Tip-Up

Line Test	Weight	Angler	Location	Date
Heaviest Only	16-8	Carl Winters	Pontoosuc Lake, MA	1/9/91

The World Records
Catch And Release

Natural Musky, Rod/Reel

Line Test	Length	Angler	Location	Date
All Tackle	58	Ed Barbosa	Ottawa River, ONT	10/20/94
2	Open			
4	35	Sean V. Murphy	Chippewa Flowage, WI	5/31/93
6	36	Barbara Gilchrest	Teal Lake, WI	7/17/93
8	53	Bill Haase	Ball Lake, ONT	6/4/94
10	42	Bruce P. Huston	L. of the Woods, ONT	6/26/94
12	44	Michelle Meyer	Spirit Lake, WI	7/15/93
(Tie)	44	Larry McDermott	North Turtle Lake, WI	9/19/93
14	51	Michael H. Halberg	Pipestone Lake, ONT	8/18/94
15	50	John W. Klinzing	Trout Lake, WI	11/7/93
16	47	Ray Zakrzewski	L. of the Woods, ONT	9/17/93
17	50	Phillip Blankenship	Manitou Lake, ONT	6/20/93
20	52	Russel Ruland	High Falls Flowage, WI	10/29/94
25	56	Denise Wachelka	Ottawa River, ONT	6/19/94
30	57	Curt Fenton	Lac Seul, ONT	8/3/92
36	56	John W. Bonneville	Eagle Lake, ONT	7/7/94
40	53	Lou Eich	Lac Seul, ONT	8/11/93
45	58	Ed Barbosa	Ottawa River, ONT	10/20/94
50	55	Mike Langhammer	St. Lawrence River	10/7/94
Unlimited	57	Shawn McCarthy	Georgian Bay, ONT	8/16/92

Natural Musky, Fly Fishing

Line Test	Length	Angler	Location	Date
2	Open			
4	Open			
6	Open			
8	Open			
10	Open			

1996 Musky Hunter's Almanac

Natural Musky, Fly Fishing, *continued*

Line Test	Length	Angler	Location	Date
12	Open			
14	Open			
16	39	John Bloom	Chippewa Flowage, WI	8/10/94
17	Open			
20	Open			
25	Open			
30	Open			

Natural Musky, Pole/Line/No Reel

Line Test	Length	Angler	Location	Date
Longest Only	30	Mike Berg	Lake Michigan, IN	10/20/94

Natural Musky, Ice Fishing, Pole/Line

Line Test	Length	Angler	Location	Date
Longest Only	Open			

Natural Musky, Ice Fishing, Tip-Up

Line Test	Length	Angler	Location	Date
Longest Only	Open			

Hybrid Musky, Rod/Reel

Line Test	Length	Angler	Location	Date
All Tackle	48	John W. Klinzing	Long Legged L., ONT	8/13/93

The World Records

Hybrid Musky, Rod/Reel, *continued*

Line Test	Length	Angler	Location	Date
All Tackle	48 (tie)	Robert A. Todryk	Long Legged L., ONT	8/13/93
All Tackle	48 (tie)	Corey M. Meyer	Sand Lake, WI	8/14/92
2	Open			
4	42	Leonard J. Kouba	Chippewa Flowage, WI	9/18/94
6	32	Joseph P. Zich	Clear Lake, WI	6/27/94
8	Open			
10	40	Jeffrey Ply	Austin Lake, MI	6/5/94
12	40	Jeffrey Ply	Austin Lake, MI	7/13/93
12	40 (tie)	Jeffrey Ply	Austin Lake, MI	9/5/94
14	48	John W. Klinzing	Long Legged L., ONT	8/13/93
15	Open			
16	Open			
17	35	Michael R. Schick	Okauchee Lake, WI	7/22/93
20	48	Robert A. Todryck	Long Legged L., ONT	8/13/93
25	36	Jeffrey Ply	Austin Lake, MI	8/30/94
30	47	Gary N. Schwengel	Eagle Lake, ONT	8/19/93
36	42	Joe Jasek	Chippewa Flowage, WI	9/22/94
40	Open			
45	Open			
50	44	Dave Dorazio	Chippewa Flowage, WI	8/30/92
Unlimited	48	Corey M. Meyer	Sand Lake, WI	8/14/92

Hybrid Musky, Fly Fishing

Line Test	Length	Angler	Location	Date
2	Open			
4	Open			
6	Open			
8	Open			
10	Open			
12	Open			
14	Open			

1996 Musky Hunter's Almanac

Hybrid Musky, Fly Fishing, *continued*

Line Test	Length	Angler	Location	Date
16	45	Barry Reynolds	Quincy Reservoir, CO	8/2/94
17	Open			
20	Open			
25	Open			
30	39	Jim Matschulat	Chippewa Flowage, WI	8/7/94
40	38	Jim Matschulat	Chippewa Flowage, WI	8/17/94

Hybrid Musky, Pole/Line/No Reel

Line Test	Length	Angler	Location	Date
Longest Only	Open			

Hybrid Musky, Ice Fishing

Line Test	Length	Angler	Location	Date
Longest Only	Open			

• • •

Quotable Notable — "The musky is distributed with a careful hand, as if nature had a full appreciation of its value to an angler."
— *B. A. Bensley*

• • •

Quotable Notable — "If necessary, cut off the hook points to set the fish free. The hooks can easily be replaced; the trophy musky cannot."
— *Dick Sternberg*

THE WORLD RECORDS

A few facts you may not have known

Today's musky hunters are more "data" conscious than ever before, paying attention to the most minute details. Trying to correlate things like moon phases; perigee; sunrise/sunset; moonrise/moonset, etc. I thought it would be interesting to correlate these things to past record catches. Will it help you catch a record class fish? Perhaps, but more important than any of the above data will be water fished and "local" weather conditions. If you can get on the water during considered "prime" time, great! Combine that with the correct water, spot, weather, lure and presentation and you may be the next world record holder! For those of you who follow this type of data, find it in this *Almanac's* calendar. Good Luck!

Please turn the page for world record facts. See Pages 108-111 for even more world record information.

1996 Musky Hunter's Almanac

Date	Angler	Moon	Perigee	Sunrise a.m.	Sunset p.m.	Catch Time	Moonrise	Moonset
9/3/11	Dr. Frederick Whiting	3/4 to full	NA	5:25	6:33	Morning	12:18 a.m.	NA
9/13/16	F.J. Swint	Full 11th	NA	5:38	6:14	Morning	6:48 a.m.	NA
7/16/19	John A. Knobla	Full on 13th	NA	4:36	7:35	NA	9:16 a.m.	NA
9/30/24	Lewis Walker Jr.	New/Dark on 28th	10/2	5:56	5:44	7:30 a.m.	NA	7:09 p.m.
7/1/29	E. A. Oberland	Last Quarter on 29th	7/4	4:25	7:42	NA	12:28 a.m.	NA
8/25/29	Gordon M. Curtis	Last Quarter	8/31	5:16	6:47	Morning	9:23 p.m.	NA
7/24/31	Jack W. Collins	1st Quarter on 22nd	7/18	4:42	7:29	Morning	NA	12:33 a.m.
9/24/32	George Neimuth	Last Quarter on 22nd	10/1	5:49	5:55	Early a.m.	12:06 a.m.	NA
7/27/39	Louis Spray	1st Quarter on 23rd	7/17	4:46	7:26	10 a.m.	NA	1:39 a.m.
10/3/39	John J. Coleman	Last Quarter on 6th	10/10	5:58	5:40	Noon	9:43 p.m.	NA
8/19/40	Louis Spray	Full 17th	8/9	5:11	6:56	Morning	7:36 p.m.	NA
7/24/49	Cal Johnson	New/Dark on 25th	7/28	4:44	7:28	5:15 a.m.	2:52 a.m.	NA
10/20/49	Louis Spray	New/Dark on 21st	10/21	6:18	5:11	3:15 p.m.	4:33 a.m.	NA

A Few Facts You May Not Have Known

Date	Angler	Moon	Perigee	Sunrise a.m.	Sunset p.m.	Catch Time	Moonrise	Moonset
6/6/54	Robert Malo	1st Quarter on 8th	5/30	4:24	7:33	4:30 a.m.	NA	11:37 p.m.
10/16/88	Ken O'Brien	Last Quarter on 17th	10/23	6:18	5:13	11:30 a.m.	12:26 a.m.	8:17 p.m.

TIPS ON ESTABLISHING A KEPT FISH RECORD CATCH

provided by the
National Fresh Water Fishing Hall of Fame

When you suspect you have a fish on your line which is large for its species and may be a record catch, do not allow another person to touch your line or tackle during the encounter. More than one person involved in subduing the fish — except for help in netting or gaffing — may disqualify the catch.

Get the fish to a certified or balance type scale (one legal for trade) as soon as possible. Such scales are found in stores, post offices, fisheries, medical facilities, industry, feed mills, and often in sport shops, tourism centers or resorts.

To ensure unquestionable accuracy, use a scale to which is affixed a seal bearing a number, inspector and date of check. Spring mechanism type scales are sometimes inaccurate but may be used if they can later be verified for accuracy in case you are in a place where a certified scale is not available. Such spring scale check/verification documents would then be required to be submitted.

Weigh your fish only once in the presence of two disinterested witnesses and get their full name, address and signatures. Measure girth, fork length and total length.

Have your fish identified as to the species by a professional fisheries person. If the fish is a suspected hybrid or a potential all-tackle record, have its species identified by a fish biologist or taxonomist. Get such identifier's full name, address, signature and place of employment.

Have photos taken — color is best. Hold the fish broadside for further positive identification purposes. If possible, take a black & white picture also for future press reprint purposes. Use a good camera, take a well-lighted, clear, sharp, close-up photo. For small fish, close-up waist-up shots are best.

Do not open the fish. This may be required later to verify weight if suspicion arises. Meanwhile, keep the catch cold-fresh or frozen until status is determined. A taxidermist can mount a fish that has been frozen.

Save the first 25 feet or more of line next to the hook/bait to later send with your application for laboratory line test purposes. Wind line on a notched cardboard to avoid kinks or tangles. For fly fishing records, save about 15 inches of the tippet used, leaving the fly/hook attached (fly returned by request). For rod/line/no reel or ice fishing records, only the heaviest of species is recognized so a line sample need not be submitted. Records are updated quarterly in the Hall's official publication — *The Splash* — and annually in the Hall's World & State Book of Records, out each April.

For a world record application and rules form, write or call the National Fresh Water Fishing Hall of Fame, Box 33, Hall of Fame Drive, Hayward Wisconsin, 54843, (715) 634-4440.

For local record application contact the state or province DNR or Fish and Game Commission. All of the above services are free.

United States Minimum Size and Possession Limits

State	Type	Minimum Length	Possession Limit
Alabama			
Arkansas			
Colorado	Hybrid	30 & 36	One
Georgia			
Illinois	Natural	30 & 36	One
	Hybrid	30	
Indiana	Natural	30	Two
	Hybrid	30	
Iowa	Natural	36	One
Kentucky	Natural	30	Two
	Hybrid	30	
Maine			
Maryland	Natural	30	Two In Aggregate
	Hybrid	30	
Massachusetts	Hybrid	28	One
Michigan	Natural	30 to 45	One
	Hybrid	30 to 45	
Minnesota	Natural	36	One
	Hybrid	36	
		One lake has 30" limit	
Missouri	Natural	30	One
	Hybrid	30	

State	Type	Minimum Length	Possession Limit
Montana	Hybrid	30	One
Nebraska	Natural	30	Two
	Hybrid	30	
New Hampshire			
New Jersey	Natural	30	Two In Aggregate
	Hybrid	30	
New York	Natural	30 & 40 & 44	One
	Hybrid	30	
North Carolina	Natural	30	Two
	Hybrid	30	
North Dakota	Natural	30	One
	Hybrid	30	
Ohio	Natural	0	Two
	Hybrid	0 Pymatuning Res. has 40" limit	
Pennsylvania	Natural	36	Two
	Hybrid	36 Pymatuning Res. has 40" limit	
South Dakota	Natural	30	Two
	Hybrid	30 Amsden Dam has 40" limit	
Tennessee	Natural	30	One
Texas			
Vermont	Natural	30	Two Per Day
West Virginia	Natural	30	Four
	Hybrid	30	
Wisconsin	Natural	34	Two
	Hybrid	34 Some waters have a limit up to 45"	
Wyoming	Hybrid	30	Three

IS THIS THE FORERUNNER OF TODAY'S BUCKTAIL?

1886

UNITED STATES PATENT OFFICE

JOHN B. McHARG, OF ROME, NEW YORK

SPINNING FISH-BAIT.

SPECIFICATION forming part of Letters Patent No. 347,122
dated August 10, 1886
Application filed February 9, 1884. Serial No. 120,211.
(No model.)

To all whom it may concern:

Be it known that I, John B. McHarg, of Rome, Oneida County, New York, have invented an improvement in Spinning Fish-Baits, of which the following is a specification, reference being had to the accompanying drawings, forming part of the same, in which -

Figure 1 is a side view of a spinning fish-bait embodying my invention. Fig. 2 is a crossection on line x x, Fig. 1, and Fig. 3 is a side view showing a modification of said bait.

My invention relates to a spinning fish-bait; and it consists in the combination of a metal plate rotatable on its longitudinal axis, an opening in the body of said plate at and along said axis, and a globular reflector located on said axis within said opening, as hereinafter particularly described.

A is the axis of the bait, consisting of a piece of wire with a loop at its upper end, as shown, to serve for attaching the bait to the fish-line, and with a loop at its lower end to serve for attaching the fish-hook b.

B is a metal plate, generally highly polished, so that it reflects light, and preferably oval in outline, as shown. This plate is mounted to rotate on the axis A, having bearings a a', the axis extending longitudinally of the plate. The plate on opposite sides of the axis is reversely inclined or pitched, so that the plate will be caused to rotate on its axis when drawn rapidly through the water, as in trolling. This form of the plate is shown in Fig. 2.

d is an opening in the center of the plate and at and along the longitudinal axis, as shown. This opening may extend the major portion of the length of the plate B, or it may reach over a minor portion of such length, as shown in Fig. 3.

C is a globe or ball mounted on the axis A within the opening d in plate B. This ball is preferably of burnished metal, it being thus adapted to reflect light. Washers c c' may be employed to hold the ball C centrally of the opening d.

I am aware that glass beads have been heretofore employed as washers and bearings in spinning fish-baits; but in such cases the beads have been located at the ends or above and below the sides of the revolving bait, and, from their nature and location, have not performed the office of reflectors, and have usually been more or less obscured by the revolving bait.

I am also aware that a bait has been heretofore constructed with a longitudinal opening in the body of the revolving plate and a tubular or cylindrical reflector on the axis within said opening; but in a bait thus constructed the tubular or cylindrical reflector operates to reflect the light only to or in the direction of the sides or edges of the bait, and not, as in the case of my globular reflector, to or in the direction of both the forward and rearward end of the bait, as well as to the sides.

It is obvious that my globular reflector will reflect light radially in all directions, while, from the nature of its structure, a cylindrical reflector or tube on the central axis can reflect only in parallel lines sidewise of the bait.

I do not intend to claim herein, broadly, a spinning bait in which there is combined with the rotating plate a reflector in an opening in the body of the plate, nor the combination with such revolving plate of bead washers, whether of metal or glass, but I desire to limit my claim hereunder to the combination of the specific parts shown and described-namely, the plate B, rotatable on its axis and having reversely-inclined opposite edges and provided with the opening d, together with the globular reflector C on said axis within said opening, as set forth.

What I claim as my invention, and desire to secure by Letters Patent, is-

A spinning fish-bait composed of a plate, B, having reversely-inclined opposite edges, an axis, A, extending longitudinally of said plate, and on which said plate is mounted to rotate, an opening, d, in said plate at and along said longitudinal axis, and a globular reflector, C, on said axis within said opening, as and for the purpose specified.

Is This The Forerunner Of Today's Bucktail?

JOHN B. McHARG.
    Witnesses:
A. G.N.Vermilya,
A.S. Fitch.

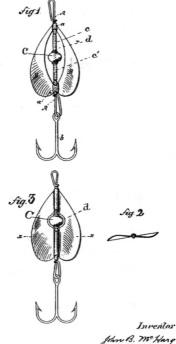

WHERE ARE THEY NOW?

History's greatest musky mounts

Super sleuths Larry Ramsell and Bill Hamblin have searched to the ends of the musky world to determine the present locations of some of history's greatest mounted muskies. Following are the results of their investigations.

- **John Knobla's 1919 World Record Tiger Musky — 51 pounds 3 ounces**

Mr. Knobla's world record tiger musky was recently remounted by Ron Lax Taxidermy in Conover, Wisconsin, and is now back on public display. This spectacular hybrid may be seen at the Minnow Bucket bait shop at 3296 Hwy. E near Phelps, Wisconsin.

- **Delores Ott Lapp's 1951 Tiger Musky — 50 pounds 4 ounces**

Mrs. Lapp's musky is second on the list to John Knobla's world record. It too was recently remounted by Ron Lax. Taken from the same body of water as the Knobla fish, it is on public display at the Pick-A-Flick Video Store on Hwy. B in Land O'Lakes, Wisconsin.

- **Ken O'Brien's 1988 Canadian Record — 65 pounds**

Mr. O'Brien's musky, caught out of the Moon River area of Georgian Bay, still tops off Canada's list of big muskies. The fish was mounted by Grant Mcleod of Toronto and remains in the possession of Mr.

O'Brien. Although the actual fish has never been on public display, a number of replicas have been displayed at major sportsmen shows.

- **Cal Johnson's 1949 World Record — 67 pounds 8 ounces**

This impressive mount may be seen at the Moccasin Bar in downtown Hayward, Wisconsin. The bar in which the fish is displayed is named after the sand and weed bar on Lac Court Oreilles off which Mr. Johnson pulled this former world record.

- **Robert Malo's 1954 Unofficial World Record — 70 pounds**

Although short in stature at 55 inches, the 32-inch girth of this fish is one of the largest on record. It may be viewed at the Dun Rovin Lodge just outside Hayward, Wisconsin, on Highway B. The fish is presented behind a wall of water, making it one of the more realistic and interesting displays you will see for a mount.

- **Louis Spray's Trio of Magnificent Muskies: 1949 World Record — 69 pounds 11 ounces, 1940 — 61 pounds 13 ounces, and 1939 World Record — 59 pounds 8 ounces**

Regrettably all of these fish were lost when Louis Spray's Rice Lake property was destroyed in a fire. "They were magnificent, I'm glad I had the opportunity to see them before they were gone." — Larry

- **John J. Coleman's 1939 World Record — 60 pounds 8 ounces**

This first ever 60-pound musky was last seen and photographed in Duluth, Minnesota. Have you seen this fish recently? Does it still exist? If you can shed some light on this mystery the editors would appreciate hearing from you.

1996 Musky Hunter's Almanac

- **Edward Walden's 1940 — 61 pounds 9 ounces**

This fish was the second 60-pound musky ever caught in Canada and remains No. 3 on the Canadian list surpassed only by Ken O'Brien's 65-pound fish caught in 1988 and Gary Ishii's 62-pound fish caught in 1981. The editors would like to know if this fish remains in existence. If you can help us please drop us a line at the addresses listed at the bottom of this feature.

- **Harold Ferguson's 1954 — 52 pounds**

This little known musky hangs in O'Brien's Bar and Restaurant, 226 Webb Street, in Clayton, New York (Thousand Islands). It was caught by the late Harold Ferguson in October and is reported to be 60 inches in length.

- **William Fulton's 1917 — 57 pounds 10 ounces**

This French River fish may be the one of the oldest musky mounts in existence. It is presently the property of the Royal Ontario Museum in Toronto, Canada and periodically goes on public display.

- **Lewis Walker Jr's. 1924 Pennsylvania State Record — 54 pounds 3 ounces**

Captured from Pennsylvania's Conneaut Lake in 1924, last reports have this fish on display at the Pennsylvania State Fish Hatchery in Linesville.

- **Gary Ishii's 1988 — 62 pounds**

Gary's 62-pound Moon River monster is mounted and hangs in the home of his brother-in-law, Gary Finkler, who was his guide for his catch.

Where Are They Now!

• **Joe Lykin's 1972 Ohio State Record — 55 pounds 2 ounces**
This fish is on display at the marina at Piedmont Lake.

• **Art Barefoot's 1989 — 59 pounds 11 ounces**
This beauty is now on display at Art's Bear's Den Lodge on Hartley Bay of the French River near Alban, Ontario.

• **Eugene Borucki's 1984 — 56 pounds 11 ounces**
This dandy from Lower Manitou Lake in Northwestern Ontario is mounted and has, in past years been displayed at the Chicagoland Sports Show. We believe it is now at Gene's home or office where he can catch it over and over again.

• **Steve Alber's 1985 — 55 pounds 0 ounces**
Eagle Lake in northwestern Ontario surrendered this behemoth. It too has been on display at the Chicago Show in past years but has been retired, we believe, to Steve's residence.

• **Angler Unknown 1982 — 60 inches**
This fish was found dead in September of 1982 along the shores of Lac Vieux Desert on the Wisconsin/Michigan border. It is on display at Ron Lax Taxidermy, 5455 Hwy. 45, Conover, Wisconsin.

If you have done some "sleuthing" of your own and would like to share your findings with Almanac *readers we would like to hear from you. We would also like to know if there are other fish that you would like us to find. Super Sleuth Larry may be contacted at P.O. Box 306, Knoxville, Illinois, 61448. Bill Hamblin may be reached at Sleuthing Headquarters, 718 Dunbar Road, Kitchener, Ontario, N2M 2X6.*

1996 Musky Hunter's Almanac

Humor
And
Poetry

POEMS

A Fisherman to His Son

My son, when you have older grown
I'll take you to a lake I've known
At midnight, noontime, dusk and dawn
I want to show you where I've gone

To find my freedom — want to be
In the boat with you and have you see
And learn from me, O! son of mine,
How to swing a fishing line.

For I've been young — too well I know
The rocky road your feet must go.
But I know too, a path that clings
To a wooded hill where the peewee sings —

Where dogwood grows and oak and pine.
And all I ask, O! son of mine,
Is to row the boat for you some day
Along that shore where the willows sway —

To be with you when first you feel
A leaping bass unwind your reel.
My son will sleep as I have slept
Beneath the Heaven's reach star swept.

I want the dawn's first gleaming dim
To waken something deep in him.
I want my boy to learn to take
His troubles to that shining lake,

And lose them there. And so I wish
O! son of mine, that you may fish.
For my boy's sake I ask it, God,
Teach him to love a casting rod.

— *Anonymous*

Pull The Rascal In

"Enjoy thy stream, O harmless fish;
And when the angler, for his dish
Through gluttony's vile sin,
Attempts, the wretch, to pull thee out
God give thee strength, O gentle Musky,
To pull the Rascal in!"

— *Peter Pindar*

1996 Musky Hunter's Almanac

Crazy Musky Fisherman

He left at daybreak. Said, "I'll be home at six."
Got home at nine, wife was having a fit.
He came home empty handed, didn't even have a strike,
Said, "I'm fishing again tomorrow, I'm sure they will bite."
He ate a warmed up dinner, and then went straight to bed.
There will be no love tonight, he's asleep like he was dead.
He hasn't seen his children, it's been several days.
Must catch a musky, late, that's why he stays.
He must score tomorrow, or the grouch may want to bite us.
Really, he is not well, he's diseased with Muskyitus.

— *The late Homer LeBlanc*

Fisherman's Wind

Wind in the East, fish bite least.
Wind in the West, fish bite best.
When the wind is in the North
The prudent angler goes not forth.
When the wind is in the South
It blows the hook in the fish's mouth.

— *A pattern conscious angler*

Murphy's Law
of Random Perversity

As it applies to musky hunters in their noble quest

1.) Left to themselves — all things go from bad to worse.
Translation — The longer a musky you want to keep is "in the swim," the better its chances of escape are! Don't however, rush it too much!

2.) Anything that can go wrong — will go wrong.
Translation — If a musky hits your figure-8 at the side of the boat your reel will backlash if you have engaged the free spool or break if your drag is too tight.

3.) If there is a possibility of several things going wrong — the one that will go wrong is the one that will do the most damage.
Translation — If you ever hook two muskies at once, the bigger of the two will usually get away.

4.) If you play with a thing long enough you will surely break it.
Translation — Play with your drag while fighting a fish and it will surely seize.

5.) If everything appears to be going well — you have obviously

1996 Musky Hunter's Almanac

overlooked something.
Translation — Just as you confidently slip the net over that 40-pound musky you have been fishing a lifetime for, you remember the hole you tore in the bottom of it carrying firewood to the cabin.

6.) Nature always sides with the hidden flaw.
Translation — Knots always hold on snags but give on fish.

7.) Mother Nature is a witch.
Translation — She always saves her absolutely worst weather for your fishing trip; or, you should have been here last week!

• • •

Quotable Notable — *"No other fresh water sport fish is quite like a musky; none other has the combined gifts of size, strength, wolfishness and dazzle. None is more difficult to find and capture on a hook — a major reason in itself why the fish is revered and obsessively pursued. A dedicated musky fisherman doesn't simply fish for muskies — he quests for them. What begins as a pleasant sport may culminate in a burning obsession."*

— *Tony Acerrano*

• • •

Quotable Notable — *What's the point in walking five miles to fish, when you can depend on being just as unsuccessful near home.*

— *Mark Twain*

This young lad is quite proud of his catch on a bamboo rod years ago.

1996 Musky Hunter's Almanac

Musky Clubs

Directory Of Musky Clubs

*I*n the 1980s interest in musky fishing expanded greatly as witnessed by the following list. How many of these still exist? How many new ones have formed?

We would like to hear from you. If you would like your organization to be listed in a directory in subsequent almanacs please mail the particulars of your club to Larry or Bill. Bill Hamblin, 718 Dunbar Road, Kitchener, Ontario, N2M 2X6; Larry Ramsell, P.O. Box 306, Knoxville, Illinois, 61448.

1. 12 Apostles Musky Club, Stevens Point, Wisconsin
2. Allegon County Big 4 Anglers, Allegon, Michigan
3. Bill's Musky Club, Wausau, Wisconsin
4. Blackhawk Muskie Club, Inc., Janesville, Wisconsin
5. Buckeye Muskie Hunters, New Carlisle, Ohio
6. Consolidated Muskie Club, Wisconsin Rapids, Wisconsin
7. Dave's Muskie Club, Kaukauna, Wisconsin
8. Dunbar Muskie Club, Friendly, West Virginia
9. Elk River Muskie Club, Elkview, West Virginia
10. Husky Musky Club of West Virginia, Parkersburg, West Virginia
11. Indiana Muskies, Dyer, Indiana
12. Iowa Great Lakes Muskie Club, Royal, Iowa
13. Kentucky Silver Muskie Club, Lebanon, Kentucky

14. Michigan-Ontario Muskie Club, Madison Heights, Michigan
15. Midwest Musky Club, Chicago, Illinois
16. Muskellunge Club of Wisconsin, Milwaukee, Wisconsin
17. Muskies Canada Inc., multiple chapters
18. Muskies Today Limited, Wisconsin Rapids, Wisconsin
19. Muskies Unlimited, Oconto Falls, Wisconsin
20. Muskies, Inc., multiple chapters
21. Ohio Huskie Muskie Club, Columbus, Ohio
22. Packerland Muskies Club, Green Bay, Wisconsin
23. Pennsylvania Muskie Society, Yardly, Pennsylvania
24. Project Illini, Palos Heights, Illinois
25. Southern West Virginia Muskie Club, Pocatalico, West Virginia
26. West Virginia Husky Muskie Club, Mt. Clare, West Virginia
27. Winnebagoland Musky Club, Markesan, Wisconsin
28. Wisconsin Muskies Limited, Delafield, Wisconsin

• • •

Quotable Notable — "Have you ever noticed how other anglers always get their big muskies because of dumb luck while us musky chasers must always resort to our expertise."

— Anonymous

• • •

Quotable Notable — "The day you become selfish in your fishing is the day you stop your fishing growth"

— Buck Perry

MUSKIES CANADA

TORONTO • KITCHENER-WATERLOO • HAMILTON
TWEED • OTTAWA-VALLEY • MONTREAL

With an increasing number of mobile musky anglers knowing how to fish the best spots on the best waters, the future outlook for muskellunge will be dependent in large part on the philosophy and ethics of the angling community across North America. Ontario and parts of Quebec sustain some fine musky fishing opportunities. However these are not without threats. Many quality musky waters in northwestern Ontario are subject to high levels of tourist angling pressure, while waters in southern portion of the province lie within close proximity of large Canadian population centers and are impacted accordingly.

Today's status quo sees all waters facing fishing pressure for trophy size musky and in some cases these waters also face encroaching development with its odious byproducts (at least from an angler's point of view) of habitat destruction and water pollution. At the same time natural resource agencies in Ontario have terminated the stocking of muskellunge. The province of Quebec still maintains a limited stocking program on selected waters.

The goal is to manage wild muskellunge populations by natural reproduction and trophy management on certain waters accomplished by regulatory changes and angler cooperation instead of intensive stocking.

In 1978, a group of Canadian musky enthusiasts formed a club called Muskies Canada. Its version incorporated the philosophy of live release as the way to prevent the indiscriminate killing of legal size musky. The goal was to protect the watery habitat and the musky stocks within. Spreading the word was indeed hard work and over the years has involved many dedicated musky anglers.

Muskies Canada is a non-profit sport fishing club dedicated to promote better musky fishing in Canada. It invites membership from the general public. Club operations are overseen by a National Executive Committee which is responsible for the administration of general club affairs and programs. The broader organization is divided up into six chapters: Toronto, Kitchener-Waterloo, Ottawa-Valley, Hamilton, Tweed and Montreal. These range across a geographical area bounded by western Quebec and southern Ontario and focus on their respective areas of interest.

Club members enjoy the company of others with the same addiction for the muskellunge. Monthly meetings, chapter trips, Muskies Canada banquets, and sanctioned live release outings furnish a platform for exploration and knowledge as well as allowing for friendship and good old fashioned fun. A 20-page club newsletter — *The Release Journal* — provides members with an effective medium

1996 Musky Hunter's Almanac

of communication and discussion throughout the year.

At the national level, Muskies Canada operates a public release program aimed at the general fishing population, both resident and non resident alike. Special Release posters are placed at participating lodges, marinas, and tackle shops. Any angler releasing a legal musky is eligible to receive a Release patch after completing and submitting the prescribed information.

Chapters carry out a wide variety of projects, many in conjunction with the natural resource agencies of Ontario and Quebec. In the recent past most work has involved identifying spawning habitat, either through visual search in the spring or through the use of radio telemetry. Many members complete year to year angling logs related to musky fishing activity on various waters. This data is utilized by resource agencies to compute catch per unit effort for muskellunge in addition to other useful information. Some chapters have moved to introduce launch ramp signs asking the angling community to support catch and release, and other basic information. On some waters chapter members have undertaken specialized tagging projects to update musky data in their region.

The educational effort continues over the cold winter months with Muskies Canada booths at various sport and outdoors shows across the great white north spreading the gospel of catch and release.

More so, the club is about musky fishing, which is different things to different people. Some people like it to be competitive, others the fellowship and camaraderie with like-minded folks, some the new angles and personal challenge, others find pure relaxation and for many its environmental contact. It could be some combination of all these reasons, it does not matter, we should all consider getting involved. Muskies Canada wishes one and all a most suc-

Muskies Canada, Inc.

cessful angling season. Please remember one thing — as musky anglers it is up to us to ensure the future of our sport.

Membership information can be obtained by writing to Muskies Canada, Incorporated, P.O. Box 814, Station C, Kitchener, Ontario, N2G 4C5.

• • •

Quotable Notable — *"Fishing is a discipline in the equality of men, for all men are equal before fish.*

— H. Hoover

"Yep ... it's a 30." A scene from long ago — note the "high-powered" motor on the back of the boat.

MUSKIES, INC.

An introduction to the world's largest musky organization

*I*t began as a dream of founder Gil Hamm in 1966 and on February 15, 1967, a handful of men signed their names to the articles of incorporation. The membership has grown from 14 to several thousand concerned fishermen and women. The organization has chapters throughout the entire natural range of the musky, from North Dakota to New York and outside the range in Colorado. Gil Hamm's dream has come true. Prior to his death in 1984, Gil received national recognition for his efforts and dedication, having been enshrined in the National Fresh Water Fishing Hall of Fame at Hayward, Wisconsin in 1981. But more important to Gil is the fact that he started an organization that puts its ideas to work!

Purposes of Muskies, Inc.
• To promote a high quality muskellunge sport fishery;
• To support selected conservation practices based on scientific merit and carried out by authorized federal and state agencies;
• To promote muskellunge research;
• To establish hatcheries and rearing ponds and introduce the species into suitable water;
• To support the abatement of water pollution;
• To maintain records of habits, growth and range of species;
• To disseminate muskellunge information;
• To promote good fellowship and sportsmanship among men, women and children.

Promote Quality Muskellunge Fishing

Muskies, Inc. is dedicated to the goal of promoting, not only the actual sport of musky fishing, but the quality as well. Although catching a musky is a thrill for most fishermen, Muskies, Inc. encourages the release of unharmed muskies in order to assure continuation of the species for future generations of fishermen.

Members of Muskies, Inc. often share their techniques, types of successful bait and tackle at monthly meetings and on musky fishing outings. Muskies, Inc. members also teach methods of releasing a captured fish in order that it may grow even larger and fight another day.

By increasing the knowledge of the muskellunge in whatever way Muskies, Inc. can, the goal to have a future of excellent musky fishing can be reached.

Muskies, Inc., Hatchery and Rearing Ponds

For the purpose of propagating the muskellunge, Muskies, Inc.

owned and operated a hatchery at Battle Lake, MN, for 11 years. That facility produced 36,000 eight- to 12-inch muskies that were stocked in suitable waters approved by the departments of natural resources. Musky rearing ponds are being developed by several chapters of Muskies, Inc. in close cooperation with each DNR. Musky fry are obtained from each DNR in June and are provided with all the forage they can eat, for about 80 days. During this time, they grow from a size of two inches to 8 to 12 inches. They are then harvested and stocked in suitable musky lakes. At this size, they have an excellent chance for survival. Muskies, Inc. members maintain these ponds and provide the forage, which is substantial. It takes approximately 2,500 pounds of forage to feed 3,500 musky fingerlings for 80 days. Other chapters purchase muskies from private hatcheries for stocking. Many new musky lakes have been created by these endeavors.

A committee assists the chapters in obtaining and operating rearing facilities. The committee also keeps records of all operational and research undertakings, recommends improvements, keeps members informed and openly communicates and cooperates with state and federal agencies.

Musky Research

Muskies, Inc. is actively pursuing a number of research projects. A research committee is continually collecting and analyzing data as it applies to muskellunge propagation and management. The following projects are examples of committee activities:

• Musky Tagging Programs — In cooperation with many state DNRs, muskies have been tagged. By tabulating information on where the tagged fish have been sighted or recaptured, a better knowledge of the survival rate, growth and movement of these fish is determined.

Muskies, Inc.

- Stomach and Scale Analysis — These samples, taken from fish in a variety of lakes, are analyzed to determine growth and diet information.
- Potential Winter Rescue Rearing Ponds — For these experimental projects, musky fry are stocked into "freeze out" ponds or ponds with low predator populations. In the fall or early winter the muskies, 12 to 14 inches in length, are seined or rescued from the ponds before the water is depleted of oxygen, thus providing a low cost method of raising muskies when a surplus of fry is available.
- Telemetry Study — Muskies, Inc. has supported radio telemetry studies conducted in northern Wisconsin, Minnesota and Ontario lakes. Knowledge of habits, movement and behavior of the muskies greatly increased from the information supplied by this research.
- Muskies, Inc. chapters have made significant financial contributions to a joint study being made by the DNRs of Wisconsin and Minnesota to determine the genetic differences between the Shoepac and Mississippi strains of the muskellunge. This study is expected to result in more efficient stocking and may answer the question of why some lakes are populated with stunted muskies.

An advisory board, established to assist the research committee in its work with the muskellunge, included such individuals as: Dr. E. J. Crossman, curator, Ichthyology and Herpetology Department, Royal Ontario Museum, Toronto, Canada; Dr. Charles N. Huver, Ph.D., curator of fishes, Bell Museum of Natural History, University of Minnesota, also assistant professor of ecology and behavioral biology, University of Minnesota; Mr. L. M. Christensen, chief, Fishery Research Section, Wisconsin Department of Natural Resources and Mr. C. Burrows, chief of fisheries, Division of Fish and Wildlife, Minnesota Department of Natural Resources.

1996 Musky Hunter's Almanac

Muskies, Inc. Release Program

Muskies, Inc. keeps records of all fish kept and released by its members. In recent years, members of Muskies, Inc. have caught thousands of legal sized muskies but less than 10% of these fish have been kept. There is a keen feeling of sportsmanship when releasing a captured fish. The released musky will also live to reproduce, grow and fight another day. Muskies, Inc.'s tagging programs have proven, that if properly handled, released muskies do survive. For each musky caught and released, a certificate and a release patch are awarded to the member.

Muskies, Inc.'s release program is a second stocking effort. This program probably does more to perpetuate this great sport than any other single program. It has been applauded by the Wisconsin DNR and by many professional guides. Many muskies over 50 inches in size have been released by members of Muskies Inc. This is sportsmanship at its best!

Musky Tournaments

Throughout the fishing season, Muskies, Inc. chapters hold musky fishing tournaments, open to all fishermen. These tournaments are release-oriented and the proceeds from them are used for the propagation of more muskies. These tournaments draw much attention from local and national sports media. But the most prestigious tournament of all is Muskies, Inc.'s annual "Chapter Challenge" tournament in which chapters compete for a coveted traveling trophy.

Muskies, Inc. Board Meetings and Annual Awards Banquet

Twice a year, Muskies, Inc.'s International Board of Directors meets to discuss the business of Muskies Inc. This is a democratic

Muskies, Inc.

organization, each chapter having equal representation on this board. At the spring meeting each year, the results of Muskies, Inc.'s Members Only Fishing Contest are announced and recognition is given to the winners. The combination of good fellowship, an excellent dinner, special guests and dignitaries and entertainment make this annual event something to remember.

Muskies, Inc. Public Education

Several times throughout the year Muskies, Inc. chapters participate in sports shows, clinics and seminars. Muskies, Inc.'s show booths are staffed by volunteer members who explain what Muskies, Inc. is all about and answer questions posed by visitors.

A speaker committee also puts on programs for civic organizations and sportsmen's clubs. Muskies, Inc.'s release programs, musky stocking programs, tackle and fishing techniques are often topics of popular discussion.

"Musky Fever" is the term often used to describe the sport of musky fishing, and without a doubt Muskies, Inc. members truly enjoy this activity. However, Muskies, Inc. also realizes a responsibility to promote and protect this valuable fishery, a responsibility which has been met and accepted with pride.

For more information, write Muskies, Inc.'s International Office at: Muskies, Inc., International Office, 2301 7th Street North, Fargo, ND, 58102.

Next year's Almanac will feature other North American musky clubs. Using this format, clubs are encouraged to submit information to the Editors.

1996 Musky Hunter's Almanac

Stories And Articles

1895

THE TECHNIQUE OF FISHING

Reprinted from the book,
The Picturesque St. Lawrence River

*I*n Governor Alvord's most interesting and instructive articles upon the Great River, he has much to say about the "men he has met," and he speaks of all of them more as beloved comrades than as mere acquaintances or as the passing visitors of an hour; but he does not say much about the technique, the appliances, the methods of fishing. Ourself an amateur, we have not failed to seek information upon the points indicated; and, like all amateurs, we try to believe that there is some "royal road to learning," by pursuing which we may exceptionally "get there" without the labor and inconveniences of learning by experience. From the great Izaak Walton himself down to our own day, and taking our distinguished Governor Alvord as one of the brightest teachers of modern times in all arts piscatorial, the methods, the little incidentals by which the agile water denizens are lured into the voracious frying pan, have been much disputed — this grand "faculty" of becoming an expert fisherman being as elusive, various, and sometimes as intricate as wooing one of the fair sex, whose moods are often as contradictory as are those of the most artful muscalonge or bass, and yet when captured, are almost "too sweet for anything." From the crookedest tree limb, with a piece of twine at its end, to the jointed and polished rod, with linen line and silver reel, the margin is wide and expensive. The poorest and the best of these appliances have each won great renown, but generally in the hands of those who know how to use them, the fish being largely democratic and as willing to take a wriggling worm from a pin-hook as from one of Skinner's best treble-arranged, feather-decorated devices. As in all good things, in fishing there are many methods; but in all fishing, good bait is an indispensable adjunct. With it you feel as a soldier feels with a good gun in his hand; it is his guaranty of probable success.

The improvements in fishing tackle have been immense during the past forty years. In 1849, the writer saw the elder Walton, long since dead, at work upon spoons that could not now be given away — yet of those rude attempts he could dispose readily of as many as he could put together. Chapman, at Theresa and Rochester, has made many beautiful and successful fishing appliances. But the most successful man in the business for the past ten years has been Mr. G. M. Skinner, of Clayton, whose goods are now known all over the United States and Canada. He began to study the art piscatorial upon the Great River itself, having been long a resident of Gananoque, Ontario, in his early youth. He finally located at Clayton, a place possessing some advantages not apparent to the superficial observer, among them being a prominent angling resort and the principal gateway for tourists coming to the river over the only avenue on the American side, viz.: the N.Y.C. System, comprising the R., W. & O., and U. & B.R.R.R. It is the distributing point for those desiring to reach, by water, the numerous islands and parks in its immediate vicinity, and, also, the fashionable resort, twelve miles down the river, of Alexandria Bay.

1996 Musky Hunter's Almanac

In this romantic and favored vicinity he served his apprenticeship in fishing and experimenting with all sorts, sizes and shapes of artificial baits obtainable. He was not content but strove to construct a spoon for his own use, which should have decided advantages over any used. As a result of such effort, two corrugated or fluted spoons were made; one being given to a fishing companion, the other he retained for his own use. In numerous practical trials, these two spoons gave satisfactory evidence of having uncommon merit, notably in the capture, by his wife and self, of a muscalonge, measuring four feet eleven inches in length and weighing forty pounds.

Mr. Skinner himself says: "I have been frequently asked, what I considered a spoon to represent, as revolving while fishing, and why are fish attracted by them to such an extent that they will seize them, even when unprovided with any other attraction save the glint of the cold metal. In reply, I offer those of an inquisitive turn my humble opinion that the motion or action of a revolving lure, unquestionably simulates or means, life — prey, to fish, and as a natural sequence, life means food — sustenance."

Mr. Skinner also relates the following: "A party from Clayton went to Hay Bay, Bay of Quinte, to fish for muscalonge. The water in Hay Bay is not very deep where the fish are caught and the weeds come very near the surface. To prevent the trolling-spoon fouling, a gang of naked hooks is attached to the line some distance ahead of the spoon, which breaks off or pulls up the weeds and allows the spoon to go free. Messrs. D. Pratt and Edwin Seymour, of Syracuse, were fishing in one boat. Mr. Seymour, in letting out line, felt a tug when the line was out but a few yards. Turning he saw the water break where the naked hook was and commenced to haul in, finding he had caught a muscalonge upon the naked or weed-guard hook.

1895: The Technique Of Fishing

"One of the party trolling with two hand lines caught a large pike under somewhat unusual circumstances. The voracious fish had captured one troll and made a race for and secured the other, having both of them securely hooded in his mouth when hauled in.

"A most unusual occurrence I would like to place on record. In August, 1883, Miss Annie Lee, at that time eleven years of age, while trolling near Clayton for bass, with a No. 3 gold fluted spoon, which size is fitted with a No. 2 hook, struck and successfully brought to boat a muscalonge weighing thirty-six pounds, measuring four feet six inches in length. In the effort to secure this large fish the guide's gaff was broken, showing the enormous strength of the fish, yet it was finally secured, brought in and exhibited with those slight hooks still fast in its capacious mouth — an evidence not only of good tackle, but of skillful handling."

Annie Lee with her August 1883, 36-pound beauty. Note the rod and reel.

Are The "Big" Muskies All Gone?

By Larry Ramsell

Oftentimes you hear conversation questioning if there are any big muskies left. That kind of talk is not new, as witnessed from the following quotes from *Forest & Stream* in 1901.

From May 4, 1901 ... "The muskallunge is the largest of our American game fishes ... The muskallunge ordinarily taken by anglers runs in weight from 5 to 50 pounds. It is said that specimens have been taken weighing 75 and 80 pounds, these giants having been captured in the St. Lawrence River in the earlier days. Weights of 50 to 55 pounds were not unusual in the early days of the muskallunge waters of Wisconsin and Minnesota. By this I would not seek too much to excite your imagination, for to-day, if you go muskallunge fishing, the probabilities are that you will rarely get a fish weighing over 20 pounds!! It is likely that in the much fished waters of the muskallunge country the weights of the fishes do not run so great as they did ten or twenty years ago. Some think that this is because the fish is becoming extinct, and no doubt its numbers are being cut down very much. Yet the fish commissioners of certain States who have set their nets in waters supposed to be nearly fished out, have in some instances taken giant muscallunge of 40 and 50 pounds weight, where it was supposed no such fish had lived for many years."

From July 6, 1901 ... "Fishing, as one would naturally suspect, is not comparable to what it was a few years ago; but ..."

Sound familiar? Yes, big muskies still exist! To borrow a phrase from John Dettloff ... "These *are* the 'good old days'!"

A day's catch from turn of the century St. Lawrence River near Clayton, New York.

Strange But True

COAST GUARD HELPS LAND A MUSKY

Reprinted from a Detroit newspaper via the late, famous Lake St. Clair guide, Homer LeBlanc

"A Detroit fisherman caught a 38-pound musky three times — once with a hook and twice with his hands. During the tense struggle, the big fish plopped the angler and a friend into Lake St. Clair and kept them water-bound for an hour until they were rescued by the Coast Guard. Victors of the battle were Arthur Smith and William Campbell.

Smith hooked a 53-inch musky while he and Campbell fished off Peche Island from a rowboat and outboard motor. Smith played with the fighter for 45 minutes before he gaffed it. A fin hit Smith as he pulled the fish into the boat. Struggling to regain his balance and hold the musky, Smith overturned the craft. Smith, Campbell and the fish went into the lake. Smith spotted the tired musky swimming at the surface. He grabbed the fish but it slipped through his arms and disappeared. Back to the boat went Smith. Then the musky bobbed up again 30 feet away. Smith swam over and caught it again for the third time. He held on to it. Campbell meanwhile, was clinging to the overturned boat. He helped Smith tie the musky fast. So fisherman and fish waited. A woman on shore saw them and notified the Coast Guard. The very tired anglers and the well-caught musky were brought to land."

And again the Coast Guard comes to the rescue

Reprinted from a photo caption in Ontario Out Of Doors

After helping with a tow, unidentified Coast Guardsman poses with musky caught by Bob Hyde of Michigan, while trolling a Pikie Minnow behind his disabled craft while under tow on Lake St. Clair. The towing Coast Guard craft even slowed down on request during the tow to give Hyde a chance to land the musky, reported to weigh 25 pounds.

• • •

Quotable Notable — *"'Taint people's ignorance that does the harm; tis their knowin' so much that ain't so."*
— *Artemus Ward (1834-67)*

DIFFICULTIES OF THE OLD DAYS

By Larry Ramsell

What musky hunters often fail to realize is how "easy" they have it today when it comes to equipment and travel to get to the highly productive areas of today and yesterday. A musky hunter of today can leave Chicago, Illinois, and arrive at the world famous Chippewa Flowage in a matter of hours (about six at "normal" speed). As recently as 60 to 80 years ago this was a two- or three-day ordeal. An overnight or all day train ride and then a two-day horse and buggy ride to get to the lake. Further back in history it was even more difficult to travel to musky water not to mention finding accommodations once they arrived. As I researched writings from the 1880s, '90s and early 1900s I found several good references to the above. Following I will quote from a few.

From *Forest And Stream*, July 3, 1890, comes the following: "The guides of the party were Bert Louk and young Blodgett, both of Three Lakes Station, Wisconsin. It is proper to say in advance that a trip to the mascallonge country, if it is to be pleasant or successful, necessitates the country is big and difficult, and a tenderfoot alone in it would be an object of pity, always supposing he wants to leave the railway and get out to where he can reasonably expect good fishing ... A boat and a few provisions were unloaded from the wagon as it passed on its way to town ... The mosquitoes fairly swarmed. Unprotected, the sportsmen in that country would have no sport. But we were not seriously put out by these pests. We used good head nets and long gloves, and applied liberally a compound of pennyroyal and vaseline. A little smudge kettle, set in the main room of the house, did much to thin the fiends out and on turning in for the night we availed ourselves one of Charlie Gammon's Camp inventions ... this was simply a wide sheet, made by sewing together strips of mosquito bar. We spread it over the whole bed, and the high head board kept it off our faces. In camp, Charlie rigged up a frame, about 2 1/2 feet high which extended entirely over the sleeping room of the tent. Over this he threw his mosquito sheet ... We rowed (no motors then) around Lake Julia ... two or three miles in length."

Continued in the July 10, 1890 issue ... "Bert and Blodgett also intend cutting a trail from Seven Mile over to Butternut this fall ... new Mascallonge ground ... for those who want to go into this region and have success, that the way to do is to pull out from the beaten track and 'stand' with men like the above mentioned, who will get to good waters where the tenderfeet are afraid to go ..."

Continued again July 17, 1890 ... "Mac and I walked half a mile through the woods ... Bert took the boat around, an hour's journey, full of mosquitoes and crooked water ... We saw the team (horses) arrive that was to take us over to town ... We now bade farewell ... and indulged in the luxury of a wagon ride over to town ... not luxurious by reason of its comfort"... "our fish had been buried in a mossy swamp with a chunk of ice over them ..."

In the February 25 and March 3, 1892 issues we find more ... "the trains brought me to Manitowish ... the dam at Rest Lake was my objective ... at about 1 o'clock I got my outfit into an old leaky boat, with a muscular guide at the oars, for a fourteen mile pull up

1996 Musky Hunter's Almanac

to the dam ... Henry tied up the boat and got out to catch some frogs for bait ... when evening came ... (we) were less than half way to the dam. But we reached a place where an Irishman ... had homesteaded at ... and was building himself the best house I saw in that country ... We reached the dam about 5 o'clock in the afternoon ... At the dam is a logging camp. In summer it is completely deserted. But Capt. Henry ... had turned this camp into a sort of a summer hotel ... With Jim Lawson for a guide I went to Papoose, some ten or twelve miles away ... to reach it there is a three-mile carry."

A musky angler from days past. Note the "steel," one-handed casting rod and old round-bottom wood boat. Good, old-fashioned elbow grease was the means of propulsion.

Difficulties Of The Old Days

Things changed rapidly in the northwoods as witnessed in the July 6, 1901 issue ... "The shores of the larger lakes are nearly all dotted with summer resorts, where comfortable lodging and good wholesome food may be secured ... Fifteen years ago it was considered a hazardous undertaking to travel from one lake to another ... Nowadays most of that wilderness has disappeared and well beaten trails lead from one lake to another ..."

So you see, modern day musky hunters, you have it easy compared to 100 or more years ago. Enjoy it; protect it; release it!

• • •

Did You Know — That BIG Muskies can be caught in non-traditional waters. For example, Wisconsin's last two 50-pounders came from "non-traditional" waters; Bob LaMay caught a 50-pounder from High Falls Flowage which is considered a Class "B" water by Wisconsin DNR. Robert Grutt's 50-pound 4-ounce came from a lake not even classified as a musky water. It had been stocked only twice! — LR

• • •

Quotable Notable — "There is no other fish like a musky. It is diabolical in its cunning, maniacal in its rage, unpredictable in its habits. It is the most awesome of all freshwater fish, a creature that captures the imagination, fires the spirit, and — alas — break the hearts of fishermen by the thousands, by the hundreds of thousands every year."
— William O. Johnson

Did You Ever Dream?

By Larry Ramsell

*I*n a popular outdoor magazine, a compilation by one of its writers stated that a female musky can produce 22,000 to 180,000 eggs. While this may be the range for the smaller species of musky, the maskinonge (lake strain), the larger of the two species, the muskellunge (riverine strain), contain far more. This was known as far back as 1897 (May 29 issue of *Forest and Stream*) when a 36-pound female yielded 265,000 eggs and not all of them were taken. I suspect the balance were not yet ripe, as Dr. Bernard Lebeau discerned that muskies spawn twice. In the most recent large specimen of the larger musky species, Ken O'Brien's 1988, 65-pounder, Dr. Lebeau found over 850,00 eggs.

Facing page — Ken O'Brien with his Canadian Record. No doubt this amount of eggs contributed greatly to her 30 1/2-inch girth. Photo by Dave Sault

Strange But True

FISH KNOCKS OUT WOMAN

Philadelphia — August 5, 1987

A 19-year-old Bucks county woman remains in critical condition at Lower Bucks Hospital after being knocked out by a 20-pound musky that jumped over her fishing boat in the Delaware River yesterday, a hospital spokeswoman said.

Leigh Malloy, 19, of Andalusia, was in a bass boat traveling about 40 mph when the fish jumped "three or four feet out of the water and nailed her in the head," said Chief Mike Plebani of the Bucks County Rescue Squad.

"It was the weirdest I've ever heard of," Plebani said.

Malloy was unconscious when her male companion brought her into the Neshaminy State Park marina at 5:30 p.m. Thursday.

She was admitted to the hospital for head trauma and was in the intensive care unit, said Charlotte Rebuck, a hospital spokeswoman.

Strange But True

LIGHTNING STRIKES TWICE IN THE SAME PLACE!

By Bill Hamblin

I remember the day well. I was fishing Muskies Canada's season opening derby on Pigeon Lake. Pigeon is one of the popular Kawartha Lakes in south central Ontario, known for its fine population of muskies. My Dad was along and we were both looking forward to the weekend's fishing. If we boated a musky, well that would be just fine; just being on the water was enjoyment enough.

Pigeon Lake is a long, narrow lake, very shallow and weedy at one end and deep with better rock structure at the other end. I opted for the deeper end, hoping to tie into one of the larger muskies Pigeon was known to give up from time to time. As the morning sun warmed the 16-foot cedar strip we'd rented for the weekend, I settled into a comfortable troll in 25 feet of water running down the side of appropriately-named Big Island. Its the only island of any significant size on the lake. I was rigged with a black and yellow jailbird Believer with about three ounces of lead for added depth. I can't remember what Dad was using, but as this day would develop it wouldn't seem to matter. Fate seemed to be on my side.

Sometime around mid morning I was jolted by a hefty strike. I

1996 Musky Hunter's Almanac

knew we were into a good fish because she stayed down and wanted to do battle deep. Just as I was prematurely accepting the plaque and congratulations that are presented to the angler with the derby's largest fish, my line went slack. As quickly as it started it was over. To make matters worse, as I slowly wound in my line it was apparent I had not only lost the fish but it had absconded with my bait. The snap had opened. The fish had beaten me fair and square.

By prior agreement I had arranged to meet a friend for shore lunch. Mark Sauder and I have shared many a fish, in many a boat, on many a lake in our pursuit of North America's musky. It only seemed appropriate that we should meet over lunch to compare notes on the morning's events. Dad and I arrived first at the preset location and got out to stretch our legs. A short time later Mark and his partner for the day pulled in. Eager to tell my tale I headed down to his boat to muster whatever sympathy I could.

Barely had I a word out when Mark announced "You'll never guess what I found around the other side of Big Island."

Knowing full well this is where I lost the fish and the lure I took a stab at it. "Let me guess. A black and yellow jailbird Believer."

"How did you know?" he said in disbelief.

"Because I lost it on a good fish over there this morning." Reluctantly giving up his prize find, Mark returned the bait to my tackle box. This lure had to be destined for greatness.

No sooner had we hit the water after lunch and it was back on my line probing the same depths it had that morning. As I approached the area where I had already done battle and lost I couldn't help but think how I had been defying the odds all day. What were the chances that I would hook into a potentially derby winning fish with 45 other boats on the water competing for top honors. What were the odds of losing a lure to a fish only to have it throw

Lightning Strikes Twice In The Same Place

the lure to be found by another angler. The chances were roughly 1 in 90 that it would be found by my friend. Was it just coincidence that he found it so quickly and that we had arranged to meet for lunch or were the musky gods at work? We were about to find out.

By now you can probably imagine, in the words of a popular radio spot, "the rest of the story." Yes, I did hook another fish in the very same place. Yes, on the very same bait I'd lost that morning. Yes, at 47 inches it was large enough to win the derby. And yes, lightning does strike twice in the same place.

• • •

Hambug's Hint — If you are a novice with baitcasting equipment there is no better lure to use than a safety-pin style bucktail. Most beginners have difficulty getting the blade on an in-line spinner moving on impact with the water because there is a delay in engaging the reel. A safety-pin style spinner begins to work immediately on impact because it flutters on the drop. Start your kids out on them. They are also big fish catchers.

• • •

Quotable Notable — A true sportsman is one who can catch a large fish, release it, and never tell anybody.

— Charles Pickens

Strange But True

MUSKY JUMPS INTO THE BOAT

By Dean Bortz
Reprinted from the Lakeland Times — August 11, 1989

Watch out. Muskies are jumping into boats on Lakeland area lakes. Until recently, that old line passed out among fishermen was a figure of speech. But the Markham brothers can say that without spinning a fishing tale.

Adam Markham, 6, and his brother Neil, 7, were fishing with their father, Kent, of Kohler, when Adam "boated" his first musky, a 30-inch sub-legal musky that was returned to Lake Minocqua.

"He still can't say that he caught a musky, but he did bring one into the boat," said his father.

The two brothers were tossing crankbaits with their father and grandfather on Lake Minocqua last week. Adam had just made his third cast and was retrieving the green Cisco Kid when his father, who was standing next to Adam, looked behind the bait.

"I usually watch their baits because the boys often forget to watch for a follow. They also forget to do a figure-8 now and then," said Dad.

Kent saw a musky come up behind Adam's bait, but before he could tell the first-grader to do a figure-8, Adam lifted the bait out of the water.

The musky followed.

It jumped out of the water after the bait. It slammed into the steering console and fell, flopping, to the boat floor.

"I was standing right next to Adam and I just watched this musky jump into the boat. I couldn't believe it," said Kent.

Adam couldn't believe it.

Nor could Neil.

"I was so excited I think I stopped breathing," said Adam.

Neil said he nearly stepped on the fish.

"I turned around and saw the musky flopping on the floor. I almost stepped on it when I turned around to see what they were yelling about," he said.

Although the moment was unusual and exciting, both boys said they could give up some of their musky fishing and pursue panfish instead.

"When you're panfishing, you only have to wait a few seconds for a crappie," Adam said. "Musky fishing can get boring," said Neil.

Well sure, fishing probably does seem slow if the muskies aren't jumping into the boat.

• • •

Did You Know — The average number of boats stolen each month in the United States is one thousand! Ten percent or less are recovered. — LR

MUSKYOLOGY

This article, reprinted from the April, 1936, edition of Hunting and Fishing *magazine, goes a long way to explain how some of today's myths actually got started and perpetuated many years ago.*

The muskellunge, to many anglers, is still a fish of mystery and there are probably as many misconceptions abroad as to the habits of this sweetwater fish as there are about any other fish that swims. Hardly any angler that has not heard time and again that muskies "teethe" in midsummer and hardly an angler who has not aligned himself on one side or the other of the old argument as to whether or not the muskellunge, when teething or suffering from sore mouth, will strike at a lure.

Stove-pipe leagues all over the country will have nothing left to talk about when that one is settled!

The fact is that twice a year muskellunge make what to all appearances is an absolute fast. During these periods they apparently eat nothing at all. The first fast begins when the big fellows go on the spawning beds, usually about May, and when they are on the beds neither male nor female will strike at anything. As the season everywhere is closed at this time this fact is of secondary interest to the angler.

As soon as 'lunge finish spawning they go on the feed in a big way. Fasting and listening to love stories has left them looking as Mae West does not, and they will hit at anything. Suckers are the principal food of muskellunge when they can get them and these are always the best bait; but when they first start feeding they are not too fussy and anything that looks as though it might be good to eat is meat in the pan.

The habits of the fish when taking its food are of interest to all anglers who go after them with live bait. The musky always attacks its prey sideways and does not swallow what it has caught immediately unless it is a minnow or a lake chub. Most of the bigger fish, at least, and probably the smaller ones as well, have their own private dining rooms and when they catch a good mouthful they carry it back to this dining room before turning it and swallowing it head first. This business may take anywhere from five or ten minutes to a half hour or so and a good many musky strikes are missed by overanxious anglers who attempt to set the hook before the bait has been swallowed.

It is generally believed that muskellunge scale their prey before swallowing it. They often do so but may not do this always. In livebait fishing, line must be left absolutely slack from the moment the fish first strikes until the meal is finished. After taking the bait the 'lunge usually runs a short distance back to the "house," which may be and generally is a hole in some weed bed. Then there will be no movement to the line for some time. When the fish again begins to move it is time to set the hook.

In July and August the fish prefer to lie in or close to weedbeds, preferably the so-called "musky grass," and this is where to look for them. The baitcaster will be successful with bait-size spoons and plugs. Larger lures are better for trolling although I think it is a mistake to use those that are too large, especially in lake fishing.

Soon after the middle of July muskellunge begin to lose their teeth and begin their second fast of the year. But there is an important difference between this fast and the spawning fast. While they eat nothing they will hit at a plug viciously all through teething and when hooked will jump more and fight harder than at any other time of the year.

Two or three years ago a party of Harvard scientists made a study of the mouths of muskellunge at Little Vermilion Lake, far up in northern Ontario, to see if the "sore mouth" had any relation to similar human ills. They found that the teeth of the fish are attached only to the skin and that new teeth grow where the old ones break off. They also found, as many others who have done a lot of muskellunge fishing, that the stomachs of the fish are not only completely empty at this time but that the entrance is entirely closed and knotted.

It is no hearsay as to the fish striking during this period. During the past ten or twelve years I have caught, and released, a great many 'lunge. They will not strike so frequently as they will a little later on when they are feeding again, but it is possible to get some very good fishing all through August.

Towards the end of August feeding again begins and the first fish caught will be found to have a green, slimy substance in the stomach. This probably is something they find among the weeds or may be from the outer skin of the fish itself. It may be an old family remedy to take the place of sulphur and molasses.

Early in September the fish leave the weedbeds and begin to work out into open water. This is the time to fish for them over reefs and in shallow or deep bays. By the end of the month they are well on the move and may be found anywhere in the lake or river. Warm September afternoons often find muskies in the shallows where they roll and sun themselves. They are not feeding when doing this and it is useless to fish for those that are spotted on the surface, with rare

Muskyology

exceptions.

September and October are the best months for muskellunge fishing and it generally stays good until the season closes.

Larry's Note: I contend that muskies eat more and digest faster during the hot summer months when their metabolism is higher than they do in the fall! They are however, harder to find, but should be easier to catch if you find them.

• • •

Quotable Notable — Here's to fishing — a grand delusion enthusiastically promoted by glorious liars in old clothes."

— *Don Marquis*

This Wisconsin beauty was taken in the 1930s.

Old Musky Ads

Musky anglers have been trying to outwit the great fish for over 100 years. Here's a brief sampling of the advertising and products of yesteryear

Not exactly a sensitive musky stick! From Hunter Trapper Trader *magazine, September 1937.*

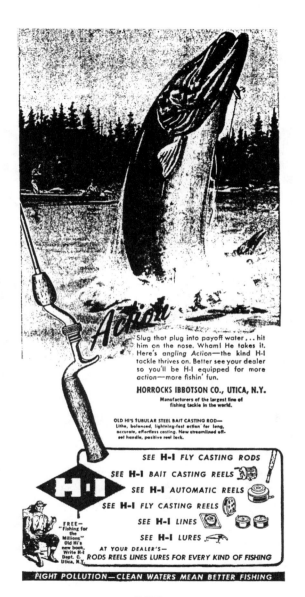

Old Musky Ads

SKINNER EXTRA LARGE MUSCALLONGE SPOONS
FINISHED IN CHROME, COPPER, BRASS, OR WHITE ENAMEL
— EXACT SIZES —

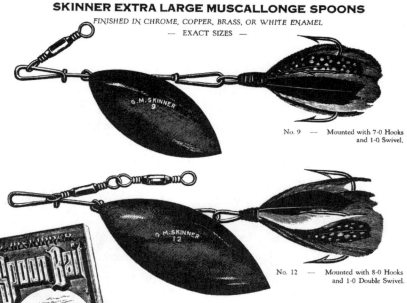

No. 9 — Mounted with 7-0 Hooks and 1-0 Swivel.

No. 12 — Mounted with 8-0 Hooks and 1-0 Double Swivel.

"My first effort showed me that I was on the right track. This was in the year 1874, and the first Bait made was about the size of my now No. 5. . . . The outcome of my making this Bait has resulted in the G. M. Skinner's Fluted Bait . . . a Bait of exceptional quality, finish and workmanship. "The idea of the Fluted Spoon [is] to increase the reflection, thereby multiplying the attractiveness as well as to strengthen the spoon without increasing the weight.

"On a bright sunny day, in clear or cedar waters, a copper spoon may be used to the best advantage; on a cloudy day of when the water is rough, a brass or chrome plate is better.

"For fishing in dark waters, the Enamel Spoon cannot be equalled by anything."

Superstition — It's Garbage

Don't let "Hambug's Curse" get you!

By Bill Hamblin

I've never really been a superstitious person. Friday the 13th comes and goes without a thought. Black cats are cute but a little boring. I jump on sidewalk cracks. Heck — occasionally I'll even go out of my way to walk under a ladder just to spite it. None of the conventional superstitions bother me.

Why then, you would wonder, am I superstitious about garbage — that's right — garbage!

Now this isn't your everyday garbage. I walk it down to the curb like most other husbands without any severe aftereffects. The garbage I am talking about is the floating kind. The stuff thrown into our lakes, rivers and streams by uncaring fishermen, irresponsible campers and thoughtless vacationers. You know it when you see it — floating pop and beer cans, sandwich bags, chocolate bar wrappers and the two biggies — empty bait containers and cigarette butts. Oh how I hate cigarette butts!

It's not the garbage itself that bothers me. It's the thought of where it is, why it's there, and what it might do to my fishing should I choose to ignore it and just let it float by.

In other words, show the same disdain for our environment as the person who first dumped it into the water.

I view the consequence of such an act in two ways. First, every piece of garbage I don't pluck from the water costs me a musky. That is, I will catch one less musky than I was otherwise destined to catch before I passed up the garbage. Secondly, and particularly if I am trolling, if I don't troll over and pick up the garbage I will pass up the opportunity to catch the musky that is undoubtedly suspended under it with an inquisitive eye.

More simply put, its the old adage, you "reap what you sow" or is it you "reap what you throw." You can't sustain the resource for generations to follow if you take from the environment without contributing back to it in equal or greater measure.

Like most superstitions it seems rather petty. There is no basis in fact or scientific evidence to substantiate it. It's just a gut feeling — or maybe more appropriately — a fear, for without human fears there would be no such thing as superstitions.

Are you superstitious?

Well we're going to find out because as of this moment you have been inflicted with the dreaded "Hambug's Curse." Feared by fishermen the world over its black magic is quite simple. Litter a lake and lose a musky. Troll by trash and lose a musky.

Cast a blind eye to floating refuse and lose a musky.

There is no escaping it!

Dare you take a chance?

I'll be watching!

The Musky Trip
Of A Lifetime

By Mark Sauder

"Mark is an avid musky angler of 18 years with a passion for sampling as many of Canada's and the United States' musky waters as possible. Following he chronicles, what to many, including myself, is the musky trip of a lifetime. Join Mark as he takes you back to the heart and soul of musky fishing, northern Wisconsin, and the personalities, waters and fish that kindle the passion for musky fishing in all of us."
— *Bill Hamblin*

Residing in southwestern Ontario, a short three hours from Georgian Bay, one would think that a "Musky Trip of a Lifetime" would include a stop at these world famous musky waters. To the contrary, waters with a history of big fish are not necessarily the first thing that comes to mind. Rather, I prefer waters with a big fish history. If you want to fully experience the sport one must travel back to its roots and traditions. And no area better embodies all that is musky fishing than northern Wisconsin and its legendary bodies of water, fish and fishermen. Let's not waste any time.

First stop should be the town of Eagle River. If at all possible try to schedule your trip for the third weekend of August and the

National Championship Musky Open. Covering five groups of lakes (Eagle River, Three Lakes, Big Lakes Family, Western Family, Sugar Camp Chain) there is plenty of water for the 800 musky anglers who enter this "release only" event each year. After the day's fishing there are evening seminars that offer a great opportunity to learn from the local pros and exchange ideas with other competitors.

Good accommodations can be had at either the Eagle River Inn or the American Budget Inn. A visit to George Langley's Eagle Sports Shop that first evening is a must so you can stock up your tackle box with all the latest baits that are hot on these waters. After enjoying dinner at Captain Nemo's and viewing the fish on display in the aquariums a good night's sleep is the order of the day.

Saturday morning you'll want to be up at 6 a.m. for an all you can eat smorgasbord breakfast at Betty's Eagle Cafe. After a good day on the water, dinner that evening is a short trip to St. Germain and Spang's Italian Restaurant.

Sunday, after an early morning stop at Ron Lax Taxidermy to view some of his beautiful musky mounts, we're off to fish Lac Vieux Desert where the world record hybrid of 51 pounds 3 ounces was caught by John Knobla in 1919. This fish can be seen locally at the Minnow Bucket baitshop. The Edgewater Beach Resort is a good place to launch at a nominal fee. This body of water sits on the Wisconsin/Michigan border and is famous for its hybrid muskies. Fishing can be tough due to the thick cabbage weed that covers most of this lake. Ask someone to point out the "Valley of the Giants" on your map.

It's now time to do some more driving across the state to Hayward. If you're traveling via Hwy 70 make sure you stop at Blink-Bonnie Restaurant between St. Germain and Woodruff for a steak dinner you won't forget. The jaunt from Eagle River to

1996 Musky Hunter's Almanac

Hayward is a little over 100 miles so you will probably arrive in the dark if you stop for dinner on the way. There are many fine accommodations in Hayward. My choice has been the Cedar Inn Motel for its hot whirlpool. A quick dip before bed is just what the doctor ordered for loosening up those muscles that have stiffened up from the last two days of continuous casting.

Monday dawns on a another new body of water, Lac Courte Oreilles. This lake is one of the few in northern Wisconsin that you can troll. It is also one of the clearest lakes that you will fish in this area. In 1949, Cal Johnson caught a world record, 67-pound 8-ounce musky on a weedbed called the Moccasin Bar in this lake. If you're nostalgic you may want to toss a few baits there. Lunch is at the Anglers Haven, just a short distance from the bar. It is visible from the water because of the large wood carving of a musky at its docks.

While visiting the town of Hayward there are numerous sites to see. The biggest and most visible is the 144-foot long musky that stands 4 1/2 stories high at the National Fresh Water Fishing Hall of Fame. Many famous fish and fishermen are documented at the hall. Stops at the Musky Museum and the Moccasin Bar are also a must to view many of the area's most noteworthy musky mounts. If you have the time you might also want to take in Hayward's world famous lumberjack show. This town caters to the musky fisherman.

Hopefully you will still have the strength for dinner and some evening entertainment. A short trip to the Dun Rovin Lodge on the Chippewa Flowage for dinner is recommended. Here you can view Robert Malo's unofficial 70-pound record musky in a truly unique display.

Well, it is now Tuesday and you're only halfway through your dream musky trip. Today we're fishing the Chippewa Flowage where

The Musky Trip Of A Lifetime

the current world record musky of 69 pounds 11 ounces was caught by Louis Spray in 1949. Breakfast is at Herman's Landing, the local watering hole of many of the flowage's fine guides. A registry of all local musky catches is posted here that's sure to whet your appetite for the day's fishing. After discussing the day's tactics with several other anglers you're off to the water. All the traditional areas are fished — Fleming's Bar, Pete's Bar, Three Sisters Islands and, of course, the spot Louis made famous — Chapel Point. Lunch is at Indian Trail Resort which is owned by Pat Dettloff and her son, John. John is a famous musky guide on these waters and is also a renowned musky historian who has written many articles on various world record muskies and their authenticity. Ask Pat to tell you of some of the great stories about the Chip, particularly the one about a ghost sighting that was featured on a television show a few years back. She may even show you the video.

Dinner this evening has to be at a restaurant called the Blue Heron. It's just down the road from Herman's. Here you may expect to find one of the best prime rib dinners you will ever experience.

Wednesday is another short trip by car to Park Falls and the St. Croix Rod Company. This is a great opportunity to pick up a new musky stick or make note of the latest in musky rods for your Christmas list. After a short visit to Park Falls it's off to the Turtle-Flambeau Flowage — home of famous musky guide Bill Tutt and his long time nemesis, Big George. This flowage needs to be traversed at very slow speeds by the first time angler as there are numerous rock shoals and logs submerged just under the surface in most areas. Fishing pressure is very light on this flowage. It also has very stained water and you can easily lose numerous lures on the underwater timber. (Sometimes this is necessary to appease the musky gods.) It can be very rewarding for those not intimidated by its hazardous waters.

1996 Musky Hunter's Almanac

That evening it's time to check in to the World Musky Hunt in Minocqua, an invitation-only (you can make an application to compete) tournament held yearly in late August. The Hunt is a stark contrast to the Open event that kicked off the week. Thriving during a time when fishing tournaments are contested for large amounts of cash and prizes, the World Musky Hunt remains true to old fashioned fishing values of bringing people together for fish, fun and fellowship. Seven teams of three members from across North America compete for bragging rights. Accommodations are at the Concord Inn.

On Thursday, past contestants of this tournament meet and fish whatever bodies of water they so desire in the Minocqua area. In past years I have chosen a lake called Big St. Germain between the towns of Woodruff and St. Germain. A guide is provided free for this day (as they are for all days) by the tournament. Dinner that evening is at Bosacki's in Minocqua, the headquarters for the tournament. A great time is had renewing old friendships and making new ones. Friday, fishing starts for the contestants at the crack of dawn. The event is contested on three lakes — Minocqua, Tomahawk and Kawaguesaga. Lunch is a magnificent walleye fry served at Indian Shores Resort and a casting contest is held on shore to see who is the "Master Caster." Yours truly had the good fortune to win this event on a previous trip. After all boats reconvene at Bosacki's to tell their day's tales, a dinner is held that evening in honor of past contestants. Many return year after year.

Time from fishing has to be taken in Minocqua to visit the Arthur Oehmcke Fish Hatchery where they raise musky fry to be stocked in the many lakes in the area. If you still haven't got enough fishing tackle, Rollie and Helen's carries a huge selection of musky lures and equipment.

The Musky Trip Of A Lifetime

Saturday, the final day of fishing for the dream trip, is back on the same bodies of water as Friday. The Beacons Resort Boat House is the location of this lunchtime meal. That afternoon, while the contestants beat the water to a froth in search of that one winning fish, past contestants usually take this free time to pack up luggage and do last minute shopping. The awards dinner for the World Musky Hunt is held at the Minocqua Country Club that evening. Fun and laughter prevail as the dead fish award is presented for the best blooper of the tournament and each team takes their turn at the podium to offer their excuses for coming up short.

Sunday morning brings fisherman's withdrawal as the long trek home begins. This a great time to look back on the week's experience and contemplate how you'll improve it the next time you return to northern Wisconsin. The combination of the musky history and tradition, the food, the drink and the many friendships that are made make this a trip of a lifetime. If you stay at first rate motel-hotels, eat well and replenish your fishing tacklebox while there, you will spend close to $1,000 in U.S. funds in just over a week. But I can guarantee you this will be the Musky Fishing Trip of a Lifetime that you will never forget.

• • •

Hambug's Hint — Are you constantly tripping over the cord that runs from your electric trolling motor to the foot pedal? Try using a piece of cord conduit. This is the soft plastic covering you will find offices using to run electrical cord along the floor between work stations. Mark it in one inch graduations. Its a quick way to measure a fish that you plan to release. You'll find cord conduit at any full service office supply store.

The Field Trip

By Bill Hamblin

*H*aven forbid, should you ever be in the Hayward area and grow weary of fishing, you may want to consider an afternoon's field trip such as good friend and fishing partner of 15 years, Dave Jantzi, and I took on our most recent excursion to Hayward.

For years I have enjoyed exploring our mutual pastime's animated history with the same enthusiasm I have pursued the fish. Unfortunately, living in Canada much of this history seems somewhat out of reach but for the periodic articles in my favorite musky magazines and Larry Ramsell's Compendium, which for years, was a permanent fixture on my bedside table. What better opportunity then, than an afternoon in the "Home Of World Record Muskies" to research the life and times of some of its more celebrated musky fishing personalities.

Perhaps none is more infamous (I say that respectfully) than former resident and current world record holder Louie Spray. I had always wanted to gain a greater insight into this remarkable individual, hoping that some of his musky magic might rub off on me. Having learned at an earlier date that Mr. Spray had committed his memoirs to paper in an autobiography titled *My Musky Days*, we were eager to seek out a copy.

What could be simpler, we thought. Surely in a town he helped make famous it would be a staple on any bookstore shelf. Much to our dismay we found this was not to be the case. We visited a number of bookstores without success and it became apparent that the book was no longer in print. Ultimately we were directed to a store that specialized in used and rare books. The proprietor was most helpful and well acquainted with the work. In fact, he had been asked by the National Fresh Water Fishing Hall of Fame to appraise a copy they had in their possession. He was confident a value of $100 was a reasonable estimate of its worth. Our task was more formidable than originally thought — but then, that's not new to seasoned musky fishermen. If we were to be successful we would have to change game plans. We would proceed to plan B.

After reinforcing our resolve with a draft beer at the Moccasin Bar and a must look at their many prize musky mounts, we set out for the Carnegie Library a few short blocks away. We were confident of finding the book here but the question remained. Would they let us check it out — to Canada? I didn't really think they would but at this point just a look a the book would do for the time being. Something like getting a follow from a 50-inch musky. You may not catch your prize but you still go home satisfied.

The library had an old-time flavor all its own, reminiscent of the small piece of history we were in search of. The shelves were lined with new books as well as old, ones that belied their true worth by virtue of their thumb-weary pages and fatigued bindings — just what we were looking for.

We proceeded directly to the main desk for assistance. While initial inquiries concerning the publication were met with some skepticism by library staff, we were escorted to a shelf where we would be most likely to find the book. With our heads tilted and our eyes anxiously perusing the vertical titles on hand, not even the library

1996 Musky Hunter's Almanac

staff was prepared for the hidden treasure we were about to find. The book was there in good company with other classics such as *Muskie Fishing as Told by Three Old Guides*. I removed it from its perch and slowly began thumbing through it, back to front, glancing at the pictures quickly as they passed by. As the last page slipped beneath my thumb, I couldn't believe my eyes. There on the inside jacket was Louis' personal signature. We had not only found his memoirs but what may be one of the only personally autographed copies in existence. The library staff was no less amazed. It was quickly realized by all that the general book population was no place for this highly valued collector's item.

Nonetheless I had to ask. With my tongue firmly embedded in cheek — Can I check this out? I was not surprised and actually relieved with the response. Henceforth the book would be added to the library's resource department and removal from the library prohibited. There it would remain for all to enjoy, for all of your field trips.

In retrospect Dave and I never did get to read Louis' story, but true to form, all musky fishermen must be patient and that time too will come. For the time being we'll have to be content with the knowledge that maybe somewhere Louie is looking down, appreciative of the small role we may have played in preserving his place in history.

Louie, if you're watching, how about sending down a little bit of that musky magic to tide us over!

Bill's Footnote: I thank Betty and Stephanie of the library staff for all their help that day. While we were not able to check the book out they did make numerous calls on our behalf to learn more of whether the book was available through another source. We are very appreciative of

The Field Trip

their efforts.

We did learn that the rights to the book were now in the hands of a new publisher and although there were no immediate plans to republish it, a new edition at a later date could not be ruled out. The book is listed as Item # 00312612 in the United States Library of Congress. The Carnegie Library is located at 108 Iowa, Box 512, Hayward, Wisconsin, 54843.

If you drop by tell Betty and Stephanie that Bill and Dave say hi!

• • •

Humor — A musky hunter I knew died. His last request was to be buried at "sea". (His favorite musky hole) His two musky fishing buddies drowned while trying to dig his grave.

• • •

Did You Know — John Alden Knight, in his book, Moon Up Moon Down, *says the Solunar Theory can be summed up in this way. "Other conditions not being unfavorable, fish will feed, birds will sing and fly from place to place, in fact, all living things will become more active, more alive, during Solunar periods than at other times of apparent equal value." — BH*

• • •

Hambug's Hint — Some of today's Hydrographic Charts represent quite an investment at upwards of $25.00 a set. Consider having them laminated. (I often have two done back-to-back.) They will last for years, be totally weatherproof, and, as I've learned from personal experience, will float while you run around looking for where they blew out of the boat.

Strange But True

THE MUSKY THAT COULDN'T STOP EATING

By Kurt Krueger
Reprinted from the Vilas County News-Review — October 15, 1980

What's more unusual than catching a 40-inch musky on a live sucker by hooking a musky plug already embedded in the musky's mouth?

Answer: Bringing in the big musky and finding out the sucker and hook are gone, but the line is wrapped around the treble hooks of another plug in the musky's mouth. Then going home and discovering the plug in the musky's mouth is your neighbor's 30-year-old homemade lure.

That's what happened to Ben Machura of Chicago, Illinois, September 30. Machura, a summer resident on Dollar Lake in Eagle River, was fishing for muskies with a live, eight inch sucker.

The bobber popped down, Machura waited a short time, and then set the hook. After landing the 40 1/2-inch, 15 1/2-pound musky, he found sucker and hook were gone and the line had tangled around two of the treble hooks from a red and white bass plug embedded in both sides of the musky's mouth.

But that wasn't the end of an almost unbelievable story because Machura took that musky to his neighbor on Dollar Lake to show him what had happened. Upon meeting Mel Jacobs, Machura was amazed to hear the words, "Where did you get my homemade plug?"

Jacobs had loaned the homemade plug to his son-in-law in July, and his son-in-law had lost the plug on Dollar Lake after a musky snapped his line.

Jacob's son-in-law said a "good-sized" musky had snapped his line during a fishing trip in early July. Nearly three months later, Machura caught the same, apparently well-fed fish with the plug in its mouth.

"I opened the musky up and found it still had a line of fat inside," he said. "It was feeding with the bass plug covering almost the entire mouth opening." Machura said the old belief that hooks dissolve in a fish's mouth are false, because the hooks were unrusted and in perfect shape after three months in the musky's mouth. He said the mouth lining was beginning to grow right over the hooks.

• • •

Quotable Notable — Anglers who aren't skunked occasionally lose the most powerful catalyst for improvement.
— Author Unknown

Strange But True

WOULD YOU BELIEVE A HUGE PET MUSKY?

By Harvey Duck
Reprinted from the Chicago Daily News — June 21, 1993

SAYNER, Wis. — A 40-pound, 54-inch musky is a fish to respect — not to pet. It has teeth like railroad spikes and when angry can chomp a good-size walleye in half — let alone what it might do to a fellow's hand.

So, I was skeptical as a Watergate prober when Neal Long reached over the dock behind his home on nearby Plum Lake, stuck his right hand into the water and said: "Watch how my tame musky lets me pet her. She's as gentle as a kitten."

A minute or two later a shadowy figure as big as a submerged log drifted out from under the dock and began muzzling Long's fingers. It hovered, just below the surface, as Long tickled the chin and stroked the massive forehead. The great eyes, round as half dollars, focused on me and I would have sworn the fish was smirking.

"I don't tell many people about this" said Long, a veteran taxidermist in the area who knows as much about musky habits as they do themselves.

"But, for three years now, this same fish has returned to my dock early each June and spends the summer in the area. I know it's the same musky because there's a small dimple on her back that I recognize.

"It's female because I've seen perch hovering around feeding on her dropped spawn. For some reason, the perch know when it's safe to approach her. I'd guess she's past her fertile stage and is probably around 15 years of age."

"I measure her each year. She's so tame that she lets me run a tape measure right down her back. My figures show that she grows about one inch a year.

"The local conservation warden, Ben Bendrick, who used to play football for the University of Wisconsin, helped me measure her the last time. He didn't believe it, either. until he saw me pet the fish.

Long said that he has learned a lot from watching his pet, which he hasn't named "because I can't think of an appropriate name.

"The fish actually changes color" he said. "Sometimes the back is a solid dark green. Other times it has stripes and patterns. There must be something about the water and light conditions that prompts it to adapt to the surroundings.

"She is never tempted by a lure, probably because she feeds on northern and she's always full when she shows up. There are usually lots of northern around the area except when she's here and then you can't find any.

"I know I could catch her, just by snagging the jaw with a hook, but that wouldn't be fair. Besides, it's too smart a fish and about the most perfect specimen I've ever seen.

"I used to think muskies were dumb, but not any longer. This fish, at least, understands what's going on."

MUSKY CROSSWORD PUZZLE

Questions

Across
1. World record holder
5. New York musky lake
6. Surface bait that has caught muskies verified over 50 pounds
9. One of many scientific names for the muskellunge
10. Counting these pores may give clue to identity
12. Invented the Swim Whizz
13. Weight of the Canadian record
15. These muskies are considered one of the "last frontiers" for trophy fish
17. More verified 50-pound muskies have been caught during this month than any other
19. The shape of a male musky's urogenital region
21. A release tool that's illegal in certain states
23. A deep, clear northwestern Ontario fly-in musky lake
24. They documented many of the early musky records through their annual contest
26. Potato or short for a famous flowage
28. A type of topwater bait
30. Favorite fall bait
32. Holder of the hybrid world record
34. Pike and muskies share this family
36. A brand of line used in the good old days
37. Also called a lake herring
40. Musky fishermen are said to suffer from this affliction
41. Big fish structure
42. A modern day release tool
46. Muskies Canada and Muskies Inc. compete for this each year
47. A Wisconsin lake known for its big musky but named after a different species
48. 600 pounds of muskies were caught here over a two-day period in 1955

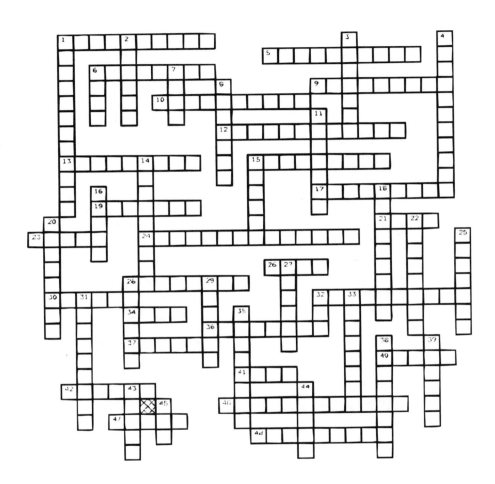

Down

1. Gweedo the guide
2. A popular structure muskies like to hang out on
3. A "release-only" Ontario lake
4. Percy Haver caught many fine musky out of this body of water
6. This Bob holds the unofficial world record

1996 Musky Hunter's Almanac

7. The shape of the female musky's urogenital region
8. Founder of Muskies Inc.
11. Its why we have so many big muskies today
14. Len Hartman
15. Lake of the Woods is considered to be this type of lake
16. A novel alternative to bucktail hair now being used on spinner baits
18. This body of water was home to the Canadian record until 1988
20. Cal Johnson caught a 67-pound 8-ounce musky off this bar
22. A peak condition for big muskies
25. Also called musky weed
27. Cross between a female musky and a male pike
28. A Canadian river and language
29. Point at which the moon is farthest from the earth
31. A bone used to age muskellunge
32. A dance or a bait
33. More and more musky fishermen are using these baits
35. This chain of lakes in southern Ontario is home to many muskies
38. Made the Mustang
39. Spook
43. Nickname for famous musky river
44. The fishing community wanted this lure banned until the inventor agreed to share it with them
45. Len Hartman called his homemade bait the Muskie _____

Word List

Apogee   Bug   Cabbage   ChallengeCup   Chautauqua   Chip   Ciscoe
Cleithrum   Cradle   EagleLake   Esox   Fever   FieldAndStream
FishNFool   Flaptail   French   FullMoon   Gaff   GilHamm   Gladding
Heddon   Homemade   HomerLeBlanc   Hybrid   Jig   John Knobla
Kawartha   Keyhole   LacSeul   LakeStClair   Larry   LarryRamsell
LeechLake   LouisSpray   Malo   Mandibular   Maskinoje   Moccasin
MudPuppy   Pear   Pfleuger   Release   Rock   Rowan   Saddle
September   Shield   SixtyFive   Skunk   Sucker   Suick   Suspended
Trout

Musky Crossword Puzzle

Answers

Across
1. Louis Spray
5. Chautauqua
6. Mud Puppy
9. Maskinoje
10. Mandibular
12. Homer LeBlanc
13. Sixty Five
15. Suspended
17. September
19. Keyhole
21. Gaff
23. Rowan
24. Field And Stream
26. Chip
28. Flaptail
30. Sucker
32. John Knobla
34. Esox
36. Gladding
37. Ciscoe
40. Fever
41. Rock
42. Cradle
46. Challunge Cup
47. Trout
48. Leech Lake

Down
1. Larry Ramsell
2. Saddle
3. Lac Seul
4. Lake St. Clair

1996 Musky Hunter's Almanac

6. Malo
7. Pear
8. Gil Hamm
11. Release
14. Fish N Fool
15. Shield
16. Skunk
18. Eagle Lake
20. Moccasin
22. Full moon
25. Cabbage
27. Hybrid
28. French
29. Apogee
31. Cleithrum
32. Jig
33. Homemade
35. Kawartha
38. Pfleuger
39. Heddon
43. Larry
44. Suick
45. Bug

Last Thoughts

Bill and I truly hope you have enjoyed this first of what we hope to be an annual *Musky Hunter's Almanac* ... its future is up to you! If you enjoyed it and want it to continue, write to *Musky Hunter* and tell them so! If you have information you would like to share or contribute, please send it to Bill or myself. If appropriate and space permits it will be included.

I am sure we will learn from this first edition and can make many changes and additions for the better next year.

While it has involved many long (and sometimes frustrating) hours to reach this completed state, I'm sure I speak for Bill when I say it's been a "labor of love"!

Musky Regards,
Larry Ramsell
Box 306
Knoxville, IL 61448

ABOUT THE ALMANAC'S EDITORS

Larry Ramsell

*L*arry caught his first legal musky at age 15 (38 years ago) in 1957, but had been exposed to "musky water" in 1949. This exposure has led to a lifetime passion of not just the pursuit of muskies, but the avid pursuit of musky history as well.

Larry has guided for muskies in Wisconsin in the 1960s and '80s and may return to it in 1996; developed the world record keeping program for the National Fresh Water Fishing Hall of Fame in the mid 1970s; served several terms as president of Musky Hunters, Inc. (now the Chicago Chapter of Muskies, Inc.) and two terms as International President of Muskies, Inc. Larry also worked as a volunteer for 4 1/2 months on Dr. Bernard Lebeau's doctoral thesis team on Eagle Lake, Ontario, in 1986.

As a youngster in the mid 1950s looking up at the mounts of Louie Spray's three world records and Cal Johnson's world record, to pictures of today's huge catches and actually holding Ken O'Brien's recent 65-pound monster, the "fire still burns bright"!

Larry has accomplished a couple of personal musky angling goals; capturing a 44-pound 4-ounce, 52x26-inch beauty from Eagle Lake, Ontario, in 1988 and the catch and release of a 52-inch "jumbo" (weighed 43 pounds with its tail still in the cradle) from

Georgian Bay waters in 1993.

Larry has written about muskies and musky history for *Musky Hunter, In-Fisherman; Fishing Facts* and *Muskie* as well as many other publications both here and abroad. His book, *A Compendium of Muskie Angling History* (now out of print), published in 1982 is a highly valued collector's item if you can find one.

While Larry has had the (mis)fortune to hook and subsequently lose a 60-pound class fish in 1969, he still hopes of one day locking horns with that "super" fish that will top them all!

Larry Ramsell and friend.

1996 Musky Hunter's Almanac

Bill Hamblin

Bill caught the musky bug in 1975 at the age of 19. At first he didn't venture far from home, honing his skills on the Kawartha Lakes in south-central Ontario, but ultimately the musky mystique had him traveling throughout Ontario and Wisconsin not only in pursuit of the fish but its animated history as well.

In 1992 Bill joined the local Kitchener-Waterloo Chapter of Muskies Canada. He went on to serve as chapter chairman for two

Bill Hamblin with a whopper.

About The Almanac's Editors

years before joining the National Executive Committee and taking over the position of editor of the organization's monthly newsletter. After a two-year term as the national treasurer he is now active at the local chapter level.

For a time Bill experimented with making his own baits, fashioned after Len Hartman's famous musky bug. They were named, by no coincidence, "Hambugs." While he no longer makes lures, the name stuck and "Hambug" is off pursuing his love of the sport in other areas.

In 1991, eager to share the magnificence of Georgian Bay with others and to try his hand at outdoor writing, he wrote an article for *Musky Hunter* magazine. The byproduct of this has been two businesses he operates under the banner of Fishermen's Depot. When not guiding clients around the treacherous waters of the Bay he serves as a sales agent for the maps developed by Canadian Hydrographic Service that have become a staple in most anglers' tackle boxes.

Bill's personal best musky is a 42-pound Georgian Bay giant but he takes equal pride in having guided two clients to catch and release line class world records (53 and 54 inches). The most recent, taken on opening day 1994, was caught by an angler in the first hour of the first day of his first musky trip. Contrary to most fishermen's concept of fishing on the Bay, both fish were taken casting.

Bill is a strong advocate of sharing one's knowledge and experiences with others. "While the fish is fundamental to the sport the bottom line is the joy and pleasure we get sharing the experience with others — both in the boat or reminiscing for months after. Musky fishing is a people thing first and foremost," says Bill.

MUSKIES! OTHER FISH ARE JUST BAIT

Subscribe to:

Musky Hunter
MAGAZINE

North America's Musky Authority—
How-to, Where-to and
When-to information
STRICTLY ON MUSKIES!

CALL 1-800-23-MUSKY

☑ **YES!** Send me 1 full year of MUSKY HUNTER for only $18.95—SAVE 25% over newsstand price OR

☐ 2 years (12 issues) for $35.00
☐ Check enclosed ☐ MasterCard ☐ VISA Exp. Date _____

Card # _____

Send to: Musky Hunter magazine, POB 147, Minocqua, WI 54548

Signature _____
Name _____
Address _____
City _____
State/Zip _____
Phone Number _____